TO DREAM OF PIGS

BOOKS BY CLIVE LEATHERDALE

Travel
To Dream of Pigs
Travels in South and North Korea (Desert Island Books)
The Virgin Whore – and Other Chinese Characters
Travels & Traumas (Desert Island Books)

Literary Criticism
Dracula: The Novel & the Legend
A Study of Bram Stoker's Gothic Masterpiece (Desert Island Books)
The Origins of Dracula
The Background to Bram Stoker's Gothic Masterpiece (William Kimber)

International Relations
Britain and Saudi Arabia 1925-1939: The Imperial Oasis (Frank Cass)

Sport
England's Quest for the World Cup – A Complete Record (Methuen)
Scotland's Quest for the World Cup – A Complete Record (John Donald)
The Aberdeen Football Companion (John Donald)

Education
So You Want to Teach English to Foreigners (Abacus Press)

TO DREAM OF PIGS
Travels in South and North Korea

by

CLIVE LEATHERDALE

Distributed By
HOLLYM INTERNATIONAL CORP.
18 Donald Place
Elizabeth, N. J. 07208 U.S.A.
Tel: (908) 353-1655   Fax: (908) 353-0255

**DESERT ISLAND
BOOKS**

www.hollym.com

First Published
in 1994 by
DESERT ISLAND BOOKS
31 George Street, Brighton, East Sussex BN2 1RH
United Kingdom

British Library Cataloguing-in-Publication Data
A catalogue record for this book is available from the British Library

ISBN 1-874287-02-3

Printed in Great Britain
by
Antony Rowe Ltd, Chippenham, Wiltshire

www.hollym.com

CONTENTS

Pages

map of Korea   viii & ix

SOUTH KOREA

1 A SOUL IN KOREA – Culture Shock and Jet Lag   11
2 GODS AND WEIRDOES – Generals, Shamans, Millionaires   30
3 A FRIEND FOR LIFE – Trains and Boats and Rains   49
4 SORAKSAN – Typhoons, Monks, and a Peep into Hell   65
5 THE FAR EAST – A Bath and the Famous Professor   82
6 ULLUNG-DO – Magical Mystery Island   102
7 KYONGJU AND PUSAN – Treasures and Pleasures   118
8 THE DEEP SOUTH – Angel Boats and Turtle Boats   141
9 CHEJU-DO – 'An Adventure into Paradise'   158
10 THE WILD WEST – The Taxidermist and the Thug   176
11 PANMUNJOM – Where North Meets South   194

NORTH KOREA

12 A DREAM OF *JUCHE* – The Mind of Kim Il Sung   213
13 PYONGYANG – Inside the Land of Fantasy   229
14 A BID FOR FREEDOM – Escape from my Minders   245

   Glossary   255

'My first journey produced the impression that Korea is the most uninteresting country I have ever travelled in, but during and since the war [with Japan in 1894] its political perturbations, rapid changes, and possible destinies, have given me an intense interest in it; while Korean character and industry ... have enlightened me as to the better possibilities which may await the nation in the future. Korea takes a similarly strong grip on all who reside in it sufficiently long to overcome the feelings of distaste which at first it undoubtedly inspires.'

Isabella Bishop – *Korea and her Neighbours* – (1898)

This book is the result of journeys around South Korea undertaken in the summers and early autumns of 1987 and 1990, and to North Korea in 1990. I am indebted to all those I encountered on my travels whose hospitality and thousand kindnesses made this book possible, and which enabled me, however so little, to learn something of Korea. To protect confidences, names have on occasion been changed and identities muddled. In 1992 I returned to Seoul to write this book.

Clive Leatherdale – June 1993

NORTH KOREA

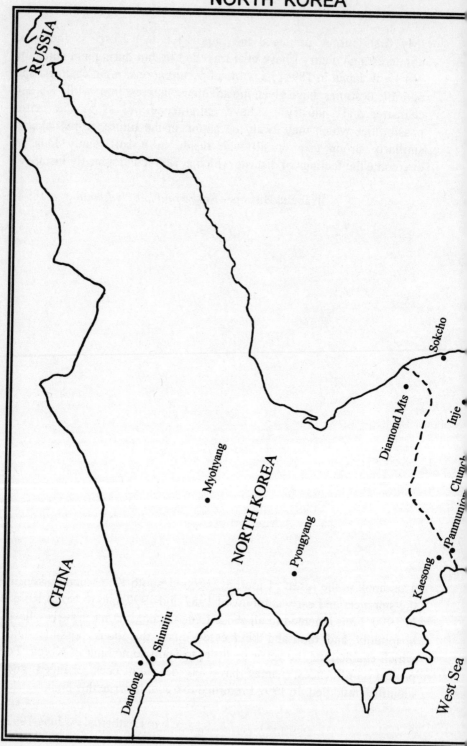

RUSSIA

CHINA

Dandong

Shinuiju

Myohyang

NORTH KOREA

Pyongyang

Kaesong

Panmunjom

Chuncheon

Inje

Diamond Mts

Sokcho

West Sea

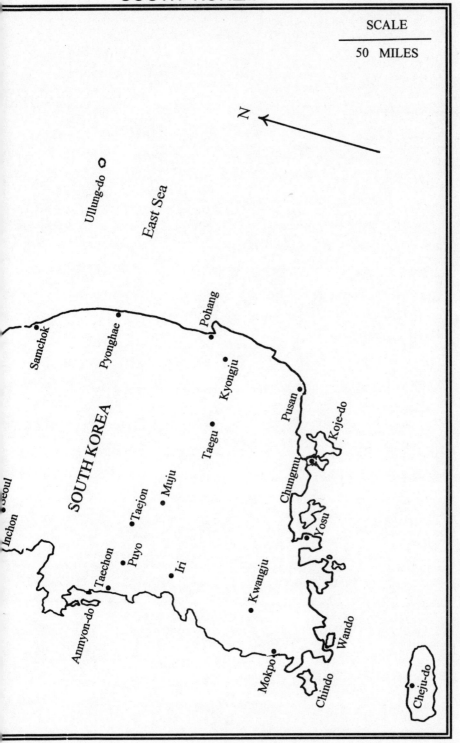

SCALE

50 MILES

N

Ullung-do

East Sea

Pohang

Samchok

Pyonghae

Kyongju

Pusan

Koje-do

SOUTH KOREA

Taegu

Chungmu

Seoul

Muju

Taejon

Yosu

Inchon

Puyo

Iri

Kwangiu

Taechon

Anmyon-do

Wando

Mokpo

Cheju-do

Chindo

1

A SOUL IN KOREA
Culture Shock and Jet Lag

I shrink from describing intra-mural Seoul. I thought it the foulest
city on earth till I saw Peking, and its smells the most odious, till I
encountered those of Shaoshing ... The monotony of Seoul is
something remarkable. Brown mountains 'picked out' in black,
brown mud walls, brown roofs, brown roadways, whether mud or
dust, while humanity is in black and white. Always the same
bundled-up women clutching their green coats under their eyes ...
the same string of squealing ponies spoiling for a fight, the same
processions of majestic red bulls under towering loads of brushwood, the same coolies in dirty white, for ever carrying burdens,
the same joyless, dirty children getting through life on the gutter's
edge, and the same brownish dogs, feebly wrangling over offal.
Isabella Bishop – Korea and her Neighbours – (1898)

HARD TRAVEL plays tricks with the libido. For some it is
enhanced, the novelty and exhilaration of the journey arousing
without exception the senses and appetites. New sights, new
sounds, new tastes ... new partners. Life is lived to the full.
For others, physical yearnings are simply washed away in the multi-
tude of exotic experiences, or left on the shelf after a knackering day
on the road. Not to mention the practical difficulties. In a Western
context the signals of sexual attraction are socially learned for the
benefit of all. Sometimes these are parodied – the lady's dropped
handkerchief, the invitation to 'come up for coffee'. These clues, these
hints of availability, enjoy limited currency in the East. It is all too easy
to flounder, misreading signs, seeing a come-on that was never there.

I was journeying on South Korea's remote east coast. Tired and
hungry I returned to my otherwise deserted hostel for a shower and to
rest my aching feet. On entering the lobby I was startled to find
stretched out in armchairs two comely women. One favoured shorts,
exposing a measure of smooth, shapely thighs. The women turned to

take in my arrival, and their casual hellos provided a further shock: they spoke good English. I was set for my first proper conversation in some weeks. I accepted their invitation to sit with them, selected a chair at what I hoped was a discreet distance, and thereafter sought unsuccessfully to avert my eyes from that golden flesh.

My new companions were nurses, picking up their English from cassette tapes and American Forces broadcasting. They had not long returned from a stint working in Saudi Arabia, a country I knew well, and we exchanged anecdotes and memories of desert oases and bedouin encampments. The nurses had blown much of their tax-free earnings on a rail trip round Europe, and been fleeced in London by a grubby hotelier near Victoria Station. I tut-tutted in sympathy. These days they worked in Seoul, and had been taking advantage of accumulated leave to tour the country. They were now heading back to Seoul, but offered instead to escort me to Soraksan National Park. I had no thought to refuse.

The morning dawned bright and clear. When the bus pulled up it was overflowing – the seats with bums, the floor with cabbages, radishes and unidentifiable vegetables wrapped in cloth bundles. We had barely room to plant our toes among the greenery. A shawled woman offered me her seat, and when I declined reached out with gnarled fingers to relieve me of my shoulder bag. This was heavy with fruit and cakes I had brought along for sustenance. Had I been new to Korea I might have snatched it away from her, but I was now wise to this particular courtesy. She wished merely to rest my bag upon her lap, that it might not burden me unnecessarily.

The previous night had been punctuated with amorous dreams, prompted no doubt by the unexpected stimulus of female company. I considered Miss Choi – the one with the thighs – undeniably and increasingly desirable. She favoured a floppy hooped sports shirt, and her long wavy hair, billowing over her shoulders the night before, was now tied up in an undisciplined pony tail. The laughter lines around her mouth were easily explained by the smile that seemed her constant companion. I was seduced by her looks, her ivory skin, vivacious manner and veiled humour. Alighting from the bus she pointed a grace-ful finger at my ankle, to a triangle of reddening mosquito bites exposed by my sockless feet.

'It must have been a female mosquito,' quipped Miss Choi. Then, with a twinkle, 'a very strong female!' My new friends had also been disturbed by mosquitoes in the night, though neither had been bitten.

'Ours must have been females too,' she explained, positing a theory of heterosexual mosquito activity that I had not previously considered. The conversation was harmless in itself. In any case, I had quickly attuned myself – hookers and hostesses aside – to the absence of innuendo in Korean women. In the West her words would not have raised an eyebrow; in present circumstances they sounded intoxicatingly precocious.

We climbed down from the bus, purchased glossy entrance tickets at the gate, and strolled into the park.

'It's a lovely day,' said Miss Choi, throwing back her head and airing her tanned face. They were the first words she had uttered for some minutes. She had been ousted from my side, though not from my thoughts, by her bespectacled friend, who had somehow latched on to me and was reliving the painful break-up of a recent relationship.

'I finished it because I loved him,' she was saying. 'To meet each person is to prepare to separate' (this being a loose translation of a Korean proverb).

This sounded a mite heavy when I had hedonism in mind. I tried to pay attention, exasperated that the confidences were not coming from Miss Choi. Relief was at hand in the shape of an ice cream stall. I made straight for it.

'*Sam*' (three), I said, leaning forward and indicating the delicious, plastic-covered ice cream cones that were one of Korea's unexpected joys. As I handed over the money I flinched as something feathered my arm. I looked down. There was Miss Choi. I had not noticed her approach. She was standing by my side, finger and thumb extended, casually removing flecks of ash or dust from the hairs of my forearm, lifting each speck in turn to her mouth and blowing it away, as delicately as if blowing a bubble from a soapy ring. The mere proximity of a hairy arm may have intrigued her, for the upper bodies of Koreans are generally hairless. She did not appear to notice my wilting gaze, or the said hairs stiffening from their rapidly goose-pimpling roots. She made no move to stop and I made no move to stop her.

Viewed from my restrictive Western preconceptions, her touch was drenched in eroticism. In a trans-Atlantic context there would have been little ambiguity about its intent. The pre-eminence of touch among the senses has been eloquently captured by Clive James's lyric: *When in a later day, little of the vision lingers, memory slips away, every way but through the fingers.*

But this was Korea. She was Korean. And I'd already had ample evidence of native barging, poking, shoving. What was she up to? On her territory, on her terms, Casanova himself would have floundered.

Three was by now a suffocating crowd. I finally lost patience with her friend's emotional complexes. It was wrong to do so, for strangers often prove therapeutic listeners, and she had willingly unburdened herself to me. I, however, could neither look nor think beyond my own beautiful stranger. My resolution to travel alone around Korea was not above compromise. There was no time for prevarication. Straight out I asked Miss Choi if she was free to spend a few days with me.

She put her ice cream to her mouth and gave it an innocently sensuous lick. For some seconds she did not speak, but I discerned no embarrassment in her eyes. She wiped her lip with the back of her hand.

'I'm sorry,' she smiled, laughter-lines tightly creased. 'I must go back to Seoul. I have not seen my boyfriend for a week and I miss him very much.' A moment later, after a hurried confab, the two nurses announced they were returning, otherwise they would not reach Seoul by nightfall. With a jolly wave they set off to catch their bus. I sat on a log to finish my ice cream and watched them go. For a few minutes loneliness sat heavily on my shoulders. Failure being one of life's great teachers I knew that, however slightly, I was a wiser man for the rejection.

~

'Your 747 comes in over Korea's East Coast at dawn ... Ridge after ridge of smoky-blue mountains march in rugged ranks against a pink morning sky, the valleys still misty with morning fog. Korea is an oriental painting in subtle pastels ... and the mountains give way to green paddies, brown hills, and the red-tiled roofs of farm villages. Just east of the Han River, Seoul sprawls in a bowl of steep rocky hills.'

That's what the guidebook said. After nineteen hours cooped up in a silver sausage nothing looked that good. My biorhythms were messed up. They were geared for breakfast, but the time in Korea was 5 pm, nine hours and two meals into the future. The first half of the journey, over the North Pole to Anchorage, had been pleasant enough. Constant daylight, mind-numbing Arctic views, and the company of boisterous Germans off fishing in Alaska. I'd earned their gratitude by demonstrating that the 'l' in salmon was silent. The second half was wretched, more constant daylight, nothing to see but water, and passengers disproportionately weighted in favour of Korean mothers and their sleepless babies.

Maybe the Land of Morning Calm was not at its best at tea-time in August. As I peered down, instead of subtle pastels all I could see was monotone muck. From time to time I snatched glimpses of a river, coiled and looping like a snake. The Korean woman next to me took time off from her squawking infant to daub her mouth with repellent pink lipstick.

'Han River?' I enquired, pointing down through the clouds. She either didn't understand or was too shy to answer. She smiled a *please leave me alone* smile. I turned back to the window. White tapeworm clouds wriggled among bald and untidy hills. The air looked disgusting. Over Seoul the view disappeared completely, to be replaced by a sickly void without depth or substance. It was a polluting smog to rival London's of yesteryear, or Athens's today. The ground only reappeared near Kimpo Airport, swampy rice fields succeeded by lines of perimeter lookout posts, from whose platforms gun barrels peered menacingly.

Curiosity had brought me to Korea. Morbid curiosity, perhaps. The country's past wars and present tensions attracted headlines but deterred visitors. Those that came were comparative neighbours, from Japan mostly, or the United States. Korea was off the track for most Europeans. Besides, in the popular imagination she offered little that was enticing and much that was not. At best, according to viewpoints canvassed, Korea might be a lacklustre Japan, lacking her neighbour's glitter and sparkle. At worst, all kinds of horrors sprang to mind.

Mostly they sprang from the Korean War and its aftermath. The TV series M*A*S*H, for example, serves in the eyes of war veterans to trivialise a non-trivial war. It had been nasty and brutish, and anything but short. When Ian Fleming wrote his James Bond novels he capitalised on Korea's unsavoury reputation when creating the villainous 'Odd Job'. The Bond-connection even extended to Korean airliners, for example the shooting down by Soviet fighters of KAL Flight '007'. Nor could real-life Koreans escape a reputation (deserved or otherwise) for malignity, either as POW camp guards under the Japanese in World War II, or as a result of atrocities mutually inflicted during Korea's civil war. And what about the weirdoes, typified by the Reverend Moon, founder of the Moonies cult? Religious cranks, devilish climate (typhoons in summer, bone-chilling winters), and inedible pickled food fertilised by human excrement all suggested good reasons for staying at home, or going elsewhere. And, lest we forget, the United Nations did not win the Korean War. Failure begets forgetfulness, as a result of which Korea was banished to the sin-bin of the mind, there to be joined by Vietnam. The very words 'Korea' and 'Vietnam' are stained by disillusion, and were until recently largely brushed from our conscious lives. How many of us, I wonder, correctly identify the North Korean capital – Pyongyang – or, prior to the '88 Olympic Games, could confidently pronounce the South's capital One of the world's most populous cities was so little on our lips that it answered variously to Sool, Say-ohl, or See-ool. Seoul, (it means 'capital'), comprises two Korean characters fused in speech into a simple diphthong. Seoul rhymes with soul.

Hidden amongst Korea's extensive debits one discovers a tiny anomaly. North Korea – exemplar of reclusive, reviled Stalinism – had in 1966 sent her soccer team to participate in the World Cup in England. The players found themselves patronised like so many cuddly dogs. The British public (Korean War veterans aside) took these tiny, valorous, unknown competitors to their hearts, all the more so for beating Italy and taking a 3-0 lead against mighty Portugal. Players such as Pak Doo Ik and Li Dong Woon enjoyed fleeting and expected fame. But it was not just the Koreans' cuteness and unforeseen success that provoked living-room murmurings. The team provided a glimpse into a strange but somehow less cynical world. Brian Glanville of *The Sunday Times* summed up the observation of many: 'The Koreans played with splendid spirit and refreshing sportsmanship: the kind of professional foul to which the World Cup exposed them clearly filled these straightforward little men with pained surprise … Alas, they would sink back into their strange isolation, leaving us with memories of their courage, their talent, their generosity.' One wonders whether kinder sentiments have ever been written about North Korea. Twenty years later, during the Mexico World Cup, no comparable epithets were merited by the South Korean team. Their ruthless professionalism was the equal of any.

But if Korea remains largely unknown today, a century ago she was barely emerging from international eclipse. Invasions by the Japanese and Manchus in the late sixteenth and early seventeenth centuries devastated the country and imbued its people with an abiding fear of foreigners. Its doors slammed shut and the Hermit Kingdom, as Korea duly became known, shunned all contact with the outside world. Not until the 1880s did Korea sign commercial treaties with the United States, Britain, and other Western powers. Its treaty ports thereafter served as the swing-doors for the influx of missionaries, consular representatives and private travellers, whose largely wretched and disparaging portrait would act as the lodestar for my own journeys.

Korea emerged from her long hibernation only to find herself brutally annexed by Japan. Freedom from the Japanese in 1945 was accomplished at the cost of dividing Korea into communist north and capitalist south, a condition unaffected by the outcome of the Korean War (1950-53), and which prevails to this day. Korea, in other words, has endured a century of oppression during which – Korean War apart – the international spotlight shied away. Being graced with the Olympics, however, thrust Seoul among a select list of exalted cities (among them London, Tokyo, Moscow, Los Angeles) to have hosted the modern Games. South Korea, Asiatic by geography and culture, Western by politics and circumstance, opened its doors to the world's media and in its wake the world. The Games' opening ceremony, in effect, constituted a *rite de passage* through which South Koreans saw themselves as coming of age. Lingering traces of international innocence would soon be swept away. I felt compelled to see this hitherto obscure little peninsula before it was changed in permanence.

I crammed into my backpack a couple of travel guides and, more importantly, the records of pioneering travellers from a century ago. Pride of place went to *Korea and her Neighbours* (1898), the compelling journals of a plump physician's widow. Isabella Bishop (née Bird) was already in her sixties and destined to be the first woman elected to membership of the Royal Geographic Society. She witnessed Korea as I would have wished to, for as the world shrinks within range of the package operator its challenges and rewards diminish. My token defiance was to get there before Korea's last corners were fouled by tourist coaches bound for luxury tourist hotels.

~

Mr Ock had a stammer, a weak chin and a noseful of blackheads. He designed computer screens for Samsung, one of Korea's vast multinational conglomerates. We met at the arrivals hall at Kimpo Airport. He was waiting for a relative. The relative didn't show. I did, and he seemed happy to switch his attentions to me.

'My car is outside', he said. 'I will take you downtown.' I jumped in, unable to believe my luck, for I was sufficiently tired and out-of-sorts to be dreading the hassle of the taxi ranks.

Thankfully, Mr Ock was too shy to bombard me with questions and permitted me to stare out of the window. Seoul and London are not dissimilar in size, though the former is rapidly expanding, the latter contracting, and both are bisected by a major river. The original settlements of both cities lay on the northern side, so that southern districts have little focus and are historically less enticing.

The River Han, however, is most unlike the Thames. This I learned sometime later when taking a ride along it in the company of Mr Ock. The futuristic-minded Koreans had named one of their pleasure boats *The 21st Century*. It had two decks linked by spiral staircase, and expensive drinks served by cooing hostesses in plumed hats. The girls' good looks and passable English qualified them as perfect guides, though they doubtless earned a pittance. 'Take Out with Dry Hands' declared the instruction on my boat ticket. I pondered this riddle for some minutes before locating a sliver of paper soap. It was hidden inside the ticket.

The trip commenced from Youido Island, a lump of priceless real estate projecting into the Han, and site of the National Assembly Building. Mr Ock drew my attention to the circular-domed building.

'It brings b-b-bad luck to Korean people.' This, he explained, was a matter of *yin* and *yang*, masculine and feminine, interwoven with an arcane art known as *pungsu*, a kind of geomancy. The building occupied the southern tip of Youido, with the river forking either side. It was positioned in anatomical terms as a vagina, sited between the two legs of the river. To be auspicious, an object or building should be 'masculine', like Youido's sixty-three storey, gold-windowed, tapering office block that towered phallically above all else. Somewhere on the far, northern shore of the Han lay the ghost of Mapo, the long-vanished river port of Seoul.

The river was empty. I had read somewhere of the Han being 'a lifeline for Koreans', functioning like 'a mother's breast'. Such intimacy was hard to fathom. What used to be carried by river now goes by road or rail. A couple of rowing eights and a dredger provided my only sight of river life. The Han was devoid of motion and energy. No barges, no freight, no fishermen, no jetties. As for its colour, the misnamed Blue Danube is notoriously brown, but no browner than the Han in August, swollen with mud and silt from summer rains.

Stretches of the fortified banks had been dignified with the name 'Riverside Park', and been transformed into endless playing fields, soccer pitches, tennis courts and cycle paths. It was a weekday afternoon and they, like the river, were deserted. The towpath had nothing to tow, nor lovers to tread its length. Exposure to these treeless wastes, battered by noise and doused with fumes from the eight-lane Olympic

Expressway running alongside, was clearly not to everyone's taste.

The Han's lack of boats was easy to explain. They had, said Mr Ock, nowhere to go, except up in smoke. Thirty miles down river, where the Han joins the Imjin, South Korea meets with North. Nothing sails past the gun emplacements and ensnaring nets of the lower Han, which means that Seoul is effectively cut off from the sea. This does not constitute much of an economic sacrifice. The Han has always been testy about humans and their silly boats, as Isabella Bishop noted:

> It eventually occurred to some persons more enterprising than their neighbours to establish steam communication between [Seoul and the sea]. Manifold are the disasters which have attended this simple undertaking ... For the steam launches are only half-powered for their work, the tides are strong, the river shallows often, and its sandbanks shift almost from tide to tide. Hence this natural highway is not much patronised by people who respect themselves, and all sorts of arrangements are made for getting up to the capital by 'road'.

It was clear that the deserted river serves no useful function to the people of Seoul. They don't look at it, don't need it, and don't even talk about it – except in times of summer flood. So far as I could tell the river was a supreme irrelevance, even a nuisance, something to be crossed and nothing else. The original city had not been built on its banks, but three miles to the north, snuggling behind the slopes of Mt Namsan. Only as the population of Seoul multiplied after the Korean War did its suburbs first extend to, and then over the Han. The overwhelming uselessness of the river, which is once again alarmingly polluted, has been rubber-stamped by the dams ('barrages') that throttle it somewhere upstream from the capital. A garrotted river, fit only for producing electricity, yet inviting sightseers. Cruising along was like being given a ring-side seat at an execution.[*]

~

Markets have lost their meaning in the West. They have diminished in size and scope and no longer provide the economic backbone of the community. Elsewhere they continue to function as the hub of social and economic exchange. Such is their vitality that visitors are drawn not only to buy but to watch. Markets are where the action is.

---

[*] Despite the pollution menace, picnickers brave the Riverside Parks at weekends, and a few paddle- and row-boats now brave the river itself.

Heading nowhere in particular one hot and humid morning I stumbled upon Namdaemun (South Gate) market. The network of streets and alleys hummed with life and vigour. Vendors stacked their wares on tables, or made do with barrows, carts, buckets, or even bits of cloth spread on the ground. The size of Namdaemun is overwhelming, as is the variety of produce. In the space of a few yards I passed coils of wire, broom handles, a sleeping man cradling his head on a stack of inner-tubes, grapes, brushes, mops, spades, fancy jewellery, tights, shoes, mushrooms, all manner of live and dead fish, nuts, shellfish, trousers, eels, motor cycle wheels, more eels – these in an aerated tank powered by primitive, clanking generator – Rubik Cubes, lacquered wardrobes lying on their backs, antlers. Next to the antlers was a line of pigs' heads decorated with coloured tinsel. Snuggled by a doorway sat an old woman with sightless eyes. She was gripping a small blue dish into which I peered. Inside was a 100-*won* coin (less than one penny).

She was the first beggar I'd seen in Korea. Over the next weeks I encountered many. Few like this old woman sat still and begged. Mostly they had to sing for their bread. Literally. I grew accustomed to men with hideous injuries crooning into hand-held microphones, the sound amplified by means of mobile loudspeakers. Those unfortunates with leg deformities, or without legs at all, wrapped their lower quarters in lorry-tyre inner tubes. They moved by scraping themselves along the ground, or on wheeled trolleys, one hand clutching a microphone, the other manoeuvring an amplifier. The blind used a white stick, or hung on the arm of a sighted but otherwise cruelly handicapped accomplice. One or other would sing or play a harmonica.

By a zebra crossing I came upon a begging mother cradling her child. She did not sing or play, but even she understood the requirement to provide a service. She was crouched by an amplifier larger than herself, which reverberated to a cheery cassette tape while her begging bowl vibrated emptily on top. Amplified music, it seemed, is as much a part of Seoul's destitute as is the private jet to the oil sheikh. Those beggars without tongue with which to sing or hands with which to play resorted to shock tactics. Artificial limbs were unscrewed to expose the jagged stumps of limbs, and on one occasion I was exposed to an eye socket gaping wide.

The Korean philosophy of begging, I reflected, is unlike that encountered, say, in Spain, where it is common to see an otherwise healthy man kneeling for hours on concrete pavements, bearing a placard listing the number of his underfed children. He has no physical injury, therefore he publicly inflicts suffering upon himself, in the form of bruised and bleeding knees, and bears his pain with an expression worthy of the Madonna. In Korea, as elsewhere in the East, it is physical injury or disfigurement that tugs at the heart-strings.

Ahead of me pedestrians stepped abruptly into the kerb. They were avoiding a beggar more disfigured than most, whose mutilated form scuffled along like a crab. He had lost almost all means of independent motion. His right leg was severed at the thigh. The stump was matted with dirt. The other was horribly twisted: it curled round his body like a lobster claw and was sheathed in a black inner tube, secured top and bottom by string. His left arm was missing at the shoulder. With his right he alternated between pushing a wheeled loudspeaker and levering his body forward a few inches at a time. On his head sat a yellow sunhat.

Photographs, unless posed, must be instant. He who hesitates takes bad pictures, or no pictures at all. For that reason I wore my automatic camera on my hip like a six-shooter. It was a simple matter to draw, aim, and shoot without pausing to weigh the ethics of the shot. My design, I told myself, was not to partake of life but to observe it, the more bizarre or pitiable the subject the better. Alas, I was no hardened photo-journalist. I had already ripped open the Velcro casing when the beggar's eyes speared mine. My hand froze. It was as well this was not the OK Corral, for my hesitancy would have been fatal. Having been caught in the act I could no longer press the button. Absurd questions flashed though my mind. The beggar wanted money: I wanted his photo. Should I 'buy' it, appeasing my nagging conscience by tossing a few coins in his plate? Would he have willingly sold his picture, given the choice? Probably he would, but already the opportunity had passed. I walked on, wallowing in bothersome ethical confusions.

Seoul's beggars were seldom where I expected them, for I saw none favouring palaces or other sites on the tourist trail. But begging, I was informed, was illegal: clampdowns came and went with fluctuations in the political temperature.

~

Seoul, I quickly discovered, has egg-white but no yoke; burgeoning new suburbs without the focus provided by an old town centre. The Korean War saw to that. Few old buildings still stand, save for occasional palaces, shrines, pavilions, and ancient fortified gates that survived the centuries and were excused the ravages of battle. These form the hub of Tourist Seoul, together with post-war attractions – museums, amusement parks, and luxurious shopping complexes.

The most luxurious of these is the Lotte complex in the heart of downtown. The Lotte is the Harrods, Claridges, and Paul Raymond's of Seoul, all under one roof. It boasts around thirty bars and restaurants, some one thousand hotel rooms, its own swish night-club, Annabelle's, on the thirty-somethingth floor, and even its own exit at the nearby subway station. Riding one of the Lotte's escalators I pondered the weight of a nineteen-layered chandelier. (I later learned that a second Lotte complex, south of the river, boasts what the Guinness Book of Records confirms as the world's largest chandelier, weighing 10.5 tons, with dimensions of 12 x 6.6 metres.)

The Lotte Department Store catered for most tastes, provided they were expensive – though it also sold picture postcards, a rarity in Korea. The mannequins in the fashion departments were strictly Caucasian – baby-doll dummies with lily-white skin, long legs, wide-set eyes, and bubbly blonde hair. White is beautiful. West is wonderful. Likewise the cosmetic and fashion commercials on TV. The Korean female is exhorted to regard herself as aesthetically second-rate, unable to command respect and admiration until she lightens her hair and disguises her oriental eyes or, better, submits to 'double-eyelids' being surgically implanted. A stroll around Lotte's provided a peep into, for me, a distasteful aesthetic revolution.

It was the same with clothes. In a single generation the Korean appearance has changed beyond recognition. Traditional costume (*hanbok*) is distinct from that of neighbouring countries, and unlikely nowadays to be worn except by the old, or on special occasions, or for TV historical dramas. For men, short waistcoats peep out from under jackets secured round the chest by tapes, while baggy trousers are drawn in tightly at the ankles. The vivid colours of the long, flowing, female *hanbok* are offset by the more restrained creams, browns and mauves of male costume. TV soap operas show the otherwise obsolete headgear once worn by the male upper classes. An inner hat, black and tight-fitting like a skull cap, within a peculiar outer hat of horse hair, conical on a flat brim, sits perched on the top of the head like a tiny bird table. The whole apparatus served no functional purpose that I could discern, either by keeping warmth in or rain out, and to compound its futility looked liable to topple from the head at any moment.

An old man in *hanbok* sits facing me on the subway. Even he has made concessions to modernity, with his Panama hat and patent-leather shoes. He nevertheless appears to belong to a different century from the high heeled, short skirted city girls about him. Among the young, stone washed denims and unlaced baseball boots are all the rage. Teenage girls drape themselves around one another, linking hands and arms in displays of innocent friendship that exceed even the Korean male's capacity for tactile comfort.

The breast, I was assured by a reputable book on Korean mores, plays little part in Korean fashion or eroticism. The back of the neck and the upturned big toe are regarded as more provocative. Plunging necklines are all but unknown, and brassieres introduced only during the Western cultural invasion. Previous generations of Korean women strapped down their breasts, though the elderly permitted them to hang freely beneath a short bodice. As their bodies were otherwise clad from head to foot, this meant that only the breasts were browned by the sun, like a sunbather in negative. But when I raised the subject of breasts with trusty Mr Ock, he expressed a keen eye. Korean men did indeed cherish ample bosoms. Korean women, alas, did not possess them.

~

The city centre is an inelegant mass of tower blocks and traffic whirring by on eight-lane thoroughfares. Step back a few blocks, however, and one might enjoy the city's peccadilloes. A boy saws through a cubic metre of ice propped on the rear of a bicycle. A moped growls past, labouring under the weight of a wardrobe. The rider hunches over the handlebars trying to maintain balance, unable, because of his cargo, to see behind him. With space at a premium, whole neighbourhoods are crammed with tiny supermarkets, restaurants, tailors – each establishment, as often as not, backed by a small room furnished with TV and mattress. There appears to be an epidemic of earthenware jars, measuring up to a metre in height. One sees lines of these jars on every balcony. They will store the *kimchi* – the fermented cabbage, radish, garlic, and pickled side-dish eaten with every meal – to feed each household in the winter months ahead. I never won the battle with *kimchi*, though I quickly overcame reservations about dried cuttlefish, ghastly, shrivelled, milky brown, flat things with tails, looking less appetising than a bog-preserved corpse. Koreans eat them as snacks (as we might potato crisps) tearing off small strips at a time. The texture suggests salty, rubbery, fishy, chewing gum. Like chewing-gum, once in the mouth cuttlefish stays around a long time. As it neither dissolves nor disintegrates, I found it prudent to tear off and sample the tiniest morsels.

In Mr Ock's capable hands, Seoul's most noticeable foibles were easily deciphered. I remarked on the numerous photography shops. These are highly conspicuous, for their windows exhibit naked babies. Always male – privates proudly displayed – the plump babies perch on tiny chairs and beam with health. The portrait records the 100th day of life, a time for celebration in view of the heavy infant mortality of the past. When his first birthday arrives, an eldest son swaps his birthday suit for full sartorial swagger. He sits draped head to toe in the blues, reds and greens of traditional costume, and poses behind a table festooned with rice-cakes, sweetmeats, pears and grapes. Judging by his unsmiling countenance, he finds his predicament irksome, and would prefer to snooze with his dummy.

The child's health will already have been charted by a fortune teller, whose untutored cousins tout for custom by the roadside, in underpasses, on bridges, squatting with their phrenology maps and palm charts. These public soothsayers are busiest in the evening, alongside tents and canopies that adorn the suburbs at dusk. At first glance these shelters look like the temporary refuges of gas or electricity engineers, but turn out to be mobile eateries. Most permit space for just a single trestle table and bench. Each tent is illuminated by a solitary bulb, the silhouettes of those inside dancing eerily on the sheeting.

One morning, approaching noon, I chanced upon an eager commotion. Thirty or forty men stood huddled inside an alcove. My height permitted me to see over their heads, to where a man in brown jacket and red tie was marketing sex aids.

I hadn't expected this. At least not so openly. Though his onlookers shielded him from public view, he retained a lookout on the pavement. The audience was engrossed. Upon a table were spread various clip folders, each containing snaps of men and women in provocative poses. One folder was entitled 'joy graph'. The folder opened to reveal a pictorial account of 'How to make your penis grow bigger in six weeks'. The diagrams were mightily impressive.

With the swagger of someone selling Wedgwood china for a farthing, the salesman was building up to a practical demonstration. He reached into a drawer for a yellow dildo which with the aid of a bicycle pump he inflated to the size of a water melon. Gasps of admiration accompanied this apparently conclusive test. The salesman opened a magazine at its nude centrefold and dabbed the sultry model's nether regions with his water melon, waving his raised forefinger in triumph. QED.

His audience watched throughout in rapt attention. No nudging and winking, no ribald running commentaries. And for a considerable time I went unnoticed. When someone finally turned and saw me the communal trance was broken. Heads turned to follow his gaze, and from that instant I was pivotal to the entertainment. Every joke from the salesman, every new centrefold upturned, every component part of the 'penis' explained, produced an instant check on my response. Heads switched from dildo to me, from me to dildo, as if following a rally at Wimbledon. It was the reactions of a foreigner to sexual gimmickry that intrigued them, as if he was more qualified and worldly than they, and they delighted at my obvious amusement.

I had learned my lesson with the deformed beggar. This time there would be no fatal delay. The salesman had the inflated dildo between his legs as I whipped my camera from its case. The minder saw me and came running, giving me a hard warning prod on the shoulder. Too late for him, the photo was safe.

I told Mr Ock about the dildo salesman.

'Asian m-m-men have small penis' he whispered, adding conspiratorially: 'I think that is good. Small brooms reach all corners.'

~

It was Sunday. A day of rest in Britain but seemingly nowhere else. In Korea the banks might be closed, but otherwise life appeared only marginally less hectic. Round about noon on my first Sunday in Korea I chanced upon the street they call Itaewon.

Itaewon is to Seoul what Soho is to London, 42nd Street to New York, and Shinjuku to Tokyo. Its location accounts for its existence, for the Yongsan district of Seoul also houses the United States' Eighth Army headquarters in South Korea. Itaewon developed initially by providing the bars and brothels that flourished parasitically upon the influx of GIs during the Korean War. Not so long ago the general seediness of the area deterred respectable Western visitors. Seoul had been under midnight curfew till 1981, something of a dampener to the night reveller. Those final minutes had been marked by desperation – drink up, hook up, and get home. Nowadays the city hums at all hours. Itaewon has given itself a spring-clean and is no longer a name to whisper under your breath. By day Westerners flock there to shop; by night for whatever else takes their fancy.

Itaewon enjoys a reputation for cheap shopping. Leather and eelskin are a speciality, as is amethyst, smoky topaz and jade. Sports shoes come in all shapes and sizes. Famous brand-names, including Nike and

Reebok, are 'Made in Korea'. Shirts come Extra-Large, and Extra-*Extra*-Large to cater for the beefier GIs. Street traders line the kerb, their tables stacked with grapes, sunglasses, baseball gloves, porcelain trinkets, cuddly toys, T-shirts. Especially popular are the fancy tasselled wall-hangings (*maedip*), bearing images of the Manchurian crane – a traditional symbol of longevity. A ship's wheel and some rusting Sousaphones stand propped against 'The Cute Little Store', whose shutters are drawn. A notice says 'Closed Sunday – Come to Worship with us'. I hadn't imagined biblical exhortations in Itaewon.

The shop names tried to impress. They included the 'Oxford Custom Tailor – Successful Businessman with Oxford Wardrobes', 'The *Wonderful* Shop', 'The Mong Blang Variety Shop' [sic], 'The Windsor Restaurant', 'The Honey Bee Club'. Itaewon's storekeepers don't appreciate leisurely window shopping. They work on the hard sell. Their hirelings stand outside as if touting for strip-clubs: 'Hello sir, would you like to try an eelskin jacket?'

I pause to observe a Buddhist mendicant, head shaven, clad in grey sackcloth, carrying a bell in one hand and alms tray in the other. He stands in every doorway, tinkles his bell, waits hopefully, then turns away empty handed. Ahead looms the American Bible Belt. Two crop-haired blacks march sprightly towards me, kipper ties flapping outside their buttoned-up maroon suits, rolled umbrellas in their right hands, bibles clutched in their left. As we pass their faces dissolve into dazzling toothpaste smiles.

'Good morning, sir. We're off to church. Are you?' Their message might have been better directed at the scruff behind them, whose T-shirt proclaimed *No I ain't got no fucking money*. Other T-shirts were more esoteric, like that which declared *The Screwing you get from the screwing you got.*

'Hi, what are you doing?' There was something unbiblical about the voice. I turned to confront a pouting creature in navy dress and violent pink lipstick. She was chewing with a ponderous circular motion, her head cocked slightly to one side. The subtlety was breathtaking.

'What are *you* doing?' I replied.

'Waiting for you,' came the practised riposte. Her twangy American English was sufficiently fluent to suggest she'd long abandoned any Korean upbringing.

Some travel writers store the day's events in their head and regurgitate them into their notebooks at night. After an eventful day this means much writing and, inevitably, much forgetting. I preferred immediacy.

Most of the time my notepad lived in my hand. Like now, and I had no intention of putting it away. I stood my ground and attempted to jot down her remarks verbatim.

Excuse me, could you repeat that slowly please?

I was aware of her nuzzling up close. She stood on her toes to inspect my notepad and read out

'Hi ... what ... are ... you ... doing? Her eyes clouded. *What kind of jerk is this?* She no longer looked so confident. The pout subsided, the chewing gum ground to a halt. She replaced what she took for sensuousness with directness. She tapped the camera on my belt.

'What's this?' It was a dumb question and got no reply. In any case, her product did not appeal. Her hand slid down my leg to my thigh pocket, within which nestled my wallet and passport.

'What's this?' she repeated. Alarm bells rang in my head. Her hand located the wallet, feeling for its outline, permitting the pout to refuel itself. I terminated our relationship abruptly, walked a few paces and took down some notes. When I looked back she was gone. I was no loss to her. She would have found no shortage of custom, even on a Sunday afternoon.

I took one of the by-ways that led up and away from the bustle of Itaewon. A kitten licked its hind quarters while chained to a door-post outside Dr Seo's Animal Clinic. From a wooden post numberless telephone lines radiated in all directions, like some grotesque electronic tree. Before I'd gone fifty yards Itaewon seemed to have been left light years behind.

My route took me to Paekpom Plaza, an enclosed park lined with willows and statues of famous Korean patriots, including the eponymous Paekpom. On three sides the park afforded immense views of the humming city below. Locals were out in force, to relax, admire the view, eat lunch. Middle-aged women commandeered benches as kitchens, pots and pans piled nearby. The equivalent of 50p bought me a bowl of *pipim-pap* – rice with fried egg, spinach, bean-sprouts, bluebell roots. What to me was a welcome meal was transformed into a public event. Passers-by nudged one another and nodded in my direction. A passing family stared as if I was naked, and sat themselves on a verge for a better view.

Feeling uncomfortably conspicuous I finished the *pipim-pap* and moved to a bench shaded by an overhanging willow. I opened my notepad and began to write, turning a blind eye to a member of my earlier audience who had risen to his feet and followed me. Although I was seated at one end of the otherwise unoccupied bench, he sat himself down so close as to warm the air between us. Maybe Koreans had different notions of privacy, or maybe none at all. I had read that they maintain psychological distance by mentally switching off at moments of potential embarrassment. What to the average Westerner may only be done in private may be performed publicly in Korea in the knowledge that what the eyes may see the brain does not. Psychological walls replace physical ones.

I suppose I should have indulged in pleasantries. But he was too close for comfort. He was of pensionable age and looked to have a bullet hole on his inner forearm. At last he spoke.

'Okay, me educated,' he began. He was clearly establishing his credentials. 'Elementary school, okay; middle school, okay; high school, okay.' He paused to gather together the remnants of his English. He was either being friendly or this was a prelude for me to part with some money. At last he made his play.

'Me make sketch people in my house. Okay?'

Go up and see his etchings? He surely couldn't know the English joke. But what did he want? In descending order of probability, my money, my body, both, or neither.

'No thank you,' I said, with what I hoped was a gentle inflection. He had already started touching me in an intrusive but as yet inoffensive way, leaning into me with his shoulder and poking me with his finger at various points between upper arm and knee. Now he placed an arm around my shoulder and began to tickle my beard, fondling it as might a babe in arms who'd never seen one before. His other hand commenced roaming my thigh. Like the Itaewon madam he discovered the bulge of my wallet. To discourage him I abruptly resumed jotting down the notes his approach had interrupted. He became even more inquisitive. He, too, leaned over to see what I'd written.

'You want beer?' he rasped, pointing over to his original seat, where a sleazy female sat by a pile of bottles, stockings rolled down to her ankles. Her cigarette spent more time in her mouth than between her fingers, and her general air was so unseemly that I speculated upon the contents of the unmarked bottles. In any case, I wished to extricate myself.

'No thank you!' Refusing offers of alcohol, especially free alcohol, was clearly unforeseen.

'American?' It was a statement rather than a question. What else could I be? And everybody knew all Americans drank beer.

'English!' The one word had a remarkable effect.

'Ah, English ... sorry, sorry.' He got stiffly to his feet, bowed and shuffled back to his place alongside his fag-puffing, bottle-swigging companion.

His sudden departure left me less satisfied than I expected. Instead of relief I felt a flush of embarrassment. I was behaving like a Little Englander. Why had I not gone with him? I had come to explore Korea, to climb inside its soul, to expose myself to whatever experiences came my way. Yet here I was running scared at the possible ulterior motives of an old man. I should have accompanied him, to see where and how he lived. And if he did want money, so what? He could want. As for my absurd reaction to physical contact, I'd grown used to it in Arabia and Japan. Touching was invariably an unselfconscious expression of simple friendship. I was being an ass. I could no longer blame my disorientation on culture shock and jet lag, and I determined to guard against such foolishness. The next invitation, from whatever source, I'd accept.

2

GODS AND WEIRDOES
Generals, Shamans, Millionaires

[Koreans] are not only unattractive and unsympathetic to a Westerner who feels no spiritual interest in them, but they appear more and more to be lazy, dirty, unscrupulous, dishonest, incredibly ignorant, and wholly lacking in the self-respect that comes from a consciousness of individual power and worth. They are not undeveloped savages; they are the rotten product of the decayed Oriental civilisation.

George Kennan – *The Korean People* – (1905)

I N 1894 Isabella Bishop arrived in Seoul through the port of Inchon – Chemulpo as it was then known – thirty miles west of the capital on the West Sea.* Inchon later attained international fame as the site of General MacArthur's amphibious landings that changed the course of the Korean War.

The Han River does not connect Seoul with Inchon, but meanders north-west through the capital and empties into the West Sea north of the port. Nowadays the lower reaches of the river divide North and South Korea and are therefore barred to vessels. In any case, the overland route between Seoul and Inchon is quicker. And safer, too, having regard to the river's natural, as opposed to military perils. Mrs Bishop had not trusted to the efforts of steam launches, preferring to be carried in a chair for seven hours by 'six bearers, jolly fellows, who joked and laughed and raced the Consul's pony'.

I rode the elevated subway to Inchon in the company of Mrs Bishop's memoirs. Developing nations like Korea enjoy league tables as a way of demonstrating progress. Seoul is one of the world's four most populous cities; Korea ranks tenth in the number of telephone lines, and second only to Japan in shipbuilding. The POSCO steelworks in the south-eastern city of Pohang constitute the world's twelfth

---

* The West Sea, separating China and Korea, is otherwise known as the Yellow Sea, on account of the vast silt deposits bequeathed by China's Yellow River.

largest steel mill. Seoul's subway ranks seventh in terms of mileage and is currently being extended.[*]

The subway is modelled on Japanese lines. The blind benefit from pimpled yellow strips along the platform edge; the deaf from shrill oscillations announcing approaching trains. Flimsy advertisements flap from carriage ceilings. The ads are never torn. Nor are the velour seat covers, for Korea is refreshingly free from vandalism. The 'Subway Information' maps above the doors are misleading, for most are entirely in Korean. Foreigners must rely on station numbers, as if Victoria was 1, Pimlico 2, Vauxhall 3, and so on down the Victoria Line.

A ticket to 8, please.

In the rush hour bodies are wedged solid. The heat is oppressive. My ride to Inchon was not so fraught, for I was heading away from the city in late-morning. From somewhere my ears were assailed by a familiar jingle, *Frère Jacques*. The refrain intensified until, barging his way through, a lad appeared in blue overalls and peaked cap bearing a pile of newspapers. The music was emitted by a pocketed cassette-player. The choice of melody, when the boy would not have known a *dormez-vous* from a *ding-dang-dong*, seemed at the time a minor oddity. But of course the tune was incidental: it was the sound of music that signalled the approaching newspaper boy.

Shortly afterwards my ears discerned yet more distant notes. Mournful. Unlike the newsboy, their source took time to appear. The notes were produced by a beggar, with dark glasses and white stick, who shuffled along with tiny footsteps. He clutched a plastic bowl with one hand and fingered a melodica with the other. The keyboard instrument hung round his neck like a chequered bib. A few passengers stared, most pretended not to notice, and no one fed his bowl.

Two more blind beggars came through in shifts, one carriage apart. The first played a mouth organ, the second sang. An old woman played d'Artagnan to the Three Musketeers, taking up the rear when any charity on offer had assuaged itself. She knew better than to ask something for nothing. She was selling chewing gum, or hoping to. She toured the carriage placing a packet on the unprotesting knee of every seated passenger. Nobody that I could see paid any attention, far less pocketed the chewing gum. Back at her starting point she gathered up

---

[*] This list appears endless. For example: South Korea ranks 23rd in the world in terms of population, third in population density, fourth in percentage of smokers, thirteenth in the number of civilian aeroplanes, 32nd in the number of scientific theses in international journals. Unsurprisingly, in most of the figures easy to come by, South Korea's rankings improve dramatically, like a soccer team on a winning run.

the packets, hoping now and again to find a shiny coin in their place.

An unwashed woman with a babe under each arm had nothing to offer but a piece of card, which she handed out. I took one for later translation:

> I lost my husband suddenly. My family consists of three members. They tried to commit suicide many times but failed and wandered the streets. If my body was strong I would be a housekeeper or baby-sitter. To make things worse I have arthritis so cannot work hard. So I do this job. Ladies and gentlemen, please give charity to our family. Thank you.

Beggars were not the only ones seeking cash. A shirt salesman prattled noisily while hanging fabrics from strap handles, pausing for breath only to retrieve them and barge his way to the next carriage. The 'ultra-sharp scissors man' theatrically sliced up bits of paper which fluttered to the floor in his wake. I was wondering whether these vagrants and merchants had tickets when three bespectacled women and a guitar appeared. They lined up and volunteered a hymn before touring the carriage seeking donations.

Gazing through the window was for me an exercise in time travel. Though the populations of Seoul and Inchon have mushroomed since the Korean War, until the 1970s city and port remained as discrete as in Mrs Bishop's day, when the connecting road passed

> through rolling country, well cultivated. There are only two or three villages on the road, but there are many, surrounded by fruit trees, in the folds of the adjacent low hills; stunted pines abound, and often indicate places of burial. The hillsides are much taken up with graves. There are wooden sign ... posts, with grotesque human faces upon them, chiefly that of Chang Sun, a traitor, whose misdemeanours were committed 1,000 years ago. The general aspect of the country is bare and monotonous. Except for the orchards and the spindly pines, there is no wood. There is no beauty of form, nor any of those signs of exclusiveness, such as gates or walls, which give something of dignity to a landscape.

That same terrain was now one vast urban metropolis: for Tokyo-Yokohama in Japan, read Seoul-Inchon in South Korea. Isabella Bishop's 'rolling country, well cultivated' was now an ocean of apartment blocks, interspersed with traditional dwellings whose sloping roofs were packed so tightly one might conceivably tiptoe across them all the way to the horizon. The slate roofs were uniformly brown, unlike the vivid reds and blues in Japan; the curves gentler than those of China.

I alighted at Tong-Inchon (East Inchon) station to be greeted by a platform aquarium, its complement of oversized carp wriggling monotonously from end to end. Widespread as these fish tanks are, I seldom saw anyone stop to gaze or inspect. They perform the function of wallpaper, or background music. Outside the station a woman sat selling terrapins. An unkempt character in sickly green vest waddled up to me. He mumbled something while massaging his stomach. A thin stream of saliva trickled from his mouth. I shook my head and growled *'anio'* (no), whereupon he bowed, saluted, and padded to the far end of the forecourt, where he snuggled down with a liquor bottle pressed to his lips.

I found a bank to change money. The 'Welcome' mat outside the door was back to front, welcoming me as I left. Azaleas decorated the counter, while a grandfather clock stood sentry by the door. A clerk at the back appeared to be playing a harmonica. Both hands were cupped round his mouth. Only when he chanced to turn sideways did I see that the harmonica was a toothpick. The clerkesses, like other females dealing with the public (waitresses, usherettes, bus conductresses), were kitted out in blue. Their lapel badges proclaimed '3S – smile, smart, speed'. The woman attending to me had fulsome lips. With the aid of crimson lipstick she had traced within them smaller outlines, thereby creating what might be called her own *labia minoris*. She computed the exchange rates on a calculator, then, to make sure, checked the result on an abacus. My receipt was stamped with her personalised signature embedded, it seemed, on the end of a pencil.

Compared to the one million inhabitants of Inchon today, Isabella Bishop had guessed the population of Chemulpo at ten thousand; and its harbour she described as little more than a slimy mud-flat, through which passed a narrow channel. Her photographs of the harbour showed a few idle sailing craft, stripped masts leaning crazily, rickety thatched sheds lining the water's edge. What, I wondered, had become of the Chinese quarters, with its 'rows of thriving and substantial shops, busy and noisy with the continual letting off of crackers and beating of drums and gongs?' Or Steward's Inn, where Mrs Bishop took refuge? Where were the old paths and roadways where the

Chinese once dried their animal hides and stored their kerosene tins and packing cases? What became of the Japanese merchants, whose stacks of rice bags covered the beach? As for the Korean community at that time, Mrs Bishop spared them little, for they were

> of little account. The increasing native town lies outside the Japanese settlement on the Seoul road, clustering round the base of the hill on which the English church stands, and scrambling up it, mud hovels planting themselves on every ledge, attained by filthy alleys, swarming with quiet, dirty children, who look on the high-road to emulate the do-lessness of their fathers.

The harbour guard granted me entry on pain of not taking photographs. In the water sat an improbable armada of floating odds and ends, whose construction appeared to owe less to nails than to wood, rope, and a prayer. The boats were tied four deep and more, like cars quadruple-parked across a busy street. How the innermost boats were expected to reach the sea other than by levitation was a mystery. Each boat bobbed and dipped to its own rhythm, as if on some private water-bed. Fisherfolk trampled over the decks, scrambling effortlessly from one bobbing hull to another with scant regard for handrails. The ear was assailed with the sounds of boatmen at work; the rat-a-tat-tat of hammers, the swish of ropes tossed over bollards, the grinding of winches.

But Inchon serves also as a naval base. Two Tacoma-Class Fast Attack craft, each weighing 250 tons and armed with four surface-to-air launchers, lay unsmiling and smug, just a few metres from their wooden neighbours. The attack craft were in uniform, so to speak. I glanced back at the fishing vessels and wondered how many were engaged in plain clothes duties, their innards crammed not with nets and floats but with the machinery of espionage.

Somewhere along the way I picked up a companion. He looked a kid, but said he was twenty-seven and celebrating his release from military service. He insisted I call him Leonard. He was anxious to please and took to collaring hapless passers-by for information, though he soon tired of random selection in favour of attractive girls, whose assistance was nil but who nevertheless provided welcome visual distraction.

Inchon has the gradients of San Francisco. Up an incline described in the brochures as Freedom Hill, past a line of fortune tellers with their charts (face reading, marriage partners, children's names), we came upon Inchon's memorial to General MacArthur. The statue, complete with dark glasses and binoculars, stood erect upon a column. The simple inscription states: 'General of the Army – Douglas MacArthur.' Leonard was more moved than I was. His English barely exceeded survival rations, but he knew the word 'genius' and muttered it reverentially while staring up at the inert general. Before we parted I had a favour to ask of Leonard: could he help me find a shaman? Leonard hooked his little finger, meaning 'I promise'.

~

Korea is a hotchpotch of religions and ethical systems. Confucianism is a code of life rather than a religion, but is acknowledged in every act of social intercourse. It governs relationships between man and woman, old and young, teacher and pupil. The resulting social harmony accounts for the reluctance ever to appear quarrelsome or create 'bad vibes', as we might say, either among themselves or with foreigners.

Buddhism was disestablished four centuries ago. It no longer dominates Korean religious life or inspires the country's literature and architecture, though perhaps a third of the population remain practising Buddhists. Its tolerance of competing beliefs may partly account for its decline. Even so, its presence is highly visible in the form of temples and mendicants.

Christianity – Korean-style – is even more conspicuous, and is one of the remarkable phenomena of modern Korea. Special circumstances were needed for the teachings of Christ to take root in Korea, for they have fallen largely on deaf ears in China and Japan. During the Hermit Kingdom's lengthy estrangement from outside influences a few Catholic missionaries filtered through from China. Their hopes suffered bloody setbacks. These culminated in 1866 with the beheading of a number of French priests on the banks of the Han, and the subsequent execution of thousands of converts. Not until Korea formally opened her doors in the 1880s did Christian missionaries (Protestant, in the main) flood the country. They constituted the vanguard of the Western cultural invasion, for they found a people open to Western learning. Missionaries offered education to Korean girls, hitherto housebound. By sharing Koreans' antipathy towards mounting Japanese hegemony, missionaries implicitly allied themselves to Korean resistance and, by extension, the Korean national identity. The seeds so carefully laid in time bore political fruit: the Christian faith today is disproportionately espoused by Korea's rich and powerful.

Korean churches have a taste for narrow spires and huge crosses pricking the sky. Crosses also decorate residential buildings, often perched on miniature Eiffel Tower rooftop frames. At night they are lit by red neon, flaming crucifixes burning bright, transforming the Korean urban landscape into galaxies of blazing proclamation. Easy it is for the newcomer to assume Korea to be devoutly Christian. But the Korean Church enjoys a dubious reputation among non-Christians, and among some believers. Its minority Catholic wing, in particular, assimilated indigenous shamanism, with consequent mystical emphasis. The larger, evangelical oriented, Protestant church is, to its enemies, primitive and fratricidal, preoccupied with saving souls rather than relieving poverty.

There are fortunes to be made in Korean evangelicalism. From time to time fundamentalist exponents are devoured by scandal, accused of extortion, or even of inducing mass suicide among wavering believers. Predictions that the world would end in October 1992 provoked a national frenzy of contrition and preparations for Armageddon. Unscrupulous and entrepreneurial demagogues lined their pockets in the process. And though few in the West sympathise with Christianity Korean-style, the suspicion is mutual. More than once was I told: 'Western Christians are evil: they do not believe the Bible.' Korean Christians account for no more than 20% of the population, but their numbers are exaggerated by the sight of so many crosses and the sounds of so many bells.

Koreans, someone pithily observed, acknowledge Buddhism in their philosophy, Confucianism in their social arrangements, but turn to shamanism when in trouble. Twentieth century 'enlightenment' has failed to eradicate animistic nature worship, succeeding only in displacing it. Koreans, if not tourists, know where to find a shaman. As in the past, most shamans today are female. The Confucian insistence that women belong at the bottom of the social ladder encourages some to seek status through mediation with the spirit world. In this, one finds loose parallels with witchcraft in Europe. Isabella Bishop took the term 'shaman' to apply to those

whose profession it is to have direct dealings with dæmons, and to possess the power of securing their good will and averting their malignant influences by various magical rites, charms, and incantations, to cure diseases by exorcisms, to predict future events, and to interpret dreams.

She saw Korean society as bedevilled by evil spirits:

> In Korean belief, earth, air, and sea, are peopled by dæmons. They haunt every umbrageous tree, shady ravine, crystal spring, and mountain crest. On green hill slopes, in peaceful agricultural valleys, in grassy dells, on wooded uplands, by lake and stream, by road and river, in north, south, east, and west they abound, making malignant sport out of human destinies. They are on every roof, ceiling, fireplace, kang and beam. They fill the chimney, the shed, the living room, the kitchen – they are on every shelf and jar. In thousands they waylay the traveller as he leaves his home, beside him, behind him, dancing in front of him, whirring over his head, crying out upon him from earth, air, and water ... Every Korean home is subject to dæmons, here, there, and everywhere. They touch the Korean at every point in life, making his well-being depend on a continual series of acts of propitiation, and they avenge every omission with merciless severity, keeping him under this yoke of bondage from birth to death.

I presented myself at Tongnimmun (Independence Gate) station at 6 as arranged. It was a squally evening and blasts of air whooshed down the subway steps behind me. Such is the weight of Seoul's vast population that the city's rush-hours are only marginally rushier than other hours. I tucked myself out of the crush under an awning, next to a man selling disposable umbrellas from a cardboard box. Take a length of bamboo, wrap red tape around the handle and attach blue translucent plastic to twig-like spokes and you conjure a serviceable rain shelter that sells for a few *won* and which with the onset of each summer shower decorates Seoul with innumerable squirts of blue.

Engrossed with my new purchase I missed the approach of Leonard's contact. A besuited figure stepped forward, hand extended. We battled our way against the prevailing current of homeward-bound humanity until we found an alley quiet enough to permit introductions. Initial exchanges followed the familiar pattern. His name was Mr Kim and he was forty, ten years older than I would have guessed, leading me to postulate a '+10 years' theorem for determining Korean ages. I reeled off Section 1 of my résumé – '*yong-guk saram imnida*' (I am British), plus my age, and instinctively braced myself for the next question.

'You marry?'

This question invariably embarrassed me. To Korean perceptions, only a seriously flawed adult of my vintage could be unmarried. I was still single, and therefore undoubtedly suspect. My safest option was to say yes, my wife was back in Britain with our six sons. Such an answer would have endowed me with honourable status in Korean eyes.

'No I am not married,' I said, as I always did. His jaw slackened, his eyes stared.

'No marry? Why no marry?' This from a person I had first set eyes upon barely a minute earlier. I could have resorted to a tactical retreat. Mitigating circumstances. I could plead I was a widower, or was still searching for the right woman, or that in the West marriage was no longer necessarily the done thing. Any suggestion that marriage might not be compatible with personal freedom would have been incomprehensible to a Korean. I toyed with my bamboo umbrella as the spats of rain amplified into a deluge.

'I'm still looking,' I said, 'but it is hard to find a wife when I am always travelling.' I side-stepped my predicament with a swift counter-attack.

'What about you, how many children do you have?' Mr Kim smiled weakly:

'Three. Three daughters.' His eyes hung on mine as if to detect ridicule. Having no sons was clearly worse than having no wife. The one was personal choice; the other was unfilial and showed divine disfavour. Not so long ago failure to produce a son was considered grounds for divorce in Korea, for daughters were nothing but a capital outlay. And *three* of them! Koreans say that such triple folly will topple the pillars of the home. My host carried his evident shame with dignity. We stepped back on to the street, into a maelstrom of aggressively mobile bodies. Seoulites work hard and play hard. Their 9-10 hour stint in office or factory was over for the day and now they could unwind. The alcohol would soon flow, the inhibitions would slip away, and Seoul would get sloshed.

Mr Kim and I had other business. The skies darkened and thundered as we battled our way through the crush. Ahead loomed two of Seoul's lumpy hills – on the left the bleak slopes of Ansan, on the right, Inwangsan. It was up Inwangsan that we trekked, via a narrow, steep path flanked by cramped houses jammed so tightly it was impossible to determine where the one ended and the next began. Buildings fossilised into one another with the passage of time, like a mouth with a thousand teeth. It was hard to believe that one of Seoul's main thoroughfares sprawled beneath us. It was as if someone had pulled the light-switch and turned off the sound.

A man stepped from his gate and stopped dead:

'Hi!' he cried. 'What are you doing here? We don't see many foreigners in this part of the city.'

My escort knew only the probable vicinity of a shaman. He followed the gesticulating fingers of helpful locals until the last houses had gone and the bare, rocky approaches to the summit beckoned. At length we entered a kind of forecourt, the far side enclosed by a natural rock wall. The building that confronted me was not, apparently, a temple, but a shrine. It had been moved here by the Japanese in 1925. Upon this spot witches and shamans were said to have performed exorcisms and held religious services for national peace and prosperity. From the outside the building looked like any other Korean temple, with its tiled roof and vividly coloured exterior. Rust-red columns supported the eaves, with gargoyle-like monsters leering down from on high.

Had I troubled to look closely into Mr Kim's eyes I might have perceived his misgivings. I was aware only of a slight hesitancy when he mounted the steps to the shrine, removed his shoes and stepped over the threshold. It was the dimly lit interior that distinguished the building from a Buddhist temple. Fading portraits hung from the walls, sepia images of bygone centuries. Candelabra, dusty books and ceramic statuettes stood on dark wooden trunks around the walls. Bells hung from wooden beams traversing the ceiling. The beams were daubed with loud colours, like the totem poles of the North American Indian. Two anterooms led off from the main chamber. As for the altar, Isabella Bishop had forewarned me what to expect:

The space in front was matted and enclosed with rice cakes, boiled rice, stewed chicken, sprouted beans and other delicacies. In this open space squatted three old women, two of them beat large drums, shaped like hour-glasses, while the third clashed large cymbals. Facing them was the mu-tang or sorceress, dressed in rose-pink silk, with a buff gauze robe, with its sleeves trailing much on the ground over it. Pieces of paper resembling the Shinto gohei decorated her hair, and a curious cap of buff gauze with red patches on it completed the not inelegant costume. She carried a fan, but it was only used occasionally in one of the dances. She carried over her left shoulder a stick, painted with bands of bright colours, from which hung a gong which she beat with a similar stick, executing at the same time a slow rhythmic movement accompanied by a chant. From time to time one of the ancient drummers gathered on one plate pieces of all the others and scattered them to the four winds for the spirits to eat, invoking them, saying 'Do not trouble this house any more, and we will again appease you by offerings.'

A comparable sight greeted me, with the addition of four tall, lighted candles standing guard over a roasted pig's head and bowls of apples and black grapes. Plumes of incense wafted upwards.

Mrs Bishop had been privy to an exorcism (*kut*). It was not unusual she said for a *mutang* to work herself 'into such a delirious frenzy that she falls down foaming at the mouth, and death is the occasional result'.

As we noiselessly settled ourselves on the floor Mr Kim, his voice as hesitant as his manner, whispered that we were witnessing an initiation, the graduation of a new shaman. On no account could I take pictures.

The cigarette that dangled from her mouth deprived the older shaman a little of her mystique. Her hair was parted in the middle and tied in a bun. She was a whirl of reds and greens, twirling a piece of cloth in one hand and brandishing a fan in the other.

Whether the musical accompaniment directed the *mutang's* cavortings or responded to them I could not tell. An old man in civvies blew into a thin bamboo pipe (*piri*) with double-reed mouthpiece, the effect of which was to make ear-splitting squeaks not dissimilar to those produced when blowing between the thumbs upon a stretched blade of grass. It was not so much a tune as a series of disconnected notes in more or less even time. The percussion was an hour-glass, two-sided drum (*changgo*) struck with a bent stick like half a stethoscope. Cymbals completed the trio.

The neophyte was even more exotically attired than the shaman, with billowing striped sleeves of purple, green, yellow, blue and white. Of the twenty persons present, the shamans alone were in costume.

As the music quickened and the shaman's bouncing grew ever more frantic the younger woman lifted her apron and received into it with a shovelling motion invisible offerings from her elder. A lighted taper was stuck through the pig's nostril. The gathering was silent, attentive, and respectful as the shamans seized a scarf at each end and tore it asunder. The older woman lit a scrap of paper and after waving it furiously above her head stepped to the open door and flung it outside, either to cast out unwelcome spirits or because it was about to burn her fingers.

The show was over. The shamans disappeared to discard their costumes, leaving the musicians and hangers-on to pack everything away, including the food. As none had been consumed, apart from that upon which the invoked spirit had presumably partaken, this took some time. The pig's head was rudely dumped into a cardboard box, and the lavishly decorated cakes hastily wrapped in foil and squeezed inside a cake tin. Someone picked up a broom to sweep up the crumbs.

It is customary in the healing arts of magic for a portion of the sacrificial feast to be offered to the afflicted, but I was not expecting a bowl of succulent grapes to be placed before me. No one else was offered anything. My instinct was to eat, both because the grapes looked inviting and because I was loath to give offence, particularly on an occasion such as this. I reached towards the grapes, only to have my wrist grabbed with unexpected force by Mr Kim. I threw him a puzzled look and saw alarm in his eyes.

'Over and out,' he hissed, in a comical gesture of finality. He motioned me outside. We put on our shoes and moved away. Behind the shrine a rocky path led yet higher up the exposed slopes of Inwangsan. From his drooping head and fidgety manner I sensed an explanation was coming. In his own time.

High above Seoul the wind gusted angrily, protean thunder-clouds squalling across the evening sky. Driving rain sandpapered the cheeks. Near a Buddhist grotto illuminated by flickering candles two squatting women fingered beads and mumbled incantations at inscriptions daubed upon a rock face. Further up the mountain two other women scrubbed pots and pans and tried to press upon me bits of cake 'for good luck'. So many faiths staking their claim for a share of Inwangsan's holiness.

Mr Kim was ready to explain. He was suspicious, he said. Like many Koreans he could not help believing in shamanism. His country, he admitted, was tolerant on matters of religion. There was no alternative: three or four deities may be worshipped within a single family. His own was an example. He proclaimed himself a Christian haunted by the ghostly presence of his grandmother. We sheltered behind a deserted temple daubed with tiger images while he gathered his thoughts.

She was not his true grandmother, for his father had been an adopted child. She had professed to be a 'Buddhist nun'. The words were spat out as if concealing an obvious subterfuge. *Not all Buddhist nuns are what they seem, you know.* She had died during the Korean War, inside a Buddhist temple.

Two men came to shelter near us. By the time the wind had relented sufficiently to tempt them back outside, Mr Kim had grown more composed. Despite his Christian faith, he said, Buddhists were to be admired because their beliefs were rational and their lifestyle disciplined. But shamanism was neither rational nor disciplined. For reasons he could not explain he was sure his grandmother had been a *mutang* – a sorceress. Again he paused, as if expecting a contemptuous riposte.

Mr Clive had to understand that even today many Koreans believe their lives to be controlled by the spirits of their ancestors. He, Mr Kim, could not rid himself of the fear that his grandmother's spirit somehow influenced his.

But what had that to do with his reactions at the shrine? That evening, he explained, a shaman had consecrated food to the spirit world. That food had accordingly, for good or ill, been exposed to the spirits. He would therefore have put himself at risk if he ate it.

But no one had asked him to eat the grapes. Why had he stopped me doing so?

He had not meant to. It was the proximity of spirit-contaminated food that had alarmed him. It was himself that he was afraid for.

Why, then, if he harboured such fears did he volunteer to bring me? Had he never attended a shaman shrine before?

No, he hadn't. This was the first time he had knowingly come near a shaman. It was his courage he had wanted to test. He had been happy to escort me, observe with me, translate for me, but on no account would he participate. He never said as much, but I guessed he held his grandmother responsible for his lack of sons.

It was dark by this time, and the wind threatened our footholds on the exposed rock. The noise and neon of the street seemed all the more contrived when set against the dark sky and dark secrets of Inwangsan. I hoped I had not in any way angered the mountain's spirits, though I fear I had, for on descending a flight of rock steps I lost my footing and slithered a dozen steps until coming to rest against a tree. Bruised buttocks were the price I paid to Inwangsan's aggrieved gods.

~

I was soon to leave Seoul for the Korean interior and required a better map than the tourist map freely available. Its scale was 1:1 million and its makers had never heard of the Korean War. You'd think, from the map, that Korea was still undivided. There was no hint of any demilitarised zone (DMZ). I appeared free to stroll northwards, whistling a happy tune, until I chanced upon a land-mine.

Chatting to some students, I'd asked about the missing demarcation. It was not deception, they insisted. It was a matter of security. Also, it was an armistice line, not a legal frontier. The division of Korea had not been sanctioned by treaty. I had already observed newspapers' habit of speaking of 'north' rather than 'North' Korea, as if the distinction was a mere matter of geography. Germany, I was reminded, had known only seventy-odd years of unity before 1945, and embraced various ethnic minorities. Korea had been unified for thirteen centuries before the Japanese annexation, and remained racially homogenous. No pockets of aliens hid themselves away, speaking their own language or following their own customs. The division of the country, I was assured, would never be accepted by Koreans, from north or south.

The students directed me to a map shop. But none of the specimens I examined acknowledged the DMZ, leaving me ignorant of where I could or could not go. I was standing at the counter bemoaning the fact when in walked a tallish, grey-haired Korean in yellow flowery shirt. He struck up an instant conversation and was, as Paul Simon might say, a Most Peculiar Man. Not frightening, but undeniably odd. Within minutes he offered to accommodate me for as long as I remained in Seoul.

'The government tells us to be kind to foreigners,' he said.

Despite, or perhaps because of, his oddity I had no thought to refuse, though finding his address required the help of the local constabulary. Korean houses are not numbered sequentially but chronologically – the oldest No 1, the next No 2, and so on, irrespective of their relative positions.

Eyeing my rucksack and deciding it was too heavy for me to carry, a policeman to whom I had showed the address tried to hail a cab. It was the evening rush-hour and all were taken. Although prohibited, doubling-up remained commonplace, drivers stopping for a second, or third fare heading in the same direction and pocketing the full amount from each. Unable to procure an empty cab the policeman hijacked an occupied one. I was not reassured by the 'Best Driver' sign on the roof. Few of my cat's lives remained by the journey's end, leaving me grateful it was not approaching midnight, when taxi-drivers drive even more maniacally in their urge to drop you off before the stroke of 12. From midnight until 4 they operate a 20% surcharge, and resent every second spent on hire at the cheaper rate. As it happened, I was lucky to find a cab at all, for drivers stop for whom they please, and foreigners appear not to please them.

The building to which the cab driver pointed left me suspecting a practical joke. Knowing the sky-high value of real-estate in Seoul, and the cramped conditions of even the most comfortable households, the spacious complex of buildings, out-houses and gardens that confronted me spoke of uncommon affluence.

I banged on the door, half-expecting a penguin-suited butler to open it. Instead, it was the man himself. He introduced himself as Mr Chung. With a wave of his arm he ushered me inside. I unthinkingly slipped off my shoes, only for my host to insist that I put them on again. 'It is more sensible,' he said. 'Taking shoes off, putting them on, taking them off, is very silly.'

I wouldn't have taken him seriously, were he not also wearing shoes indoors. In Korea the practice of removing shoes in homes is automatic. Rather than attend to laces few people bother to untie them. Shoes are kicked off when arriving and trodden into when leaving, heels permanently flattened, footwear reduced to flip-flops. Most households provide visitors with slippers. As for being 'silly', my host evidently preferred the Western habit of happily treading dirt and filth and animal excrement into carpets.

Though I never learned the source of his income, Mr Chung volunteered that he was worth 'seven million American dollars.' He eschewed extravagance. He was wearing the same shirt and grimy off-white trousers as when I'd met him some days earlier. And the 'guest room' was little bigger than a broom cupboard, without even a curtain for privacy. There was just room enough beside the thin mattress for a mosquito coil and a box of Korean matches, the size of a small toolbox, with the matches stacked vertically, heads uppermost. Peeling off the lid was to confront the helmeted heads of a miniature terra-cotta army.

The house had a single toilet. The oriental squat-down variety is rapidly being displaced in most Korean habitats. Westernisation had pervaded Mr Chung's life in most respects, but not in the matter of his bodily functions. His toilet was a straightforward hole in the ground, six feet deep. Not only was there no seat, there was no flushing mechanism either. To save expense on water, he switched it off from the mains.

We sat drinking lemonade in chintz-covered armchairs in an untidy lounge shorn of Korean fittings. He evidently shared my dislike for small-talk, for he soon raised the conversational tempo.

'I am a liberal,' he declared, as I put down my glass. We had hitherto been discussing plane schedules.

'Oh, really?'

'Yes. I should like to see compulsory birth-control introduced in Korea.'

'Compulsory?' I challenged, 'surely that is not particularly liberal.'

'It must be compulsory. The people have no sense if left to themselves.'

'Are you referring to all people?'

'No, not all people. It is imperative that well-educated people have more children. This is their social responsibility, for Korea's greatest asset is her educated manpower. But poorly educated people should not have any children. This is a social, not a biological, point. It is only well-educated people who know the importance of educating their children.'

I knew better than to risk showing dissent. Questions of *kibun*, or mood, govern Korean relationships. One must avoid loss of face. The only shame equal to losing it is to cause it in another. I did not dare attempt to undermine Mr Chung's argument, for should I win the argument I would lose his respect.

He was unmarried and had no family, further reasons to alienate him from this socially rigid society. No family, but he had a god-son, the child of a neighbour. The little brat came in at that moment. Six years old, spoiled to death, and arrogant to the point of insufferability. He was carrying some plastic bags which he proceeded to empty on the rug; toy racing car, cap pistol, chocolate sandwich cake, and various comics.

'Oh, look at him,' beamed the millionaire, placing his hand on the boy's head and twirling his hair. 'He just goes out and spends all my money. Such initiative, and he knows exactly what to buy. Last week I took him to a department store to buy a new outfit. He listened to the assistant's suggestions and said: "No, I don't want that. I want this, and this and this." So independent. What a boy!'

Mr Chung had high hopes for the child. 'He will become a world leader one day, believe me.'

I looked down as the latent Mahatma Gandhi, cum Saddam Hussein, cum Kurt Waldheim rolled his toy car hard against the millionaire's ankle. He didn't wince, just patted the boy's back and repeated: 'Yes, I have great hopes for him.'

I had fewer hopes, but did not say so. From his shirt pocket the millionaire extricated a calling card which he handed me. Korean society has become so stratified as a result of Confucian insistence that someone is always superior to someone else, that upon first acquaintance people never know how to address one another. The simplest Korean sentence may be uttered in half a dozen ways, from ultra submissive to ultra contemptuous, depending on the perceived standing of the parties.

Business cards help solve the problem. By revealing job titles and the like, the pecking order can be ascertained without the need for delicate probing and stiff formalities.

'Don't laugh,' he said, as I examined the card.

Don't laugh – that most English of expressions, wrapping within its nuances false modesty, confiding intimacy, anticipation of ridicule. But there was nothing to laugh at. The card (Korean on one side, English on the other) simply offered his name, address and, as was increasingly popular, his photograph.

'What do you mean, don't laugh?'

'The card! The quality is dreadful. The print is not level, some letters are capitals and others are not, some are bold and others faint. This is the problem with Korea. And when I complain they say I am fussy. Next time I will have my cards printed in India.'

He got to his feet. 'Tomorrow I will show you the city.' As if reading my pained vision of more palaces and museums he added: 'Do not worry, you are not a tourist now.'

He woke me at 8, looming in my broom cupboard with a tray, on which was an omelette, some buttered toast and a pot of jam. Not only was he without family, he now confirmed he had no helpers to manage his estate. I thought fleetingly of Castle Dracula, and its solitary sinister occupant, making beds, preparing meals and driving carriages for his unsuspecting guest.

The millionaire's carriage was a battered Hyundai, a product of one of Korea's heavy industry corporations which lend their names to everything from ships to automobiles. Korean roads are largely free from foreign threat due to the domestic oligarchy of Hyundai, Daewoo, and Kia. (Japanese cars were banned until 1988.)

Mr Chung did not smoke, but a previous passenger had left an empty cigarette packet on the dashboard. The back was decorated with a colour photograph of a small child, accompanied by personal details.

'Missing children,' Mr Chung explained. The child staring out in red jumper had disappeared on 30 May 1987. How children could 'disappear' in Korea and later be found was beyond Mr Chung's comprehension. Nor was it possible to check the success rate of the cigarette-packet campaign. The Korean tobacco industry is still owned by the state, as in the days of the Japanese. Government control of tobacco goes some way to explaining Korea's half-hearted anti-smoking campaigns. In effect, smokers are encouraged to buy more cigarettes in order to publicise more disappearances. Shortening some lives to rescue others: it had a distinct oriental circularity.*

Cruising through the traffic, Mr Chung began reminiscing about his early life and World War II. Born in 1930, he had been too young to work in Japanese mines or be conscripted into the Japanese army. Instead he had been compelled to perform hard labour, carting rocks on his back from dawn till dusk. It was the cold he remembered most. He gave an involuntary shiver as he recalled the thin fabric of his clothes and the rice-paper doors and windows of his home. His animus had not receded with the years. I said I had found modern Japan the least militaristic of nations, due largely to their experience of two atomic bombs. Mr Chung was unimpressed.

'They should repent, not resent, militarism.'

He was a kind but embittered man who, I noticed, had yet to say a good word about Korea or her people. He had once sought assistance in running his property and handling his correspondence, but found that those he employed had wanted to be 'spoon-fed'. He felt constantly let down by their inefficiency and lack of courtesy. He looked in his rear-view mirror, then over his shoulder, and tried to switch lanes.

'Look at this. I'm indicating left but they refuse to let me over.' He wasn't given to swearing, just muttering, as if sharing profound intimacies.

'You sound disillusioned,' I said. He didn't know the word, and had me explain and repeat it, while he practised it under his breath. A summer storm suddenly unleashed itself.

'Maybe god is angry with Korea,' he suggested. Through the spattered windscreen he directed my attention to an artificial waterfall by the roadside.

'This is an important highway. So what do they do? They build a concrete waterfall to impress the tourists. And where do they build it? On a sharp bend in the road! Drivers are distracted by the waterfall and

---

* Missing children are advertised in Korea by various means. I have before me a telephone card displaying the faces of five boys missing for over a year since disappearing while on their way home from school in Taegu.

cause many crashes. And see those gasometers? The only reason they built them so near the airport was to impress foreigners that Korea is a civilised country that uses gas and not firewood. That is the type of government we have.'

By now the rain was so heavy as to defeat the wipers. Traffic had slowed to a crawl, for which the rain was only indirectly responsible. I could make out a bridge ahead. There was a hold-up underneath, caused by two trucks sheltering side by side from the downpour. Only the outermost lane was passable. The driver of one of the parked trucks was grappling with an uncooperative tarpaulin, single-handedly trying to protect his load of dissolving vegetables. The other driver stayed put in his cab, staring out at the black clouds, oblivious to the lengthening, honking queues behind him. This was the *coup de grace* Mr Chung needed; first-hand evidence of Korean primitiveness.

'Do truck drivers in England or America hide from the rain and block freeways like this? Yes, I am much … dis-ill-u-sioned.'

3

A FRIEND FOR LIFE
Trains and Boats and Rains

Ka-pyöng ... is a good specimen of the small towns in the Han
valley. It is on the verge of an alluvial plain, rolling up to picturesque hills, gashed by valleys, abounding in hamlets surrounded
by chestnut groves and careful cultivation. The slopes above Ka-
pyöng break up into knolls richly wooded with conifers and hard-
wood trees, fringing off into clumps and groups which would not
do discredit to the slopes of Windsor ... Boats were being built
and great quantities of the strong rope used for towing and other
purposes, which is made from a 'creeper' which grows profusely
in Central Korea, were awaiting water carriage. Yet Ka-pyöng,
like other small Korean towns, has no life or go. Its 'merchants'
are but peddlers, its commercial ideas do not rise above those of
the huckster.

Isabella Bishop – *Korea and her Neighbours* – (1898)

SOUTH KOREA – properly speaking the Republic of Korea (ROK)
– occupies an area of 38,000 square miles. She is often likened
in size to Portugal or Iceland. A more helpful comparison is
with Ireland. The Irish Republic and Ulster combined are marginally smaller than South Korea, but with a similar silhouette. Both
landmasses are broadly rhomboid. Their eastern shorelines run southwards to Wexford and Pusan respectively, before tilting west by south-
west to their southernmost extremities. Both western coasts are heavily
indented with bays and inlets. The DMZ travels east by north-east, as
does the crow flying from Mayo to Antrim.

South Korea's shape encourages circular exploration. Seoul lies in
the north-west corner. The only question for me was whether to head
east and clockwise, or south and anti-clockwise. In view of the damp
heat of high summer it made sense to delay my southward excursion. I
decided to head east. First stop would be Chunchon, sixty miles from
Seoul.

I had been warned against travelling at weekends, when the capital depopulated itself in search of fresh air and exercise. It was Saturday morning, and the subway was sardine-canned with prospective hikers and trekkers decked out in knee breeches, climbing boots and colourful segmented sunhats. The waiting room and ticket windows at Seoul's Chongnyangni station were located at opposite ends of a vast forecourt. Passengers were permitted to enter the station only at departure time, there to keep company with the aquarium until the guard granted access to the platform.

Swarms of young hikers piled aboard the train. The easy mixing of sexes and the loud portable stereos told that their guiding star rose from the West. It was wise to reserve seats. Otherwise one stood – as I did. There was no space for a mobile snack trolley, but a coffee lady suddenly broke through, manoeuvring a large flask on two wheels, like a junior golfer's bag. She was followed by the conductor. I recognised him by his bright red armband which bore the two distinct words 'Conduct' and 'or'.

At the small town of Kapyong a seat beckoned and I was able to gaze out upon a soothing landscape. I rummaged in my bag to see if Isabella Bishop had ventured hereabouts. She had. The single-track railway flanked the northern branch of the Han, the river having forked east of the capital. It had taken Isabella Bishop two days to reach that fork, and a further two, by water, before she reached

> the beautifully situated town of Ka-pyöng, which straggles along the valley of a small tributary of the Han on slopes backed by high mountains which, following the usual Korean custom, are without names. The bright green of the wheat fields, varied by the darker green of clumps of conifers and chestnuts, arranged as if by a landscape gardener, and the lines of trees along the river bank were enchanting, but Ka-pyöng does not bear close inspection.

Protected by my wall of glass I could detect no smell of chestnuts. As in Seoul, the Han was the colour of molasses, muddied by summer rains. The train rattled over a short bridge, beneath which, at the mouth of a tiny tributary, a farmer crouched, fully clothed, pouring water over himself with his brimmed hat. An old couple pottered by a corrugated iron shack miraculously supported by an overhanging rock.

The train was slowing. The hills were gentler now, able to support terraced rice paddies. Isabella Bishop had described Chunchon, my first destination, as comprising three hundred men at arms garrisoned among a population of just three thousand. Nearly a century later the military presence – lookout towers and armed guards – was still in evidence. But judging from its crazy-golf courses and tennis courts, Chunchon had clearly diversified into a resort centre. Guns and games in tandem.

A tourist map dominated Chunchon Station's forecourt. It was the size of a cricket screen, like those I would find in other resorts. A line of taxis stretched up the road, their drivers huddled in idle chitchat. Perceiving a lone foreigner they wasped around the honey-pot, fingers thrust at the cricket screen and then at their cars. The honey-pot took to its heels.

It was blisteringly hot, the sky an unsmudged blue. The road into town was sandwiched between camouflaged fuel tanks and the perimeter fence of Camp Page, which like all American military bases lives a phantom existence off the map. The wire fence stretched endlessly, yet no trooper or mechanic could be seen, just a huddle of helicopters, hellish grey with rotor blades limp and lifeless, like the skeletons of huge vultures decomposing under a scorching sun.

I needed somewhere to stay. In Seoul I had been passed from contact to contact and was never further than a phone-call from assistance. Now I was very much on my own. I had been surprised by the number of Seoulites who spoke English, but I was not prepared to bank on such help out here. All I had to assist me was a precautionary list of written questions, translated into Korean, of the form *please help me find this or that*.

Isabella Bishop had had no choice on where to bed down, and had not always been favourably impressed by Korean hostelry:

The inn, if inn it was, gave me a room 8 feet by 6, and 5 feet 2 inches high. Ang-paks, for it was the family granary, iron shoes of ploughs and spades, bundles of foul rags, seaweed, ears of millet hanging in bunches from the roof, pack-saddles, and worse than all else, rotten beans fermenting for soy, and malodorous half-salted fish, just left room for my camp-bed. This den opened on a vile yard, partly dunghill and partly pig-pen, in which is the well from which the women of the house, with sublime sang-froid, draw the drinking water! Outside is a swamp, which throughout the night gave off sickening odours. Every few minutes something was wanted from my room, and as there was not room for two, I had every time to go out into the yard. Wong's good-night was, 'I hope you won't die.' When I entered the mercury was 87°. After that, cooking for man and beast and the kang floor raised it to 107°, at which point it stood till morning, vivifying into revoltingly active life myriads of cockroaches and vermin which revel in heat, not to speak of rats, which ran over my bed, ate my candle, gnawed my straps, and would have left me without boots, had I not long beforehand learned to hang them from the tripod of my camera.

Korean hostels are typically of two kinds: *yogwans* the more comfortable, *yoinsooks* the more basic. As yet I knew not how to recognise either establishment, nor what constituted comfortable or basic. I fetched the appropriate note from my pocket and thrust it into the face of a passer-by, who stroked his chin, then pointed across at a square building undistinguished in every way. I followed his finger and strode inside.

'*Adjima*,' I called out. (Korean women above a certain age are addressed as *adjima*. It translates roughly as 'auntie'. Younger, unmarried women are termed '*agassi*', pronounced as for the 1992 Wimbledon tennis champion). A woman appeared and showed me a standard hotel room with bed. This I declined in favour of a bedless, Korean-style room next door. I cleaned myself up and took a stroll to the waterside. Chunchon owes its military and leisure value to its strategic and scenic location by a river junction. South Korea has erected memorials to the sixteen nations who fought on her behalf under the flag of the United Nations. That for Ethiopia is in Chunchon, next to an up-market coffee shop known as Ethiopia House. It was late-August, and the tourist season already seemed dead. Nobody bought from the women attending the ice cream carts by the marina; there was no one around to buy. But I took my chance at one of the kerbside gaming tables, throwing darts at a revolving wheel for cigarette prizes. The waterside was dotted with candy-striped-roofed floating cafes, devoid of customers. Swan-shaped paddle boats, secured one to another like kite tails, swirled off into mid-channel.

Children scampered to a patch of wasteland commandeered as an impromptu fairground. They were attracted by a miniature Big Wheel, ten feet high and with space for just six seats. It was attached to a trolley and turned by hand. The operator was an old man, an urban nomad, who harnessed the Wheel to his shoulder and worked the streets in search of custom. His friend operated a rocking-horse frame, like a mobile bicycle shed. Youngsters gee-upped their steers, bulls, and camels, urged on by the Korean musical equivalent of *The Lone Ranger* from a cassette player powered by a twelve volt car battery.

Adult street games were more cerebral. Old and older men huddled over their *paduk* ('Go' in Japanese) boards, tossed dice in the form of *yut* sticks, or played *hwa-too* (otherwise known as Go-Stop), with tiny playing cards. These cards depict flowers or shrubs – orchids, irises, maples – and are slapped noisily upon the playing surface. Such games are played anywhere, in doorways, on waste ground, inside stalls after trading hours, or, just as likely, on the pavement, the players oblivious to pedestrians having to step into the road to pass by.

Elsewhere I was distracted by the snick of bat on ball. The sound emanated from a baseball practice court, wire-caged and fully auto-mated. By inserting a 100-*won* coin into a slot, aspiring Babe Ruths are permitted ten swipes with an aluminium bat at softballs hurled from a self-loading catapult. Youths dropped in for a spot of macho exercise, dreaming of the big time, each successful swipe eliciting a smirk of manhood.

The following day I hoped to take a river-boat to Inje. Assuming that was possible. But how to find out? I extracted my notepad and sketched a sailing boat on rippling water, alongside INJE in bold letters. I was wandering around the bus terminal, wondering to whom I should exhibit my artwork, when up stepped the same young man who had found me the *yogwan*. He stood before me, smiling shyly with arms stiff by his side. I handed him my diagram. He reached out and helped himself to the pen poking out from my shirt pocket. *Perfectly normal, reaching into other people's pockets*. He wrote English better than he spoke it, and we conducted a merry conversation via my notepad, passing it from one to the other in full view of the bus station's bemused passengers.

My new friend wished to introduce himself. He scrawled his name in large wobbly letters. He was Mr Kim. Another one. He was twenty-seven, unmarried and lived in Seoul. He might have told me his life story but I was fast running out of notepad: he liked a clean page for each message, irrespective of its brevity.

He went and fetched the sailing times I needed, then pointed to himself. He wished to accompany me. Not content with that, he wanted to pay. He dragged a fistful of notes from his pocket and waved them under my nose. He turned a fresh page in my notepad and wrote: 'I want Mr Clive with tour.' On yet another page he scribbled the single word 'Pay'.

The prospect of a day out with Mr Clive seemed to excite him greatly. He jumped up and down, and after arranging to meet at my *yogwan* at noon the next day he turned and sped down the street like some little boy desperate to share his joy with his mother.

~

At nightfall I wandered out in search of dinner. I'd only gone a few yards when I was overtaken by a sporty young man in red vest, outsize rucksack on his back and beads of sweat dripping from his nose. His right hand worked a springy hand-strengthener.

'I want talk with you,' he growled. It was his way of saying hello. He'd hiked all the way from the east coast and had tigers on his mind.

'Where are tigers in England? In London? In palace of queen?'

I told him we had no tigers. He gave me a withering look as if to say that's what you think. He insisted I eat with him, and we found an upstairs restaurant by the market. He too saw nothing amiss in reaching into my breast pocket, from where a small map protruded.

'You spare time, you spare time?' he asked. He was seeking some English practice. I gave him an hour before heading for the bright lights around Camp Page. Near the main gates and up a darkened flight of stairs I discovered the Seven Club. The music could be heard in the street, yet the club was almost empty. A solitary pool table sat marooned in the centre. The dance floor danced with itself under the flashing lights. A couple of GIs slouched against a wall. I crossed to the bar and was swooped upon by a swish of yellow. There beside me, materialising as from nowhere, was a long-haired Korean beauty. She favoured a lemon, sleeveless dress, and eyed me up like I was Clark Gable.

Hostesses in Korea, as everywhere, existed purely to lubricate the flow of cash. Pockets that were not deep were not welcome. Mine were not deep. When all you wanted was a quiet drink, the presence of these hostesses could be irritating, not to say expensive. I bought a beer to test the prices and drank from the bottle as no glass was provided. Beer came late to Korea, via the Japanese early this century. There exist two indigenous brands – OB (Oriental Breweries) and Crown. Most establishments serve one or the other. To the non-connoisseur, OB and Crown are not dissimilar, though each claims its loyal adherents. 'Crown too much f-f-f-filtered, too much viscosity,' Mr Ock had earlier informed me.

The hostess clicked her fingers to the barmaid, who poured her an iced tea.

'Hi, I'm Mimi,' she said. She'd obviously seen too many films about Pacific islanders in grass skirts, picking on a name like that. Nothing seemed to me less Korean than Mimi. (In this I was mistaken. The character 'Mi' appears in several Korean names: the equivalent Chinese character means 'beautiful'.)

'What made you choose Mimi?' I asked. She didn't answer, but rolled the cogs of her brain forward to the next question.

'Where are you from?'

How easy it is for women to ridicule male chat-up lines. Mimi was not above needing some lessons in originality, but then she had the looks to compensate.

'You are from England? Oh, how wonderful. You are English gentleman.'

I don't know where Koreans learned about gentlemanly Englishmen, but flattery would get her nowhere if she hoped to refill my glass.

'What do you do? Really? You are astronaut who went to the moon? No, I only work here part time. I am student: I major in English literature.'

Her English was good, but then it would be if she worked in a GI bar. Her face, however, retained traces of innocence and naïveté, not like some of the hostesses I would meet later. Mimi was less assured when the conversation turned to her.

'Why do you do this, encouraging men to buy you marked-up drinks that you don't want and they can't afford?' She was not programmed to deal with that kind of question and she fell silent. She had twice asked me to 'have another'. I had successfully changed the subject each time, and now she asked no more. A GI sauntered over for a refill: 'and one for the lady,' he suffixed his order. I drank up my OB and left, kissing the back of Mimi's hand in mock imitation of an English gentleman.

Approaching the town centre an elderly man scuttled by clutching a handkerchief to his nose and mouth. Then two youths similarly distressed. Heavy pollen-count perhaps. Suddenly my eyes began to smart, as if from a whiff of ammonia. I noticed a policeman ahead. Then another beyond him. Then police cars. Ahead in the darkness I perceived what looked like shapeless sacks crawling over one another in the road.

The sacks transformed into fifty uniformed riot police. They lay on the ground, relaxing, smoking, laughing. They had removed their nightmarish Darth Vadar helmets, built with rubberised neck protectors and proboscis gas masks. It was this outlandish headgear that lent the riot police such notoriety on television newsreels.

I felt conspicuous and vulnerable in the midst of this show of state force. I had ignored a warning by my sweaty young companion earlier in the evening to stay indoors tonight. Through a slobbery mouthful of eel he had warned of demonstrations to coincide with the funeral of a car worker killed by a tear-gas canister. I promised I would be careful, but inwardly had pooh-poohed the prospect of foreigners being targeted at times of public disorder. Besides, in matters of personal danger instinct and intuition weigh more heavily than the warnings of well-meaning acquaintances. I had never felt threatened in Korea. No doubt there would be no trouble, but if I was mistaken I did not wish to miss it.

Or so I had thought. Courage is so easy in the abstract. I no longer felt quite so cock-sure. I approached a policeman, megaphone dangling from his hand, and learned that a student/worker demonstration had been broken up in the past hour. But more trouble was possible. The tear-gas had dissipated sufficiently to permit the riot police to unmask themselves. But it had been my first exposure, and I was not anxious to experience a second. I pondered whether to move closer or stay out of sight.

Korean riot police are mostly conscripts, an option for young men undertaking their military service. Ironically, this means student demonstrators being baton-charged by units of fellow students, classroom pals temporarily on opposing sides of the barricades.

The recurring image of South Korea to the world outside is of a violent, trouble-torn country with brutal security forces eager to stamp on dissent. The image makes good TV and good copy. The British 'quality' press was fond of running pictures of urban gung-ho, masked students tossing Molotov cocktails at lines of riot police. I would search for explanatory text and find none. The pictures spoke for themselves.

But the violence seemed so incongruous. It was like being told your mother ran a secret torture chamber in the attic. I recalled the words of one foreign correspondent who had come to check the disturbances first-hand. He filed a report to the effect that a seasoned English football thug could teach Korean street demonstrators a lesson or two in the tactics of urban terror. I recalled, too, the words of a friend in Seoul whom I'd phoned from Britain at the height of the riots, when martial law seemed certain to be imposed and my coming trip placed in jeopardy.

'Riots?' he queried. 'What riots?'

I told him of the TV pictures I was watching at that very moment. A girl was being led away with blood streaming from a head wound. A riot policeman looked to be on fire.

'Oh, you mean the demonstrations. We have those all the time, usually during lunch break, after morning lectures. They're just around the corner. I can see them from my window. Nothing at all to worry about.'

The riot police looked up at my approach. They showed no hostility. They lay in the road, propping themselves on their elbows, riot shields and batons by their sides. As I moved closer I could see what the TV cameras could not. Unmasked, the 'vicious' riot-troops were nothing but fresh-faced boys. I thought them about sixteen, though they must have been older. They joked with me as I came among them, practising their English greetings and farewells with unmistakable good humour.

'Hello', the nearest one shouted and waved. 'Goodbye', he answered himself as I stepped carefully over his feet. His words were taken up like a refrain as I picked my way through the sprawling bodies.

'Hello; Goodbye; Where you from? Come back; Sit down; You want woman?' I looked over my shoulder to wave farewell and fifty boyish riot police returned my wave.

~

Midday was the time we had agreed to meet. It was five past, but still no sign of Mr Kim. A chap with a shiny black briefcase stopped to speak and straight away offered to accompany me wherever I wished to go. When I told him I was expecting someone he demanded to know his occupation and how long I'd known him, as if sizing up their respective rights to my company. My answers – 'I don't know' and 'since yesterday' – led him to scoff contemptuously.

'Why you go with him and not me?' he demanded, his voice curt rather than inquisitive. 'He is not for coming.'

The same thought had occurred to me, but Mr Kim, last seen sprinting down the street the previous afternoon, now appeared sprinting towards me, breathlessly apologising. 'Solly! Solly!' The rival for my company marched off without a word. I looked at my panting friend.

The Western stereotype conjures up images of tiny Japanese men, and by association tiny Koreans. In truth, they appear distinctly taller and broader than their Nipponese neighbours. In Isabella Bishop's time the average height of the Korean male was just 5 feet 4½ inches, and with regard to their physiognomy:

There are straight and aquiline noses, as well as broad and snub noses with distended nostrils; and though the hair is dark, much of it is so distinctly a russet brown as to require the frequent application of lampblack and oil to bring it to a fashionable black, while in texture it varies from wiriness to silkiness ... The mouth is either the wide, full-lipped, gaping cavity constantly seen among the lower orders, or a small though full feature, or thin-lipped and refined, as is seen continually among patricians ... The usual expression is cheerful, with a dash of puzzlement.

Mr Kim's had more than a dash. He was also as thin as a chopstick. When seated his kneecaps protruded through his trousers in knife-edged right angles that threatened to rent the fabric. His limited English was exacerbated by his acute shyness. He had brought along his college English books. With these, and my own trusty phrasebook, he hoped to lighten our darkness. He had, I learned, been heading back to Seoul, but was postponing his return to accompany me. His motive appeared simply the pleasure of being with a foreigner. Unused to such gestures I wondered what he might want in return.

It was raining heavily at the ferry terminal. Mr Kim bought the tickets and ordered rice and chicken at the cafeteria. He picked up my rain-spotted glasses from the table and proceeded to wipe them carefully on his handkerchief. He had put down a sheet of paper, on which I could see half a dozen pencilled expressions. These included 'Shall we have lunch?' which he had asked a moment earlier with surprising facility, and 'Let's take a break,' which he uttered solemnly at intervals throughout the day.

Laying aside the chopsticks I reached over for his phrasebook. It confirmed he could read much that he could not say. This reinforced the impression I was already forming of Koreans as a whole, which helped explain why Westerners were in such demand for impromptu English lessons. Korean students are taught by Korean teachers, whose own grasp of spoken English is frequently abysmal, and who concentrate instead on the hidebound rules of written grammar.

Needless to say, Mr Kim's books taught American English. These contained such gems as: 'I goofed up,' 'it's a pain in the neck,' 'give me some feedback,' 'give me a ball-park figure,' and most useful of all 'Come to think of it, I forgot to bring my wallet.'

Mr Kim's idea of friendship had a distinct Confucian aspect. Ours was not a relationship of equals, for such does not exist. He wished to demonstrate his slavish subservience at every opportunity. When I found nowhere to dispose of my chicken bones he reached out with cupped hands. When I spilled some coffee on my fingers he wished to dry them on his pullover. When I went to settle the bill he pushed me away. And when I emerged from the 'Foreigner Only' cubicle in the toilets (the one with the seat) I found him with my rucksack already hoisted upon his back. This was too much: we compromised by letting him carry my apple.

The Soyang-gang dam, 123 metres high by 530 metres long, had been completed in 1973 and had transformed a barely navigable river into a flooded valley. It was perhaps thirty miles long with innumerable inlets and side-channels.

Our boat was a forty-eight-seater hoverfoil with ornate golden dragon prow. Mr Kim shepherded me to my numbered seat like a mother fretting over a child. A ride along a man-made lake on a high-tech hoverfoil is the Koreans' idea of fun. The waterway acts as a street. At each junction a blue street-sign announces destinations in white letters. Inje is twenty-five kilometres in this direction: Yanggu seventeen kilometres in that.

For those less enamoured with modern miracles it was not a pleasant trip. We travelled over a flooded valley whose slopes of pine and fir plunged into the depths. There was no river bank, no path, and no people. Just trees, the twisted shapes of dead and dying trees. The waterline obscured a sunken, dead, murdered forest. Unlike the tens of thousands of drowned trees, out of sight and out of mind, those that fringed the lake still clung to a kind of half-life. The leafless upper branches of submerged trees masked the view of this twilight world, thrusting above the water like the raised arms of drowning men.

Nor was this supposedly idyllic scene without its dangers. The surface was littered with the detritus of the deceased forest. Twigs and branches floated by, the pilot weaving a path to avoid obstruction, sometimes succeeding, sometimes not. Makeshift moorings could be seen up the side-channels. There weren't many boats. Like the River Han, there was little risk of running into a traffic jam. No less than with urban roadways, the habitat for much wildlife had been consummately destroyed.

Conversation with Mr Kim proceeded intermittently. He liked to rehearse his lines for several minutes before risking the air-waves. I learned that he lived with his mother, three sisters and two brothers. He was a management student. With his regimental short back and sides he presented a picture of respectability. But most Korean students looked like fledgling city slickers. No long hair or patched denims for them. Twice in the space of a mile Mr Kim tapped my arm and said: 'Good time, good time.'

Halfway to Inje the wooded slopes flattened and patches of deforestation signalled rice-paddies and, here and there, a remote settlement. A rowing boat snuggled against the bank. A couple of ducks flew noisily in a wide arc overhead.

Without warning the engine cut and the hoverfoil gently belly-flopped into the water. The co-pilot had been occupied with sporadic guide duties: we had just crossed the 38th Parallel, the original dividing line between North and South Korea. Now he turned mechanic, moving aft to the padlocked engine room. On re-emerging he paused to admire himself in a mirror slung on the wall and deftly evacuated the contents of a spot on his cheek.

'Too hot,' explained Mr Kim, pointing back at the engine. The vessel reared phallically out of the water, ejaculating spray through my open window. The channel passed close to a bank, where strips of wire looped from tree to tree to restrain detached branches from floating away. The hoverfoil pulled into a pier and a waiting bus drove us into Inje.

Inje lay in a hollow, flanked on one side by the upper Han, and on the other by Mohican haircutted hills stripped of trees on their lower slopes. At my request Mr Kim found me a *yoinsook* – hostels so down-market that the tourist authorities feign ignorance of their very existence. Mr Kim couldn't resist a shudder when he saw inside. Mr Clive probably nose-dived in his estimation.

A series of doors fed off a concrete tunnel, which opened out upon a small courtyard with yet more doors. My room was perhaps ten feet by seven. It was as empty as a room can be, apart from a rolled up, thin, foam mattress (*yo*), padded quilt (*ibul*), and a cloth-covered wooden pillow (*pyogae*). A row of clothes hooks was nailed to the wall, next to a small mirror and a faded price chart. The floor was covered with greenish oiled paper. The wallpaper's only patterns were the stains that spattered it from floor to ceiling. In the far wall was a small, barred, prison-like window, with an apology for a curtain that sagged below the height of the glass. The *yoinsook*'s washroom was tucked away in the courtyard, and was crammed with empty boxes, buckets and pails. A solitary tap, cold water only, protruded from the wall, with an attached hose-pipe that flew off when distended with water. The toilets were by the entrance, three unlockable wooden doors leading to three unlit cubicles. Each had a hole in the centre of the floor and, in the absence of taps, a few sheets of grimy torn newspaper shoved into cracks in the door.

'Perfect, I'll take it,' I said, reminding myself that I had pledged myself to see the Korea the tourists didn't.

Goodbyes were difficult for Mr Kim. He was the gentlest and most sensitive of men and had been evidently dreading this moment. He had spent the last hour of our journey making notes from his dictionary. Now I learned why.

'You are friend for life,' he told me, articulating each syllable with care so as not to be misunderstood. He asked me to sign his Korean-English Dictionary. As he boarded his bus back to Seoul he turned and said 'I am heart-bro-ken.' He left me feeling embarrassed and tongue-tied. Months later, upon my homecoming, a letter from Mr Kim awaited me. It must have taken days to compile. He wrote

... my mind is very good. Your an itinerary finished and come back safe and missed a calamity so I was peace of mind ... I feeling lonely and emptiness in my heart at this time. Sometimes I go on a travel by saving money. This time I saw you. I during the travelling, I feel the first impression. It's I feel unegoistic and a sense of duty and a good man. I have a great esteem for you. I am very glad to know you.

His sincerity matched my bafflement at reading words like itinerary, calamity, egoistic, and esteem from a man with the active English vocabulary of a child.

Inje was the sort of one-horse town I later found to be typical of provincial Korea. Shaped like vertebrae, it had one main street with side roads that seemed to do nothing, go nowhere, and peter out after a few yards. It had the same twelve-inch paving stones, laid diagonally to the kerb, that I'd seen in Seoul (these are rarely flush, inviting the incautious to stub their toes and stumble); the same church-top crosses scraping the clouds; and the same preponderance of men-at-arms. South Korea has 600,000 men in uniform at any one time, and with every male serving three years military service, it was hardly surprising to find off-duty conscripts in the coffee shops and bus terminals of the smallest town.

It was a drizzly evening and few people were abroad. The river bed was flat and stony, a couple of rivulets winding feebly through the pebbles. Reddish cows roamed untethered among youngsters dismantling a tent from a sandbank. Just then my ears perked at a distant siren, and into view sped one, two, three ... eleven bus-loads of soldiers. The convoy was topped and tailed by headlight-flashing jeeps, and roared through Inje like a train. The silence that descended in its wake was palpable.

An elderly man, drunk possibly, incontinent certainly, was being half-carried, half-manhandled by a younger man and woman down a muddy slope towards a rickety shack by the river. I caught up with the struggling threesome and did my best to assist. For my pains a pair of gristly, sinewy arms was flung round my neck, hands clinging on for dear life, without thought to my own. Choking for breath, I helped carry the still incontinent man through a gate, whereupon we lowered him upon some steps. A sheet of red peppers was sheltering from the rain under an awning, beside a water pump and the familiar complement of metal and plastic basins. When I turned to leave, the younger man sprang to attention and saluted.

That evening I ate somewhere near the bus terminal. Korea is glutted with trendy eating places for the young. They reminded me of Britain's coffee bar craze in the 1960s, basements and first floors reappointed to cash in on the adolescent market. Dim lights, soft music, alcoves and partitions pander to the need for privacy. Some restaurants go so far as to install curtains, or even swing doors, transforming an alcove into a booth, the waiter summoned by private telephone.

The menus in these establishments are restricted (shallow bowl of cream soup, pork cutlet or hamburger, rice or bread, curls of white cabbage, diced pasta, pickled yellow vegetable called *ranaska*, all drenched in ketchup or mayonnaise). Ashtrays, I noticed, are either half-full of water or lined with soggy paper.

I settled into an alcove. The table was laid with shallow spoons whose heads were wrapped in tissue. The rain beat upon the windows in waves. I was alone and far from home, yet Charlie Chaplin portraits adorned the walls and I sat upon Union Jack cushions with 'England' emblazoned upon them. The background music was designed to wreck a sentimental heart. I had not been surprised by the internationalism of

Seoul's musical taste, but never reckoned on hearing Jim Croche's *Time in a Bottle*, Joan Baez's recording of *Falling in Love with You*, and Georges Moustaki's *Le Facteur* in a never-never place like Inje.

The novelty of a foreigner in these restaurants was frequently rewarded with free coffee; in Inje it was a free gin and tonic. I hung around afterwards waiting to settle the bill, but nobody came and all was quiet. I walked to the counter, peered around, and saw from behind the fridge a hand running though a swathe of black hair. I turned away and coughed, and an apologetic and dishevelled waitress stumbled to her feet, combing her hair with her fingers.

I splashed back to the *yoinsook* to write my notes. The house-slippers I had left outside my door had been propped up against it. The *adjima* appeared and handed them to me, taking my own muddy sandals without a word and hosing them under the tap in the courtyard. She looked puzzled that I could wear sandals without socks, for this was not the native custom. She must have thought I lacked stockings altogether, for she pressed upon me a pair of new sports socks. She then led me by the elbow into a room hardly bigger than my own to join her family eating fruit and watching television.

When I finally got to my room, awaiting me was a copper kettleful of *mul* (or *boricha*), water boiled and flavoured with barley, giving it the colour of anaemic urine. My night-kit was completed by a mosquito coil withdrawn from its packet and perched on its stand.

No sooner had I lit the coil than there came a frightful squawking from outside, as of a bird being savaged by cats. From my window I could see nothing through the driving rain but a bulldozer, a wooden ladder, and a flower pot piled with leather thongs. I retrieved my sandals, dashed outside with shoulders hunched against the lashing rain, and traced the source of the disturbance to a chicken shop. Rows of wire cages greeted me, stuffed with chickens, claws and beaks pressed pitifully through the wire. Bowls of reddish water slopped beside a tree-stump chopping block, its surface spotted with fresh blood. A blooded hatchet lay on the stump. Against a wall stood a pot of boiling water, into which the newly killed bird had been popped that it might be softened for plucking.

Western culture is unaccustomed to this openness of death, its abattoirs and slaughter-houses shielded from public view. The butchery is done in private, for fear of driving further millions towards vegetarianism. To the less squeamish, or less hypocritical, a chicken shop is a shop like any other. To one side a florist sat watching TV among her blooms, to the other a young girl busied herself with a steam iron. Neither had come running at the sound of death.

I squelched back to my room.

4

SORAKSAN
Typhoons, Monks, and a Peep into Hell

There is assuredly no single view that I have seen in Japan or
Western China which equals [the twelve thousand peaks] for
beauty and grandeur. Across the grand gorge through which the
Chang-an Sa torrent thunders, and above primæval tiger-haunted
forests with their infinity of green, rises the central ridge of the
Keum-kang San, jagged all along its summit, each yellow granite
pinnacle being counted as a peak ... [These] weathered into silver
grey, rose up cold, stern, and steely blue from the glorious forests
which drape their lower heights ... then purpled into red as the
sun sank, and gleamed above the twilight, till each glowing
summit died out as lamps which are extinguished one by one, and
the whole took on the ashy hue of death.

Isabella Bishop – *Korea and her Neighbours* – (1898)

LL NIGHT the storm raged. Thunder clapped and lightning
flashed. Rain water poured through the streets with a harsh,
metallic roar as it rattled over the thick plastic sheets hastily
tossed over crates of sodden cabbages and fruit.

There was no let-up by morning, when I took the bus to the east
coast. I rested my head against a white antimacassar stamped in fading
blue letters with the words ARNOLD PALMER MANHATTAN. I
wondered if the legendary golfer knew or cared that his name adorned
Korean buses. Breakfast was a steaming hot corn on the cob bought
from a woman who wandered up the aisle, saw a foreigner sitting alone
at the back and turned away. I had to call her back.

The rain had temporarily called a truce by the time we arrived at the
coastal village of Naksan. I descended the bus in search of its youth-
hostel. Just off the main road I found a line of funfair stalls. A few
remained open, defying the weather and the lack of custom. Shooting
ranges and bows and arrows tempted stray visitors with prizes: 4 hits =
three packets of cigarettes; 3 hits = a book of postcards; 2 hits = a key-

holder; 1 hit = a ball-point pen. When I photographed the archery range a man dashed out to remonstrate, waving his arms and yelling 'Why picture?' Maybe unlicenced archery ranges were illegal. I walked on to the village, a jumble of corrugated-roofed dwellings with no line or shape, linked by dirt alleyways too narrow to take a bicycle. Homes were fronted by raised verandas, precarious wooden pillars supporting the awnings. A dog, tethered to a post, lifted its head as I passed: two chickens pecked at scraps. Peering inside an open sliding door I inspected rooms small and bereft of furniture. They were warmed by the traditional *ondol*, underfloor flues from kitchen or boiler, and fuelled by cylindrical charcoal briquettes. The floor being the warmest part of the house, the household sit, eat, and sleep upon it. They not infrequently die upon it, too, as a result of *ondol*-induced carbon monoxide asphyxiation.

Down by the beach a parade of open-fronted restaurants forlornly awaited passing custom, chairs propped forwards against tables as if in mourning. Each restaurant had a tank of eels, the creatures crammed in such numbers that they could barely move. All pressed their heads into the corner away from the intrusive aerator. The eel at the bottom of the heap was, for the moment, reasonably safe. I wondered how long it could survive, presuming the tank was restocked before it was down to the last eel. I watched as a luckless creature was scooped out, taken inside and spilled upon a chopping block. Like a charmed snake it raised its head and danced, temporarily frustrating the angle of the blade, which fell the moment the eel took a breather. The knife stopped short of severing the head, and the body twitched and arched in reflex as the gutting commenced. A chicken shop and an eel! I had witnessed more violent death in two days than many in our cocooned West ever see.

The youth hostel was shrouded under a canopy of trees at the top of a flight of steps. It was not a youth hostel of my teenage acquaintance. From the outside I took it for an exclusive hotel. It was framed with topiary and oleander. In its leafy setting it might have been the chateau frequented by German High Command in *The Dirty Dozen*.

'FRONT DESK' said a sign over the front desk in huge gold letters. I wasn't a youth hostel member, but successfully scaled that small barrier.

'How many people are staying?' I asked the bob-haired receptionist, for the key rack was full. She pointed at me. It was still summer and Naksan youth hostel was empty. Instead of *The Dirty Dozen* chateau I had found myself in the *Psycho* motel. Thankfully I was not asked to share with dead grannies, just dead spiders. The bunk beds were no larger than children's cots. The hostel's toilets stank of ammonia. In the washroom I precipitated a stampede of frogs, big and small, leaping about, quite rightly annoyed at my intrusion.

In view of the inclement weather and lack of companionship I was grateful for the TV in my otherwise empty dorm. The Korean networks put out dubbed movies: *African Queen, Rumpole of the Bailey*, and a French movie about Ferdinand de Lesseps, *L'homme du Suez*. I switched over to the education channel, to find two American instructors acting through this dialogue:

'Are you having any special problems at work?'

'Actually, I think I may be fired soon.'

'Fired? You must be jumping to conclusions.'

'I don't think so. I saw an attractive man and I told my boss that I'd like to be introduced to him.'

'There's nothing wrong with that.'

'But the man turned out to be my boss's husband ...'

The cultural assumptions seemed so crass. Korean women were not conditioned to make advances to men. I wondered if it was the intention to teach them that American women were not so constrained. Any intended humour was probably drowned in cultural misunderstandings.

Inaugurated in 1950, American Forces Korea Network (AFKN), broadcasts alongside the Korean networks. AFKN could only be received near US bases, not here on the remote east coast. This was a pity, for I had grown fond of its evening News and 'Talk Tip', the daily Korean lesson for linguistically minded GIs. A phrase a day was on offer, like 'please give me another one'. Knowing the problems of cultural isolation, AFKN arranges for servicemen to 'spend an evening with a Korean family'. AFKN specialises in army psychology. Troopers sweating on field exercises warrant a deep-throat voice-over: 'infantrymen don't mind the hard training. They'd rather sweat in peacetime than bleed in war.'

AFKN enjoys no advertising. Instead it interrupts programmes with nauseating dollops of patriotism, military heroics, and paternalistic meddling. To encourage soldier literacy, a series called 'American Treasury' bombards viewers with snippets of history, such as the origins of the expression 'Bakers Dozen' or 'the furlong' or 'Mesa Verde'. The item signs off: 'it's a fact in the Library of Congress. Learn more about weights and measures [or whatever] in *your* library.'

Social correctness is instilled with the help of slogans: 'Girls who *know* don't get into cars with men that are drunk;' 'Cigarettes, they're enough to make you sick.' To encourage sympathy with the host culture, army wives smile into the camera: 'Every country has its own way of doing things. Not right or wrong. Just different from what we're used to. It's a lot more fun to be inside the culture than outside.'

My favourite military advice explained how to avoid personal attack. 'Try not to stand out from the crowd,' says some smart-ass. 'Don't wear uniform on public transport; don't write your rank on baggage labels.' He omits to point out that soldiers advertise themselves to any would-be assailant by their haircuts.

Unable to enjoy AFKN, I settled for a juvenile heavy-metal guitarist with skin-tight trousers and Cliff Richard glasses who whooped it up, performing arm windmills and aerial leaps. He stopped short of smashing up his amplifiers. TV is becoming indistinguishable the world over. Nubile girls perform as hostesses on Korean-style game shows, operating the spinning balls and selecting the lucky numbers. The game show was followed by aerobics. The time is surely not far off when women from China to Colombia, Khartoum to Korea will be obsessed with their waistlines, donning leotards to stretch and bend to the rhythms of Status Quo. Such individuality as Korean TV possesses is restricted to soap operas (much wailing and gnashing of teeth), and ponderous historical dramas where only the costumes lighten the solemnity.

Korean TV apes American TV in its countless commercial breaks. A soft-drink shows children drinking from bottles – no straws, no glasses – or munching cereal while kitted out for American football. Disco-dancers advertise a wrist-watch. A beauty preens herself in the bath with a bar of soap.

Nine o'clock. Time for the evening News. Never mind that I could follow only the pictures. What was this? A typhoon? 'Typhoon Dinah' it was called. Satellite images showed Dinah to be sweeping north from Taiwan: she had already inundated parts of southern Korea. Dinah was presently three hundred miles south of Naksan, but where was it heading? I couldn't tell. I switched off the set and went to ask the desk girl. She was reading a magazine.

'Ahem. Will it rain tomorrow?' I spoke slowly to make sure she understood. 'Is the typhoon coming to Naksan?'

'Yes,' she said firmly, looking knowledgable. I cursed inwardly, then on a hunch –

'Will it be sunny tomorrow? Is the typhoon going away?'

'Yes,' she said, looking and sounding equally sure of herself.

Koreans, I had learned, have an unnerving habit of saying 'yes' when you least expect it. Sometimes it means 'I hear you' rather than 'you are right,' as in their probable reply to being told that their mother is particularly ugly. 'Yes' they will say, and then pause to work out their response. Alternatively, as with the receptionist, it is a simple reluctance to say no to anything, preferring to warm the listener's ears by affirming whatever he wants to hear. It is not seen as lying, or dispensing misinformation, for answers serve the ends of social harmony rather than truth. Nor do Koreans wish to lose face by professing ignorance. Unable to learn more about Typhoon Dinah I went to bed and waited for the morrow.

I awoke to the sounds of trees groaning and bark snapping. In the foyer I peered out on a forecourt littered with twigs and small branches. The sky was black and the rain a horizontal blur. I was thankful the hostel had been built on the leeward side of a coastal promontory. I went to order breakfast but struggled with an incomprehensible English menu. Comprehension was not helped by the grumpiest Korean I'd yet met. He was, I gathered, the manager, though his duties included waiting at table. He had a booming voice, but was stubbornly silent with regard to the menu and the typhoon. He brought me coffee and powdered coffee creamer.

Weeks later I met a couple who'd stayed in the same youth hostel. They remembered well the 'grumpy bastard', for they had had the temerity to ask to share a dormitory.

'You are married?' asked the bastard, knowing full well the answer because he was holding their passports.

'No'.

'You are good friends?'

'Er, I think so.'

'Do you normally share a room together?' He wanted to turn them away altogether, but eventually relented – for one night only.

'Tomorrow you go.'

I was stirring my coffee when into the dining room ambled a Buddhist monk. He must have checked in late last night, unless he'd braved the storm to pop by for breakfast. He sat down at a distant table, sideways to me. He was thick-set, with boxer's jaw, and his square, shaven head dropped vertiginously at the back. His baggy sackcloth trousers were drawn tightly about his ankles. His feet were adorned by dainty, white ballerina slippers. The solemnity of his appearance was not helped by a collarless shirt that might once have been white. Suddenly he got up, came over and sat down beside me.

'Me Mr Soo.' It was a relief from all the Kims and Lees. He said he was twenty-seven, which made me suspicious. Everybody of a certain age insisted they were twenty-seven. I figured it to be a psychological age – rather like thirty-nine in Britain – a refuge against encroaching middle age. Either that or there must have been a baby-boom in the mid-1960s. By Western reckoning Mr Soo was twenty-six, for Korea's system of age-accounting considers an infant to be one year old, and sometimes two, at birth.

Mr Soo was a disciple of somebody or other. The Korean equivalent of Zen Buddhism is called 'Son', and Mr Soo lived at the Son Institute in Seoul. He had a mole on the left corner of his mouth, from which two wire-like hairs protruded in opposite directions, like antennae, the innermost curling itchingly inside his mouth. He had completed his three years military service before becoming a monk, and divided his life nowadays into three-monthly stints of study and travel. He asked if I travelled alone.

'Always', I said.

'Very good,' he said. 'But today no. Typhoon tomorrow finishy. Today you come temple me.'

Later that morning Mr Soo collected his sack-cloth jacket and brown shoulder bag, and together we battened ourselves against the elements and marched up the hill to Naksan temple. A ticket office adjoined the entrance. I fished in my pocket for some money, but Mr Soo intervened.

'No, no. You with me. No pay.' This was useful to know. *When short of a penny find a monk.*

Mayayana Buddhism, of which Zen, or Son, is one form, arrived in Korea from China in the fourth century AD. It constituted the official religion until supplanted by Confucianism a thousand years later. From that time onwards the strength of Korean Buddhism declined. It no longer determines affairs of state, nor shapes the country's artistic landscape.

Korean temples are not solitary buildings but vast complexes. The pagoda at Naksan comprises seven storeys, and is towered over by a fifty-foot-high statue of *Avalokitesevera*, the Goddess of Mercy, built in 1977. In the company of Mr Soo I received the red carpet treatment, with sample demonstrations of Buddhist worship. These he performed with the aid of a bell and small, hollowed wooden pot (*moktak*). The pot was struck with a stick lightly but with increasing speed, producing a sound like a spinning coin coming to rest on a hard surface. My guide led me to the cage of the four devas, or guardian kings, whose duties were 'to safeguard Buddhist teachings and subdue devils'. Each deva measured fifteen feet, with flowers crowning a broad chiselled face expressing either anger or amusement, depending, I suspected, on the mood of the beholder. One deva guarded each point of the compass. North clutched a pagoda, symbolically linking earth, heaven and the cosmic axis; South wielded a sword; East plucked a lute with which to control the elements; while West grasped a dragon in one hand, a jewel in the other.

Buddhism emphasises the world beyond verbal explanation, which was just as well in view of Mr Soo's limited English. He compensated by touching me. A painted circle adorned one exterior wall, whose purpose Mr Soo explained by tracing with his finger an 'O' round my chest, with the explanation 'same, same, open mind'. He touched or prodded whichever part of me seemed appropriate to make his point. I had visions of body mapping at work, a secret sign language. For all I knew, he targeted my chest when uttering a profundity, rib-cage a profanity, upper arm a joke, lower arm a secret. There came a jolting prod in my chest.

'You know kungfu? Same, same.' He struggled to find the word 'dead'. It eluded him, so he settled for 'sleeping', coupled with a mime whereby he pinched his nostrils between finger and thumb.

'Dead?' I suggested. He performed a jig of joy, as if guessing right on a TV game show.

Mr Soo's gestures were more impressive than his lectures. They were certainly more entertaining. From time to time he would interrupt himself, cup his palms upwards and sit bolt upright, eyes closed. At first I thought him in a deep trance, in intimate contact with his maker. Then he would open one eye and give me the cheekiest wink, look down at his hands, and wink again.

Lunch time. As an outsider I was forbidden to enter the inner sanctum with the other monks, and ate with my host in a small anteroom. We were waited upon by a nun. Mr Soo dropped a grain of rice into the folds of his trousers, which he plucked up skilfully with his chopsticks. He saw my look of admiration, began to chuckle, and promptly tipped his bowl of soup into his lap. The nun attended to him and wiped him down, consoled by his desperate apologies, while his tears of mirth dripped into his soupy lap.

The last course, always fruit, was still to come. Chopsticks are inappropriate for manipulating arcs of sliced apple and pear. One employs toothpicks, impaling the fruit like cubes of cheese at a cocktail party.

The wind was slowly abating and a margin of blue lined the horizon as we set off through the avenues of pine and juniper towards the cliffs. My host's repertoire of antics was not yet exhausted. He liked to burst into song, his favourite to date being a vigorous humming of Colonel Bogey. By the time we reached the statue of *Avalokitesevera* he had fallen back on routine sutras. Then came a poke in the biceps.

'You know Swanny River?' He opened his umbrella, twirling it *à la* Fred Astaire, and launched into the refrain. He was word-perfect, his booming voice echoing from the rocks and buildings. I looked over my shoulder, fearing that monks were discouraged from such displays of exuberance. The Goddess of Mercy, I felt sure, cast an admonishing glance upon Mr Soo.

The temple complex was protected by a jagged shore that kept the East Sea at bay.* Above the crashing waves, seemingly inaccessible hermitages had been carved into the rocks, like curve-tiled seagull nests. Unlike the West Sea at Inchon, which has a tidal range of up to thirty feet, the lunar influence on the East Sea barely exceeds thirty centimetres. It is a wild, romantic coast, with scant harbour facilities, and is much beloved of vacationers for its fine golden beaches.

That's what the tourist bumph said. What it omitted to say was that the entire coast, from the DMZ to Pusan 250 miles to the south, is sealed off by a barbed wire fence. It sweeps mile after mile over rocky headlands, across shallow caves, and looms behind stretches of sandy beach. These are accessible only by gates opened at dawn. At night they are closed, the promise of bathing replaced by the threat of the bayonet.

Real or imagined incursions by North Koreans along an exposed and under-populated coast are responsible for this scenic desecration. As fences go, it isn't much of a specimen, dog-legged outwards at the top, but not insurmountable for the determined intruder. It was erected in the 1950s and is, I learned, being replaced by a more imposing specimen. But this rusting old fence has accomplices with which to fend off foes. Concrete bunkers and steel gun emplacements line the shore,

---

* The wider world knows the East Sea as the Sea of Japan, but Koreans are not inclined to grant geographical kudos to their powerful neighbours. The only surprise was to find Korea settling for neutrality rather than the nationalistic 'Sea of Korea'.

sometimes no more than a few feet from the hermitages above them. A military encampment sheltered behind a wooden fence. That night I watched disbelieving as an arc light swept the rocks, leaping from crag to crag in search of illegals. What by day is a serene Buddhist sanctuary is by night a tinder-box of ideological conflagration.

I left Mr Soo as he prepared himself for an all-night, cross-legged meditation. He indulged about once a week, but had some way to go before matching the accomplishment of his head monk, who, he said, claimed to have gone thirty-seven years without any part of his upper body touching the floor.

~

To the uninitiated it is easy to think you've arrived not at Soraksan National Park but at the wrong place altogether. Alongside the 'Hotel New Sorak' stands the 'Mt Seolag Tourist Hotel'. Sorak and Seolag are simply different transliterations of the same name. Similarly, the city of Pusan is also spelled Busan, or even, in the hands of Isabella Bishop, Fusan. And the name 'Lee' may also be written Li, Lih, Yi, Yih, Ri, Rhi, Ree, or Rhee, depending on personal preference and custom. No matter how it is spelled, it sounds more like 'Ee', with no audible consonant preceding the vowel.*

I was by now familiar with parts of the Korean script. Korea's is an almost unique living language insofar as it is artificial, constructed like Esperanto for a particular purpose. *Hangul*, as the written language is known, was invented by scholars in the reign of King Sejong in the fifteenth century as a way of simplifying the complexity of Chinese ideograms. These ideograms are in any case pronounced differently by Koreans, the spoken languages being unrelated. Korean and Chinese are mutually incomprehensible except through writing. Moreover, only the Korean leisured class were able to comprehend the numerous and intricate Chinese characters. Ordinary Koreans were restricted to oral communication, for no written script was accessible to them. King Sejong had duly sponsored the invention of letters fit for the common people.

The result was a phonetic alphabet comprising twenty-eight letters – subsequently reduced to twenty-four. Consonants, vowels and diphthongs were arranged in clusters to produce syllables far simpler than the countless brush strokes needed to form a single Chinese character.

---

* The governments of North and South Korea have employed alternative transliterations of English names. In a spirit of compromise they have agreed that the North's preference for 'Busan' will give way to the South's 'Pusan', in exchange for all varieties of Lee, Yi and Rhee yielding to the North's preference for 'I'. In theory, Mr Lee will in future be Mr I.

To the untutored eye, *hangul* looks like Chinese writing devoid of its spider's legs. It follows geometric rather than artistic principles, comprising lines and rectangles, with fewer circles and curves. *Hangul's* comparative simplicity and phonetic structure also render the script more accessible to outsiders. *Yogwan* and *yoinsook*, for example, both borrowed the initial '*yo*' sound, which I could easily recognise as rather like '0=I'.

Those who lost out from the invention of *hangul* were the educated classes, who had no need for a new language and who feared the diminished influence of Chinese characters. Much the same debate attends the fading importance of Latin in British education. So proud is Korea of *hangul*, that following the defeat of the Japanese a National *Hangul* Day was declared. Every year the people celebrate 9 October as a national holiday.

The spoken language (*hanguk-mal*) is distinctive to the Western ear. Listening to TV or radio I could discern common sounds – *imnida*, *imnika*, *seyo* – and a peculiar, drawn out *neeeeh* (meaning 'yes'). I became sufficiently practised at varying the length of my *neh*, and glibly mentioning my age and country, that I doubtless impressed passing Koreans with my fluency in their tongue, in the same way that their flawless 'May I help you?' in bank or tourist office masked the exhaustion of the speaker's lexicon.

~

Korea's most spectacular peaks, the Diamond Mountains (Kumgang), lie just north of the DMZ. This obliges South Koreans to eulogise their own Sorak Mountains. Soraksan has come to symbolise South Korea and all her accomplishments. It is a favourite all-season playground and takes pride of place in tourist literature with its rustic autumn reds and snowy winter whites. The pinnacles, canyons, pine forests and waterfalls occupy a place in the South Korean psyche both mystical and sacred. Yet, but for the division of the country, Soraksan would have remained in the shadow of Kumgang. It was expedience that mothered its superstar status.

Korea is sometimes hailed as the Switzerland of the Far East. This is misleading. Korean terrain is rugged, but judged solely by the height of its peaks barely warrants the description 'mountainous'. The highest point on the South Korean mainland – Taechongbong (in Soraksan National Park) – would have trouble at 5,604 feet peeping over the top of Ben Nevis (4,408 feet), never mind shouldering up to Japan's Fuji (12,389 feet), far less Mont Blanc (15,771 feet). What is impressive about Korea's peaks is not their size but their knobbliness. They are not high enough to be endowed with foothills, and they tumble one over the other like a fireplace full of coal. But only in a Lilliputian world could they be considered mighty and intimidating.

I was disquieted by South Korea's attitude to her natural beauties. A century ago the countryside was free from excessive human interference, and bountiful tigers confirmed man's subservient place in the natural world. Today, the tigers have long gone. The denudation of the hillsides deprived them of their habitat, and none have been recorded in southern Korea since the early 1920s. They exist only in the collective consciousness of the people as painted images on their tea-towels and temples.

The term 'national park' is surely one of the most grotesque of linguistic deceits. Ever since the world's first – Yellowstone in Wyoming – they have been popularly promoted as open-air treasures, weekend destinations for townsfolk desiring a glimpse of the wild. They sound pleasant and inviting, suggestive of picnic hampers, safe from danger yet where life in the raw may continue untamed. More realistically, they symbolise man's exploitation of his environment and how it threatens to consume the globe. Just in time the barricades went up, parcelling up a tiny portion of the world's surface wherein endangered species might eke out their survival.

South Korea typifies this packaging of nature. Her seventeen national parks and scores of smaller provincial parks are presented as a bastion against the despoliation, urbanisation and agriculturalisation of the entire country. Admission charges are levied to sample national parks. Having to pay to experience 'raw' nature, with its squadrons of park-keepers and attendants, was for me a vision of the future little short of nightmarish, with the whole planet soon divided between urban, industrial sprawl and national (or international) parks.

The official tourist map of Korea unwittingly contributes to that vision. National and provincial parks are represented in green and burgeoning metropolises in yellow. One conceived at some future date the whole map divided into green and yellow splodges, the green no less unnatural and contrived than the yellow.

Soraksan was my first experience of a national park and I loathed it – not for what it was but for what it represented. No matter where I walked I could never forget I was in a park, not in the wild. As for the amenities, a mile after buying my entrance ticket I was still passing rest rooms, snack bars and souvenir stalls, everything you'd expect of a holiday resort. Trash cans looked like hollowed-out tree stumps, but were in fact concrete, as were the 'wooden' benches along the footpaths and the 'wooden' ranch-style railings. The trash cans were part of a Keep Soraksan Tidy campaign, yet the paths were littered with papers and ring-pulls.

Typhoon Dinah's trail of havoc had closed off much of the park's self-appointed places of interest. The cable car was out of action and several of the tracks were 'off limits'. The ridged peaks of Ulsanbawi would have been insurmountable except for a rust-coloured steel catwalk that bore the visitor after much legwork to the summit. There were drinks stalls top and bottom, and on high a chap selling trinkets off a trestle. A photographer lurked at the summit, urging punters to smile by saying '*kimchi*'.

Panting for breath against the safety railings, and denied any view on account of swirling cloud, I could not but reflect upon the distasteful future shape of mass tourism. If Australians could contemplate a monorail to Ayres Rock, then the catwalk up Ulsanbawi was surely the prelude to a chair-lift up Everest.

~

The town of Sokcho lies a few miles north, in the extreme north-east of the country. Stuck to a lamp-post outside the bus station was a Wanted poster and a blurred photograph of a fifty-year-old man with 'sports style' (crew cut) haircut. When he had gone missing he was wearing a blue T-shirt and brick-coloured trousers. He was, said the caption, mute but not deaf. His mental age was very low and he had disappeared at 6.30 pm three weeks earlier. Maybe he had gotten lost. A contact address was given. The poster was hand-written and evidently the responsibility of a relative or friend, in the way that people might seek missing pets.

Inside the bus station's toilets I found a condom-dispensing machine. It portrayed a red pepper as a symbolic penis. A thousand faces waited inside the 'pepper' to spill out into the world. The condoms were of two types, standard or pimply headed, the difference explained by helpful diagrams.

I had had no need of condoms in Korea. A young soldier, eyelash stuck to his cheek and rifle slung over his shoulder ('Made in Korea under licence, Hartford Connecticut') had greater need but little imagination. He came in and bought plain ones.

It was hot, so I cooled down with an ice lolly. It was encased in concertina plastic. I snipped off the end, put the opening to my mouth, and pulled, stretched, and twisted the casing as though milking a cow. I thought of buying a lolly for the soldier, but doubted it would enhance his macho image. But nor did his gaudy, plastic shopping bag. Printed on the side was a poem, titled: *Lines Written in an Album in Malta.*

As o'er the cold sepulchral stone
Some name arrests the passer-by
This when thou view'st this page alone
May mine attract thy pensive eye
And when by thee that name is read
Perchance in some succeeding year
Reflect on me as on the dead
And think my heart is buried here.

We caught the same bus. I tried to befriend the soldier by occupying the adjoining seat and pointing out of the window at nothing in particular. As an ice-breaking technique it worked splendidly, for within minutes he was trying to cement our relationship on a permanent basis. He spoke no English, but seemed to want me as his pen-friend. A number of English words, of greater or lesser utility, have been absorbed into the Korean language, among them taxi, bus, bus terminal, omelette (*omulretul*), buffet (*bupe*), coffee (*copy*), crayon (*kureyong*), lipstick (*ripsutik*), and cuticle remover (*kyutikul rimubo*). Maybe the word 'pen-friend', which seemed his solitary English word, was one of these handy imports.

He went so far as to slip his dog-tags over his head and present them to me. I was ill-inclined to accept. I presumed the wearing of dog-tags to be compulsory. Surely you couldn't casually give them away to a foreigner on a bus. What would happen if he strayed into the DMZ without them? A blindfold and a hail of bullets, no doubt. And what if they were found on me? The same fate with South Korean bullets? I would have declined the dog-tags but for the soldier's entreaties.

I was nervously fingering his gift when he pointed at my neck-chain. He wanted a swap. Out of the question. It had been a gift from a past love. I demurred as politely as I could, seeking to blunt the rejection by offering him back his tags. This seemed to offend him more than my refusal to part with mine, and we settled on a one-way exchange.

Ours had the making of a complicated friendship. He aimed an imaginary rifle through the window and fired it. I took him to be explaining to me his job. He wished to give me his name and address, but had nothing to write on. He retrieved his newly purchased condom packet, removed the contents, and wrote on the back of the packet. I effused thanks, tucked the dog-tags into the condom packet, and pocketed the whole.

The bus bounced over a bridge, allowing a fleeting view of feverish activity on the shore. It was the pretext I needed to step down. My soldier-friend looked back and waved until the bus was lost from sight. The bridge crossed the eastern extremity of a small lake, which according to my map was protected against the invading sea by a few yards of sandbank. At that moment it had no protection at all. The tide was high, inrushing waves breaching the sandbank and spilling into the lake. The ever-present security fence was open and an excited crowd of men and boys had gathered. Some wielded scoop-nets. I could see no sign of life in the swirl of water, but with each wave that crested the sand someone would launch himself across and scoop up his prize.

'*Paem-jang-o*' (eels), came the chorused answer to my question.

~

'I Mr Lee,' said the portly man in the livid pink shirt. There are few family names in Korea. I'd now been introduced to fourteen Mr Lees (which translates as Mr Plum), eleven Mr Kims (Mr Gold), and a fair sprinkling of Parks, Chungs, and Chois. The repetition of names was offset by the ease of pronouncing them, for none comprised more than one syllable. The 'Mr' added a note of comical solemnity, and was retained even when addressing Koreans I had come to know well. My own surname presented an impossible tongue-twister which it made sense to avoid.

'I am Mr Clive.'

Though speaking little English Mr Lee had asked to accompany me to the northernmost point of South Korea, on the extreme north-east, from where splendid views could be enjoyed of the Diamond Mountains. He presented me with a silk scarf, to thank me for letting him guide me. The gift was presented with both hands – an age-old gesture to show no weapon was concealed in the other. Koreans do not expect presents to be received with effusive thanks, but for the said gift to be placed out of sight and ignored. I fear I failed to display the required indifference, for I tied the scarf around my neck and tweaked it for his approval. If he was offended he did not show it.

We motored north into the twilight world of army checkpoints and no-go areas. The landscape was a patchwork of rice-fields, bamboo, and hillsides of pine and fir. Parallel to the road, encrusted with rust and overgrown with vegetation, lay the coastal railway severed by the Korean War. I half expected to see rusted and twisted locomotives scattered by the track. No public transport existed here, no pedestrians, and only the occasional house.

A check-point instructed vehicles to proceed in convoy. A Military Police jeep headed the column. The coastal fence to the right joined another to the left, presenting us with a tunnel of wire. Ahead loomed great grey columns stacked either side of the road. As we passed they revealed themselves as vast cubes of concrete. Detonator wires protruded, for these were tank traps. At the first hint of invasion the fragile supports would be blown, and tons of masonry bombard the road.

So frequent were the inspections it would have been quicker to walk. First-gear slaloms were needed to negotiate murderous black and yellow tripods, each with iron arrowheads protruding at windscreen height. An observation tower came in sight, atop a convenient hillock. We were closer now to the 39th than the 38th Parallel that once divided the two Koreas. During the war this, the eastern theatre, had been the responsibility of ROK rather than United States units, and so it remains. No American generals strut around up here. Soldiers in red berets strolled menacingly, or crouched in bunkers behind gas-masks.

An officious woman in check tweeds with a baton stuck under her arm lined up visitors in straight lines, like school-children at assembly. The man in front of me removed his baseball cap. Mr Lee threw me a glance and I snatched at my sunhat. After being processed we climbed the steps to the viewing chamber. I had expected a dreary scene that no amount of propaganda could lighten. Instead, from this elevated vantage point and with the aid of borrowed binoculars, I stared out upon a landscape so mighty, so inviting, so empty, yet so terrifying, that it remains an image of Korea etched indelibly on my mind. Ahead lay a wide, flat, golden beach, extending perhaps ten miles before disappearing into a barrage of hills inside North Korea, pink and grey and blue at that distance. A huddle of offshore stacks speckled the North Korean coast. Inland loomed the famed 'twelve thousand peaks' of Kumgang, the Diamond Mountains, tier after tier of progressively fainter reliefs, fading until they were indistinguishable from the sky. Among these serrated peaks and ridges meandered the parallel perimeter fences of the demilitarised zone. Whoever dreamed up that name had a black sense of humour. Far from being demilitarised, the four-kilometre-wide DMZ is flanked on both sides with space age fire-power whose capacity for devastation I had no wish to contemplate. Between the twin fences lies a no-man's land of undergrowth and vegetation untended for forty years. The fences swept down to the beach, terminating only at the sea.

A mountainous, forested coastline that in other circumstances would have graced any holiday brochure seemed devoid of life or movement. No animals exposed themselves, no scavenging dogs, and, as if in fear of this most unnerving of iron curtains, no sea-birds either. Even the waves looked frozen. It was a peep into hell.

All was illusion, of course. In the absence of man the beasts flourish. Had I peeped inside those grim barriers I would have spied upon the most unnatural of nature reserves. Deer, wildcats, polecats, Korean bears, and the famed Manchurian crane of scarlet wing and black crown live and flourish in this otherwise bleak corridor. Sensibly the animals, too, kept their heads down, lending the place the ambience of death and desolation.

Through binoculars I discerned an abandoned coastal village, while high in the hills propaganda hoardings screamed their slogans. Mr Lee wrote them down for later translation.

We are concentrating only on our security – for our lives and for our motherland – was the South's version of events.

We object to the presence of foreign powers – unification by ourselves. In other words, countered the North, Yankees go home.

This ridiculous, scary, beautiful, chilling place was summed up by the icons beside the observation tower – a Buddhist gong with wooden hammer, and a towering white Madonna, hands clasped in prayer, beaming a Mona Lisa smile towards the North. A white cross topped a radio mast. Through this public juxtaposition of faiths, South Korea proclaimed its religious tolerance. To the North, it betrayed Big Brother America's cultural and religious imperialism.

~

Back in town Mr Lee ushered me into a backstreet eatery. Pinned above the door was a fading pin-up of actress Susan George in younger days, bikinied and dangling her legs in a swimming pool. She made a change from the endless images of James Dean or Brooke Shields seen in souvenir shops, printed on towels or carved in wood. We ate in a small, private room at the back, sitting on the floor at a low table. I was still no nearer mastering the proper cross-legged posture, and stretched my stockinged feet under the table and out the other side. We tucked into a plate of tripe and cold, runny eggs, and swigged *soju* – a cheap colourless spirit distilled from sweet potatoes and sold in small colourless bottles.

The meal was not to my taste. Nor was it enhanced by Mr Lee's obvious need for a handkerchief. Korean decorum, however, frowns upon nose-blowing at table. He politely turned away, sniffed loudly, but to no avail. With a violent inhalation he snorted up the obstruction, then swallowed it with a gulp.

5

THE FAR EAST
A Hot Bath and a Famous Professor

A country thus unknown could not fail to be the centre of many marvels. It was stated that in Korea the horses were three feet high; that there were fowls with tails 3 feet long; that the tombs of the kings were made of silver and gold, and the bodies of the dead studded with precious stones; and that there were hills of silver and mineral resources of fabulous value. These stories naturally served to excite the cupidity of shady cosmopolitan adventurers.

F A McKenzie – *The Tragedy of Korea* – (1908)

I OBEY a personal rule when travelling. Never go on after dark. There is a lesser and a greater reason for this. The lesser is a matter of optics. At night it gets dark and I can't see. In Korea I lived an early to bed, early to rise routine to maximise daylight. Up at 6 and, as often as not, asleep at 9. My night life in provincial Korea consisted of a stroll down the streets or waterside, a visit to a coffee shop, and back to write up my notes and plan for tomorrow. It was an unhurried, contemplative existence.

The greater reason is more prosaic. I needed time to find a bed, clean myself up and eat. Otherwise Murphy's Law was sure to intrude. Arrive somewhere late and you could bet yourself the *yogwans* would be full. No room at the Inn. It was on such miserable occasions that I got to know how Joseph must have felt.

By British standards the summer sun sets early in Korea, and as I was heading nowhere in particular I had grown used to conferring with watch as much as map. Accordingly, wherever I was by 6 pm, there I'd alight. This, I suppose, made me some kind of time traveller.

How far are you going sir?

Till six o'clock please.

It was not much beyond 6 when I stepped down from the bus at a fishing town called Samchok, halfway down the east coast of Korea. The Taebaek mountain chain, which includes Soraksan, constitutes the

Pennines of Korea. It runs east of centre, causing the Korean peninsula to tilt towards the west. Rocky and treacherous eastern shores mean scant harbour refuges, and with the mountains so tightly packed, no major rivers empty into the East Sea. Without rivers there can be no water transport, discouraging settlement. In Isabella Bishop's day eastern Korea was the most remote and inaccessible part of the country. Neither she, nor other early travellers whose records I had brought along, came hereabouts. As I could hear no echoes of Victorian footsteps, their writings lay crumpled in the bottom of my bag till I reached Pusan.

Samchok bus terminal adjoined a long street, whose further side dropped away by means of stadium-like terracing into the bowels of the old town, over whose roofs it was possible to see for some distance. Descending the steps was to be immersed in a labyrinth of lanes and alleyways. Seeking a *yoinsook,* I was directed towards a dimly lit flight of bare concrete steps. It wasn't until I set foot upon them that I realised that the sight of stairs programmes the brain into lifting each foot by equidistant amounts. The ascent is then performed as if on autopilot. These particular steps ranged at pernicious random from three to fifteen inches, and when taken at normal stair-climbing speed induced stumbling and jarring of knees and soles.

I was assigned room No 3. That to my left was No 2, to my right No 5. No 4 did not exist. That number is considered unlucky by Koreans, for its sound is also that for 'death'. In hotels, hospitals, and other public buildings one usually searches in vain for fourth floors. Should a room No 4 exist, it will if possible be allocated to foreigners, who are likely to be ignorant of its hazards.

Room 3 faced the *yoinsook*'s only toilet and washroom. Handy, I thought, for I wouldn't have far to stumble in the night should the need arise. Come the morning I made a mental note always to avoid future proximity. My sleep had been interrupted by a constant stream of lowlife peddlers inhabiting the washroom to spit and cough. Retching is one of Korea's most familiar of human sounds. The noise was amplified by Korean reluctance ever to close a washroom door behind them. The offenders might just have well have puked by my ear.

At dawn I was woken by the sound of someone dying in the washroom. No lungs could possibly withstand those hideous gasps for breath. I nervously went to investigate and found a man, fully dressed, squatting and hosing away a pile of glutinous phlegm. He looked up and proffered a good-morning smile. He appeared in perfect health. He crabbed sideways to make space, filled a bowl for me and rinsed it after I'd finished washing. He even scrubbed out the mug I hoped to use when brushing my teeth.

Samchok's maze of streets converged on the market, which hummed with life and movement. Down an alley I found a Presbyterian Church. I peered through the window at the tidily dressed congregation, standing by wooden pews and singing gustily. The preacher was young, smart, and animated; the pianist looked like Dr Evadne Hinge.

I stepped back on to the road and nearly trod upon the largest frog I had ever seen. It is a wonder I saw it, for it was motionless in the kerb, like a dollop of mud. I bent down in admiration, for its green back was mottled with black dots, its underside bright red. The act of bending down attracted a small crowd, one of whom prodded the frog with a broom. Only then did it utter a croak of protest and paddle itself six inches from the intrusive broom. But there it stayed and would not be budged.

Rows of tiny eateries filled the market's central square. They were numbered like so many stables, (1-25 up one side, 26-50 down the other – making allowance for no number 4). Most had room for one, or at most two, tables; but each had a television. For the casual bystander this was like being outside a TV shop, scores of identical pictures, and not knowing which to focus upon.

Notebook in hand I strolled the length of this diners' den, being heartily hailed to enter each establishment. Upon retracing my steps I was balked by a dark-skinned, scruffy individual in a blue vest, who barred my way with a raised hand. In the other he clutched a bunch of black grapes, the evidence of eating them being smeared around his mouth. He had evidently been stalking me. I had half-sensed I was being followed, but this was proving such a common occurrence, so curious are Koreans, that I had paid little heed. My current pursuer spoke a little English.

'Why you write?' There was no pleasantness in his voice. Nor was he drunk.

'Newspaper?' he followed up. I eased past him, but soon found him once again forestalling me.

'You no good,' he dribbled, jabbing a grape-stained finger towards me. On reflection it must have seemed suspicious finding a foreigner making notes in this most unlikely of places. Who could possibly be interested in Samchok market, unless driven by ulterior motives? The messy grape-eater was only doing his civic duty, for this is a country

which constantly urges vigilance from its citizens in the task of appre-
hending North Korean agents. Counter-intelligence was the responsibility of the general public, and everybody knew the numbers to ring
should their suspicions be aroused.

My thoughts were thus occupied as I made my way out of the
market complex and on to a main street. A screech of brakes confirmed
my fears, for they surely belonged to the police, alerted by my public-
spirited shadow. But the screech came from a taxi. The driver had seen
a foreigner. This had set in train a simple deductive process in his
mind. Foreigner = much money = is lost = is too lazy to walk = is
desperately searching for a taxi. The driver had stood on his brakes.

I waved him away. He wouldn't go. He kerb-crawled after me. He
cocked his head at me looking baffled.

Foreigner not want taxi? he was thinking. Eventually he gave up
and sped off, spreading his hands wide in final confirmation of my
insanity. No sooner had he gone than I provoked another emergency
stop, another taxi driver unable to believe his good fortune. There
couldn't be too many rich Westerners in a place like Samchok, but by
golly he had found one. I ducked back for the refuge of the market
place.

I had escaped the grape man and the taxi drivers, only to run straight
into a tramp. It was the eye contact that was my undoing. Life's
unfortunates depend on it. A flicker of embarrassment, or vulnerability,
or guilt, is enough to set their hopes soaring. I don't know what he saw
in my eyes, relief probably at having shaken off the cabbies. He
stepped from the shadows and made to shake my hand. I obliged. The
acid test was whether or not after a few vigorous pumps he would be
willing to let go. He was not, which spelled trouble, for it meant he
wanted money. I extricated my hand with difficulty, as tramps under-
standably prefer a captive audience from whom to beg. Fortunately his
eyes were too glazed and his feet too unsteady to offer much
resistance. Like others before him he showed no resentment at not
benefiting from our brief relationship, making a gesture of apology
before shuffling away.

Appended to the market were a few night-clubs, not the ideal
location for dancing and carousing. The World Cup Club, for instance,
faced a chicken shop, whose pitiful birds were, if anything, packed
more tightly into their crates than those in Inje. Arriving night-clubbers
were doused in chicken pong before they set foot in the place. The
doorman reeked like a zoo. He agreed to let me in for a 'peep', which

was all I needed, for the place was almost empty, devoid of leeching hostesses, and peopled only by a few teenyboppers.

~

Not till later – returning to Korea to write this book – did I become fully aware of the carnage on Korea's roads. Driving insanity, after all, is a sad fact of most societies, Third World as well as First. Korea's speciality seemed to me the Confucian carve-up. The bigger dictates to the smaller and is quite likely to kill it. Buses pull in and out without regard to life and death. Cyclists and moped riders keep a wary eye, otherwise they are meat in the gutter. At the time, I discerned no deeper malaise.

How wrong I was. South Korea now boasts the world's highest mortality rate from traffic accidents. Much of the problem is rooted in Korea's rapid development. In 1945 the car population numbered just seven thousand, since when figures have spiralled. By 1981 it had reached 572,000, but by 1992 approached five million. Even so, most Koreans know more about the moon than about the motor car, and go through life blithely unaware of its responsibilities and perils. Korean traffic lights might be American (hanging overhead from wires), but their interpretation is strictly Korean. Red does not mean stop, but stop only if the car in front has stopped; green indicates not a standing but a rolling start. The late reds and early greens jam the junctions in noisy confusion. Accident statistics make grim reading. In Britain, the USA and Japan road deaths approximate to three per 10,000 vehicles. The figure for South Korea is sixty-eight per 10,000, over twenty times greater.

Newspapers are quite rightly ashamed of these figures, seek no excuses and pull no punches. 'Drivers' speeding,' I read, 'overtaking and reckless lane changing, and pedestrians' jaywalking are among the major causes of traffic accidents. Failure on the part of motorists and pedestrians to observe traffic regulations is to blame.'

I started to take note of the pile-ups I witnessed on the country's expressways, and the countless near misses. This morbid pastime was encouraged by the sight of electronic scoreboards stuck on tall poles adjoining toll booths and across major cities. At first I thought the figures referred to temperatures and precipitation. But they do not. They speak of fatalities and injuries sustained on that particular expressway or locality during the preceding twenty-four hours. On occasions I scarcely credited my eyes. 'Thirty-four deaths and 168 casualties,' just in one day? The scoreboards constitute an earnest if futile attempt to drum into motorists the hazards they face, and provoke.

After my bus crawled past one mangled wreck, the lifeless bodies of four young Koreans squashed in their seats, I turned to the passenger next to me. So far we had been confined to pleasantries. If the nation's press seeks no excuses for wretched driving practices, the same may not be said of its people.

'It is the fault of our roads. They are too narrow,' said my neighbour.

'But Japan's roads are even narrower,' I countered.

'It is the fault of a few bad drivers,' he insisted.

It is the fault of the whole damn society and its chauvinistic self-righteousness, I thought. Should two drivers negotiate a narrow road and come face to face, it appears a matter of Confucian pride that neither will reverse. Confucian teachings may encourage social harmony, but they do little for harmonious transportation.

As I write, I have by me a booklet entitled 'Manual for Safe Driving for Foreigners in the Republic of Korea'. 'Yield the right-of-way to faster moving vehicles' it declares, which speaks for itself, for it encourages the reckless to take no heed of anyone. Mercifully, the book warns that when confronted by an 'unaccompanied child or a blind person with a white cane', the driver should 'slow down or completely stop'. In Korea, should an old woman step in front of a truck, the driver hoots and she drops dead with shock, blame rests with the driver.

City buses are guarantors of high blood pressure and frayed nerves. The flip-flops, dark glasses and handbrake skids of the drivers masquerade as 'cool' and 'hip' but fool nobody. To cater for a teeming population, Seoul is awash with buses. Bus-stops, however, are few and far between. A score of buses might recharge their loads simultaneously, so an incoming bus either has to stop behind the last or pull in ahead of the first. These two points might be a hundred yards apart, with the result that pavements are thronged with watchful passengers ever ready to stampede in each and every direction.

At the other extreme, the plush, video-equipped, express buses (*kosok*), permit no opportunity to enjoy the landscape. The only relief from the monotony of Korea's expressways – accidents aside – is when portions of road are sealed off and transformed into runways for fighter practice. Most *kosok* passengers, in any case, like to draw the curtains and travel in semi-darkness. Nor may one hop on and off as the fancy arises. Your ticket specifies a seat number, ruling out any chance of chatting up the driver. Not that he is likely to condescend. In the kingdom of the Korean omnibus, the *kosok* driver is king.

I had developed a liking for *chikheng* buses, and their drivers. These 'limited express' buses connect cities with scattered towns and villages. They are liable to hurtle down an expressway one minute, and lurch over a dirt road the next. Most of the time they ply the in-between roads. These are surprisingly empty, there being little traffic outside the big cities.

Kosok and *chikheng* buses enjoyed a crew of two (an extravagance now dispensed with on grounds of economy). Conductresses perched on foldaway seats by the front door, collected tickets and fixed the destination boards in the windscreen. By travelling *chikheng* it was possible to befriend the drivers, learn something of their ways, and benefit from the generosity and kindness ordinary Koreans display towards foreigners. The drivers had earned a recent pay rise, with intriguing perks. Should they marry they are now entitled to two days paid honeymoon leave, and in the event of family bereavement an equal period of paid mourning.

The *chikheng* driver heading south from Samchok bade me sit behind him. An ornate crucifix dangled from his rear-view mirror. I reached into my rucksack for my breakfast of bean-curd cakes, peanuts and dried squid. So far I had failed dismally in sharing any of my food. I was regularly treated to a cup of this or a slice of that, but whatever I offered in return was declined. It was, then, something of a break-through when I tapped the driver on the shoulder and showed him my irresistible peanuts. He removed one of his Alice in Wonderland white driving gloves to receive them.

'*Yong-guk saram imnida*' (I am British), I added, by way of small talk, and to answer the question I knew was already forming in his mind. Odds on he took me for an American.

The southern outskirts of Samchok were marred by ugly cement works, but thereafter the road to Ulchin was a delight. Deserted sandy bays interspersed with rocky outcrops to my left, thick green forested hills to the right. Most unexpected was the absence of traffic. The roads in Seoul had been so chaotic that I assumed the disease afflicted the whole country. One day it might. But for the moment car ownership is still the luxury of the minority and bus services are admirably effi-cient. They connect the big cities at intervals of a few minutes, and even here in the outback they seemed no less plentiful. I once counted ten miles between the sight of one private car and the next.

I had earlier anticipated hitch-hiking. In Japan this had held rewards not confined to free travel. There, hitching is rare, the Japanese themselves do not indulge. This does not mean that cars do not stop: it means there are few other hikers in competition. Drivers like to feed foreign passengers at service stations and go out of their way to drop them at their precise destination.

In theory, I could see no difference with Korea. But when taking soundings I had received the thumbs down. I never did see a hitch-hiker in Korea. There are few foreign travellers, few Koreans own cars, and buses are so cheap and plentiful as to dissatisfy only the destitute. But the main reason, it seems, is one of attitude. This is a staunch do-it-yourself country in the purest capitalist mould. Welfare and charity barely exist as identifiable public concerns. Drivers, I was told, have no respect for scrounging hitch-hikers. (In the event, I did not need to hitch. Sooner or later passing cars would stop of their own accord.)

Likewise I had enquired about likely reactions to my sleeping rough, should the need arise. There were no longer any tigers to worry about, but what about attracting local resentment? The response was the same, for respect is central to all Korean relationships, with outsiders as among themselves. The message was clear: act like a beggar and you'll be treated like dirt; act like a prince and you'll be given the moon.

~

I had to change buses. We pulled in at Wondok, on to a patch of gravel that served as a bus station. The driver gathered up my rucksack and carted it to another bus, where he deposited it behind the driver's seat. Such minor incidents were enough to bring people scurrying from all points, pestering the driver for details, as if he was a wandering minstrel bearing tidings from distant parts. I did not need to overhear 'yong-guk, yong-guk' to realise that the rare sighting of an Englishman was big news.

The new driver's mascot was a furry duck. The conductress shared her popcorn with me. I stepped down at Pyonghae, from where I made my way to the much-vaunted Paegam hot springs.

'Nine hundred and fifty million won' (£700,000), said the bow-tied counter clerk, with flair and fluency. This seemed a bit steep for a quick bath. With pen, paper and patience I convinced him that the 'million' was out of order. The penny dropped, he looked grateful and accepted my 950 won, adding that if I didn't have shampoo and towel I would have to 'borrow' them. Cussedly, for I had both, I asked him if there was a charge to 'borrow', in which case I'd teach him the word 'rent'.

'Yes sir,' he replied with polite certainty, 'to borrow is thirteen hundred million *won*' (£1 million).

The thought flashed through my mind that these might be unisex baths, like they have in Japan, though even there the excitement nowadays lies more in prospect than in actuality. Too many leering eyes have driven all pre-menopausal Japanese women into partitioned-off Female Only pools. And those who remain can only be sexually identified through a near-impenetrable veil of steam. At Paegam, I knew my luck was out when I saw the arrows – men to the left, women to the right. Denied voyeuristic opportunity, I was restricted to more sentient pleasures. For all I knew, these might be sand baths, or mud baths, or volcanic ash baths.

I had had a bath in volcanic ash in Japan, and never forgotten the experience. The premises had been segregated by sex – at least in theory. But the female half was separated by a partition, not a wall. The partition was six feet high, perfect for barring Japanese eyes, less perfect for barring those of anyone standing 6 feet 4. The sight of my bearded face, obviously belonging to some unspeakable behemoth, looming and lingering over the top of the fence caused some little commotion for which I fear I was in some measure responsible. Not knowing the Japanese penalty for Peeping Poms I hastened to disrobe and bury myself under the ash.

Horror of horrors. The attendants were women. Old and past caring, to be sure, but women nonetheless. Surely I was not expected to submit my nakedness to their attentions. There were just two other bathers: I could see their heads poking up like potatoes through the steaming brown ash. One attendant, impatiently I thought, motioned me to the lockers. What was I to do, keep my underpants on or remove them? I fretted for some seconds, not knowing how many benefits of how many doubts I was entitled to.

The moment could no longer be postponed. The crone had her back to me. I strode purposefully towards her, minus underpants but with a tiny towel held out strategically that it might frustrate her line of sight. I was in no-man's land when she looked round. Her face turned ashen. I froze, unable to move, unable to think. She strode towards me and whipped my towel from my hand, depriving me of my last protection. She jabbed a finger towards a pool of steaming water I had walked past. It was not my nakedness that had offended her, but the fact that I had expected to be buried unwashed.

Properly scrubbed, I moved to the coffin-shaped trench she had in the meantime dug for me. The ash was kept therapeutically hot by rivulets of boiling water. As I lay down she heaped shovelfuls of the stuff upon me, from my neck to my toes, a mighty weight bearing down upon my chest and stomach. Deftly she piled ash into the hollows beneath my neck, waist and knees, so that my whole body felt suspended and encased in gloriously hot, heavy, moist ash. It is a measure of its luscious warmth that I was reluctant to be disentombed.

Now, in Paegam, I stripped off in an anteroom and stuffed my clothes in a locker. A white-vested male attendant sat reading a magazine. Beyond him I espied a 'health meter', otherwise known as bathroom scales, a 'height meter' with an upper limit of six feet, and a full-length mirror with communal dog-comb dangling from a length of string. The truth lay beyond the far door. I opened it. No mud or volcanic ash, just water. Plenty of water, taps, buckets, and mirrors. The room was large enough for two pools, one cold, the other, I soon discovered, hot enough to peel the flesh from my bones. There was space too for several banana-shaped mini-pools. Around the wall low taps and blue plastic stools permitted private ablutions. One corner was taken up by an imitation grotto – jagged rocks, tumbling water, plants in baskets.

I headed straight for the showers, for in Korea as in Japan public pools are for bathing, not washing. Only bodies soaped and scrubbed and sparkling clean may enter the communal pools.

But for two natives I would have had the place to myself. One was flat out on the floor, seemingly asleep, his head resting on a stool. The other was a pot-bellied man whose eyes played pin-ball with my nether parts and (modestly) hairy chest. Rather than eyeball him in return, which might have appeared hostile, or smile, which might have led to unwelcome complications, I decided to spoil his fun. I'd get out of eyeshot.

I stepped to the edge of the hot pool and gingerly immersed myself, gasping for breath and fearing for my parboiled flesh. A minute later I thought I heard the plop of spittle, and turned to find pot-belly climbing in to join me.

'American?'

Damn. He spoke English.

'*Yong-guk.*'

'Ah, you are English gentleman. You must be lonely.'

I did not feel at all lonely, and told him so. As if to tempt me he waded to the dragon's-head tap spewing out steaming water, ducked his head under it and presented me with a close-up of his hind quarters that not even his dearest friends would have envied.

He lost interest in me after a while, and went to lather and rinse himself at the taps by the far wall, where he was joined by the 'sleeper'. The two men did not appear to be acquainted, but they joined in mutual sponging, taking turns to scrub the other's armpits, the back of the neck, and between the thighs. It was extraordinarily intimate, like preening apes, and continued interminably. They were still at it when I left. It was impossible to get any cleaner. Each soap, scrub and rinse was merely a prelude to another soap, scrub and rinse. It took an ocean of water and a mountain of soap to dredge up the innermost impurities. For my part, the alternate immersions into fire and ice proved addictive. I told myself, right, just one last dip, but I was trapped in a circular web. My boiled state needed cooling; my frozen state needed warming. There was no happy medium, and the more I hopped from hot pool to cold, cold pool to hot, the more delicious my body felt and the more intoxicated I became.

~

A vagrant timed his shifty approach to the ticket window to coincide with mine. He snatched the money from my hand, thrust it through the hatch and demanded I be given my bus ticket. Assistance of this kind, whether needed or not, was an everyday fact of life. I was an exposed and easy target. There was always someone coming up to stare, to talk, to help, to beg.

Bus terminals were fast becoming part of my daily routine. Even the smallest and most run-down had a confectionery stall, selling refrigerated Pepsis, Fantas, and a local brew, much advertised on TV as giving strength and vitality to young swingers. It tasted like turps. I could also stock up with packets of wafer-thin dried seaweed, sponge cakes, marshmallows and biscuits.

I took care to keep supplied with McVitie's digestives, made in Korea and marketed as McVitie's 'Orion' Marie biscuits. Not only were they a familiar and thereby useful resort on those occasions when the prospect of *kimchi* for breakfast was more than I could bear: they were ideal for striking up a relationship with the *chikheng* drivers. Now and again I tried offering other goodies, with greater or lesser success, but McVitie's digestives were never refused. Sometimes I could get through half a packet on a single driver, passing them over his shoulder as if to performing dolphins. In between stops the drivers would pore over my maps and I would thank them profusely and pretend to be enlightened.

I could by now recognise place-names in *hangul*, but I was still liable to be misdirected. The names of Korean towns sound maddeningly alike. There is a Taejon and a Taechon, distinguished by the faintest difference in aspiration, and a Kyongju, Chonju, Chongdo, Yongju, Kongju, Sungju, Kwangju, and two Chongjus. I had quickly learned to keep my map ready and to point. Each bus entering the terminal would precipitate an undisciplined stampede. 'Women and children last' was the unchallenged ethic. That I never boarded the wrong bus, or missed the right one, I owed entirely to the care and attention of fellow passengers. Word of my destination would spread as if by jungle telegraph. Each incoming bus would be greeted with a chorus of shaking heads or frantic nods and pointing fingers.

This was just as well, for the maps of the tourist authorities delighted in frustrating helpless foreigners. National parks, for instance, have official entrances. The maps omitted them and I spent hours in a bus circumnavigating Chuwangsan National Park before I discovered its entrance.

Not that those hours proved dull or uneventful. The bus all but ploughed into a cow, led by a small child. The child was walking on one side of the road, the cow on the other. The tether, fastened to a nose-ring, stretched across the road like a tripwire. At the sight of the bus, the young cowherd should have run back to the cow. Instead he tried to haul it in. The beast stood its ground, the bus shuddering to a halt inches from the tether.

The terrain hereabouts was typically Korean, an image doubtless stemming from childhood exposure to Pathé newsreels of the Korean War, or later war movies filmed on location. The horizon was never distant. Uplands constitute three quarters of Korea. She has little countryside, as we know it, for lowland and gentler slopes have long been sowed, asphalted, bulldozed. Every inch of non-mountainous land appears to have been appropriated for agricultural, industrial, military, or urban usage.

Most striking is the way Korea's mountains rear up from a flat floor. This is not Scotland or Norway, not an ex-glacial world gouged into depths and heights. There are no depths. Korea's mountains are not high enough to have generated glaciers or ice-caps. River valleys are flat, disproportionately wide, and often − except during the rainy

TO DREAM OF PIGS

season – dry. Apologetic creeks wind through rock-strewn river beds. Tip-up trucks park in mid-river, axles dry, loading shingle.

Such landscapes foster many bridges, their construction facilitated by dry and exposed river beds. It was easy to relive the Korean War in the mind, USAF Sabres swooping over the mountain crests to strafe stranded supply convoys. The bridges encouraged the perfect ambush, so long and exposed, offering no place to run or hide. They made for good war films, but doubtless for a grisly war.

Rounding a bend the bus was halted by a roadblock. No more unlikely place could be imagined. The road led from nowhere to nowhere. Even the rice-paddies seemed unattended. I slipped my notepad out of sight under my rucksack. Just in case.

A policeman climbed aboard from an elephant stool. He stared down the bus, barked a few words and saluted someone in the back seat. Odd, I thought, because the few passengers were all near the front, the better to observe the strange foreigner. The policeman marched purposefully to the back, turned and marched back. Ten paces up, nine paces down. The heavy boot-steps stopped by me. He was amiability itself, smiling the smile of someone about to hand me a fortune. He turned again to the rear, saluted and departed. I whipped my eyes to the rear: the back of the bus was indeed empty.

Only when this ritual was endlessly replayed over the next weeks did its purport become clear. Checkpoints are sited near strategic junctions or administrative boundaries, and are designed to apprehend spies venturing on rural buses. The salute was to apologise for the interruption. I was always above suspicion and spoken to, if at all, with excessive courtesy. All of which made me think North Korea might endeavour to recruit foreigners to perform her dirty tricks. My wilder imaginings switched from being dragged away by South Korean security police, to feeling a tap on the shoulder from a trilby-hatted, raincoated, recruiting agent for Kim Il Sung.

Further south, the country became more bucolic, exposing a new hazard – an invasion of the roads by strange tractor-driven carts that spell constant danger. They are one consequence of the agricultural modernisation of the 1970s, part of the wider New Community Movement (*Saemaul Undong*), through which government subsidies encouraged rural advancement: tiled roofs instead of thatch, and tractors instead of shanks's pony.

In rural Korea these tractors swarmed like locusts in the savanna. The basic unit is a belt-driven motor, known as *kyong-un-ki*, with a headlight fitted at one end. Fix a couple of wheels underneath and a go-cart behind, and the result is an unlicensed death-trap that chugs along like a supercharged lawnmower. Here in the outback, with private cars few and far between, these 'rice-rockets' serve as sundry transport, trailers crammed with up to a dozen standing passengers.

For other road users, rice-rockets spell constant alarm. Overtaking them, for example, requires fine judgment and strong nerve. They are yet more dangerous when about to pull on to the road. Their drivers, perched way back on the trailer and unaided by mirrors, can only check that the road is clear once they have driven out and blocked it.

Our bus had notched up several near misses by the time we reached Chuwangsan National Park. The ringing of cash tills that greets visitors to Soraksan was mercifully absent at Chuwangsan. No deluxe hotels, no manicured gardens. No information in English on the 'Tourist Information Guide'. Souvenir shops abounded, but trade was poor and the park empty.

I paused by a roaring waterfall, under a sturdy oak, where I became conscious of approaching titters. I was not the cause, for the titterers were not yet in sight. A dozen women soon straggled into view, kitted out in peaked sunhats, shoulder bags, plimsolls. Filing past me they giggled all the more. This time I was the cause. I stared after them, wondering whether to follow, when the pair at the rear looked round. They didn't beckon but gave saucy smiles. The smiles said 'what are you waiting for?'

I set off in slow pursuit, like Horst Bucholtz trailing the rest of *The Magnificent Seven*, not yet confident enough to ride boldly among them. We trailed through rocky streams and past a Buddhist grotto before the women disappeared en masse into a 'comfort station'. By the time they emerged I had advanced ahead. Horst Bucholtz had made his peace and upped the Six to Seven by sharing his cooked fish. I had run out of McVitie's digestives and was reduced to a single apple, which would not go far. With five loaves and two fishes I could have thrown a banquet.

An apple it had to be. I gave it a quick polish and held it in my outstretched palm as they emerged. The sacrifice was accepted graciously, and honorary membership of the group was conferred upon me. I provided my name, rank, and number – or rather name, country and age. Upon hearing my age two women squealed, pointed to themselves and started clapping. I clapped too, rather than be thought indifferent to finding someone else of similar age. The group were on a day trip from the provincial town of Yechon. I christened them the Yechon Townswomen's Guild.

These women were closer to nature and physically more agile than their Western counterparts approaching middle age. They stepped sure-footedly over rocky streams and clung to overhanging branches while investigating plants sprouting from rock-faces. They made stirrups for one another, fingers and toes seeking purchase on the bare rock. It was so effortless they might have been scrawny kids clambering over a fence for a spot of scrumping.

I had hitherto remained unacquainted with Korean wildlife. This might be down to poor observation, but was equally the result of care-less ecology. Many species of exotic bird – oriole, kingfisher, warbler – remain extant only by banning shooting (except for pheasant and snipe in designated places). As for the dearth of trees, Korea blames Japan for stripping the hillsides when fuelling the war effort between 1941-45. It is a moot point whether the centuries of timber-gathering to fuel the *ondol* fires bear not the greater responsibility for this denuda-tion. The habitat for tiger and bear and wildcat had been destroyed long before the Japanese arrived, and the bald, bare hills of Korea drew adverse comment from Isabella Bishop and other nineteenth century visitors. Efforts are made at reforestation – each April sees a tree-planting binge – but pine and fir serves expediency, not quality, and cannot properly replace the depleted maple, juniper and oak.

National parks, it seemed to me, supported nowt but insects, for conservation is incommensurate with hordes of foot-tramping week-enders. The only creatures happy to show themselves were idle snakes snoozing on footpaths and delightful striped squirrels called *taramjis*. The squirrels seemed not in the least afraid of humans, possibly because plodding bipeds hadn't an earthly of catching one. I'd seen enough try.

At that instant a flash of brown speared across my line of vision. With the reactions of a frontier gun-slinger, a Yechon lady scrabbled up a wall of rock, pawing like a crazed dog at the crack within which the startled creature had taken refuge. Sensibly it stayed put and the woman conceded defeat. Shortly afterwards another *taramji* shot across the path and up a tree. Though perfectly visible on an overhang-ing branch, the animal thought itself safe because no Korean yet born was tall enough to reach it The *taramji* almost paid for its compla-cency, for although out of the women's reach its branch was easily within mine. Shrieking with excitement they implored me to shake it, and twelve pairs of hands craned upwards for their prize. It never occurred to me they might harm the creature, though Koreans were known to eat the queerest animals for the queerest reasons. I rattled the branch, the animal dropped like a stone through the web of hands, and vanished into the brush before anyone could recover. The Yechon Townswomen's Guild let out a collective groan, like school-kiddies losing a newt through a hole in the net.

In Seoul an old man had told me: 'In Korea a person who gives one receives ten.' Generosity, he implied, was rewarded tenfold. In a clearing by a waterfall the Yechon ladies stopped to eat. Their shoulder bags unearthed pears, peaches, bean-curd cakes, bottles of Pepsi and cider. Handfuls of each progressed from hand to hand, like firemen passing buckets, until the pile stacked before me dwarfed anyone else's. Koreans do not eat the skin of fruit, fearing fertilisers and pesticides, and I drew strange glances when I attempted to bite into an unpeeled peach. It was whisked from my grasp, peeled and returned with approving nods from the Yechon ladies.

I had exhausted my pitiful stock of Korean. The good-natured curiosity retained the good nature but ran out of curiosity, for I could learn no more of them, nor they of me. Slowly I found myself excluded from their jokes and frolics. I could only sit back and observe, no longer participating.

Or so I thought. But with consumption of the last pear and swig of the last Pepsi the picnic transformed into a ceilidh. Fruit skins and empties were tidied away. I assumed we were moving on; instead a woman got to her feet. She tucked her thumbs inside her belt and promptly started to sing. For a moment I thought she'd gone off her head. Folk-songs around a campfire are common enough. But this was something else. She was serious, as if imagining herself on stage at the Albert Hall. She screwed up her eyes, tossed back her head and sang from the heart. Strangest of all she was singing *Edelweiss* – in English, a language she could not speak. Her chums took the performance equally seriously, some humming along, others quietly singing the bits they knew. The diva sat down to rich applause and another rose to take her place. She was as animated as the first. The lyrics were instantly recognisable: 'doh, a deer, a female deer,' also sung in English. I mumbled along, too, thinking it would look better, for everyone else seemed totally engrossed.

Edelweiss and *Doh, Ray, Me*, both from *The Sound of Music*, concluded the English language contributions. The songs thereafter were Korean, and half an hour later each Yechon lady had done a turn, each with gusto, each well practised at what I assumed was their individual party-piece. I was therefore not entirely taken aback when all eyes fell on me. It was my turn. Natural reticence did not constitute an acceptable excuse. The temporary laryngitis I yearned for kept stubbornly away. By chance I had retained the words of *The Ugly Duckling* from my childhood, and in this unexpected setting aired them, complete with accompanying waddles, quack-quacks and crocodile tears. My audience paid rapt attention and laughed uncontrollably at all the wrong places, never more heartily than when the poor duckling was told 'get out of town'.

~

Pohang wins no prizes for beauty. It is a middling sized port with a population of 70,000. It is spread out, flattish and dull, with wide streets that give the town an un-oriental, Mid-West American feel about it. Its disfigured profile speaks of heavy industry, which at times lends the sky a yellowish hue.

I was here through an unlikely encounter back at Soraksan National Park, where I chanced upon the distinguished Korean physicist, Professor Hogil Kim. Our hilltop exchanges had been limited to pleasantries until it emerged that we were both graduates of Birmingham University. And from that moment I was caught up in another of Korea's enduring social customs.

'We are alumni of the same university!' The words were not mine but his. That our studies were twelve or fifteen years apart did not matter. What to me was simple coincidence was to him like finding a distant cousin. Our relationship became almost familial, producing obligations and loyalties that have their distant counterpart in the Old Boy network of Establishment Britain. He gave me his phone number and told me to ring when I reached Pohang.

His chauffeur was despatched to the bus station to meet me, whereupon I was ferried to an exclusive estate like those seen on American movies. Toytown boulevards, Noddy trees, wide pavements, and security guards patrolling every intersection, walkie-talkies in hand.

Professor Kim greeted me like a long-lost friend. Weeks of lowlife travelling had taken their toll on my appearance: my shirts were unironed, my trainers caked in mud, my trousers stained with spilled *kimchi*. If it mattered, my host was too polite to show. We passed the evening over wine and wrapped chocolates, and later that night I slept in a Western bed for the first time in Korea.

I was already familiar with South Korea's scientific and technological capabilities, evident from her Olympic facilities and from her motor, electronic, and domestic appliance industries. These ensured that virtually everything from cars to hi-fis are Made in Korea. One marvelled at the speed of the country's advancement. It is a matter of debate whether South Korea qualifies as a developed or a developing nation, for she is adept at arguing both cases as circumstances dictate. What is not in doubt is that during the Korean War the country was devastated, the capital reduced to rubble, basic infrastructure either lacking or destroyed. The technological breakthrough began in the early 1970s. Communications in such a mountainous country had hitherto been arduous and time-consuming. A network of expressways now links the major cities, and 1974 saw the opening of the first of Seoul's subway lines. To have visited the country even twenty years ago would be to stare dumbfounded today.

Faced with such progress it was inevitable that South Korea would eventually seek to cut the knot that bound her to external expertise. Professor Kim had been handed the scissors. The aim was to build a prestigious science and engineering university, research-centred, staffed by Koreans, an institution of sufficient international stature to tempt the finest Korean brains from around the world. This could only be done by providing facilities equal to anything they enjoyed abroad. It needed to tempt the finest students, too, and in so doing pledged to turn away no one otherwise eligible on account of inability to meet the fees.

In theory, a new university faced insuperable obstacles. Korean society regards the scholar as top of the social pile, and its brighter youngsters still strive to be professors rather than entrepreneurs. In what other country might the theft of examination papers provoke headlines and anguished editorials? School children and parents endure improbable sacrifices in their quest for the best grades. Competition between Korea's existing universities was already intense. The most illustrious – Seoul National, Yonsei, Korea, Ewha Women's – traditionally scoop the best students. A degree is less important than the institution that awards it, and it is not unknown for graduates of lesser colleges to forswear their place of education. A further obstacle to Professor Kim is the continuing, if diminishing, disposition of the country's best and brightest to study law or English literature in preference to science and technology.

Hogil Kim had been recruited from his chair in the United States to become the first president of the Pohang Institute of Science and

Technology (POSTECH). The enormity of its vision was matched only by the enormity of its building programme. The world-wide reputation enjoyed by Korean construction workers is not without substance. The go-ahead for the new university was given in July 1985. In December 1986 POSTECH held its opening ceremony. In just seventeen months an entire university – laboratories, libraries, lecture theatres, dormitories – extending over three hundred acres, awaited its first students. The graduate programme, facilitating research, commenced in 1988, three years ahead of schedule.

Einstein's famous words, *Great spirits have always encountered violent opposition from mediocre minds*, hung from Hogil Kim's office. It was impossible to doubt the president's pride as he contemplated Korea's first 'particle accelerator, a 2 Gev synchrotron radiation source'. He posed for my camera in POSTECH's central square, which is adorned with busts of Einstein, Newton, Maxwell, Edison. One day he hoped to erect a fifth bust, of a Korean fit to stand comparison.

Isabella Bishop never made it to Pohang. A later British female rectified the omission. The enormity of POSTECH's vision encouraged a tour by 'Madam' Margaret Thatcher during her visit to South Korea in 1986. A plaque commemorates her planting a ceremonial zelkova tree. It seemed ironic to me, British universities wilting from the same hand that celebrated their birth in Korea. How long would it take, I wondered, before British students in search of excellence fought for admission to POSTECH.

~

Hogil Kim had a favour to bestow. He placed his chauffeur at my disposal. The chauffeur spent most of his time polishing His Master's Car and staring up at the window awaiting summons. His professionalism had previously prohibited conversation with me. But now I found him anxious to quiz me.

'How old you?'

It was too much to expect anything else. Upon my answer he relaxed visibly. He was three years older, and therefore need not appear quite so deferential. I no longer held all the aces.

We drove to the traditional village of Yandong, preserved since the fifteenth century against the ravages of Japanese annexation, the Korean War, modernisation, urbanisation and Westernisation. The houses constitute a living museum, if you turn a blind eye to the washing machines, the stainless steel pots and pans, the electric cookers, and the running water. The buildings are constructed in time-honoured fashion round a central courtyard, with wooden posts and beams, sloping tiled roofs curled up at the corners, mud wattle walls covered with white plaster, oiled-paper windows, and raised wooden *ondol* floors.

The village had just one other visitor. The young man spoke good English, the result he said of living in Australia for three years.

'Australia?' I queried. 'Then you must be a cricket fan.'

He nodded, adding that he had represented some team or other which had toured abroad.

'Batsman or bowler?' I asked, warming to the conversation. He replied:

'I am a bowlsman.'

6

ULLUNG-DO
Magical Mystery Island

Foreigners on their first arrival in Corea are little troubled by the difficulty which is encountered in most other Oriental countries in distinguishing one native from another. Some faces are almost destitute of hair, like those of the Northern Chinese; others exult in rich silky whiskers and beard; others are almost hidden in a course tangle of hair. Among the gentry it is by no means uncommon to meet almost an English face, with round cheeks, small aquiline nose, well-cut mouth and chin. Even a bright blue eye is not unknown, and the hair is by no means invariably of a pure black.

W R Carles – *Recent Journeys in Korea* – (1886)

THE FERRY TERMINAL at Pohang seethed with humanity. Half of Korea seemed off on vacation, and the air was heavy with boisterous anticipation. I was asked to fill in a passenger inventory. It was a relief to know that my fate would quickly come to light should misadventure befall the boat. The fact that the clerkess, my passport in her hand, had logged me as 'Mr Clive' seemed unlikely for long to frustrate enquiries into my disappearance. Besides, it only served to confirm the identity I had willingly assumed. I even thought of myself as Mr Clive.

I found the quietest spot to await embarkation. I propped myself against a back wall, and observed a clear-skinned Korean nestling her head into the shoulder of a stubbly-jawed Caucasian many years her senior. No tourist he. We exchanged hellos later in the queue. He was a time-serving storeman from Indiana. He'd been in Korea longer than he could remember and the prospect of returning home had blurred over the years beyond hope of expectation. He was living out his days in this Asian backwater. All he'd got to show was his young Korean wife.

With American involvement dating back to 1945 and with some 40,000 US servicemen stationed in Korea, inter-ethnic marriages have become commonplace. For the GI the attractions are obvious. His loneliness is relieved only at the bar, the brothel, or the altar. Korean women are submissive and loyal, happy to honour and obey 'till death do us part'.

For her part the benefits are more equivocal. A Korean girl risks ostracism for her attachment to an outsider (*yangnom*), and for willingly undermining the purity of the Korean race. Parents or mediators are unlikely to have initiated the relationship, with consequent breakdown of tradition and trust. The girls may be despised by the wider community, for few other than bar girls, hostesses and prostitutes enjoy the necessary proximity to army camps to lure American husbands. But for many girls the risks appear worthwhile. Their generation has been brought up to revere the guiding star of the West. An American husband promises a higher standard of living, not to mention an American passport and the opportunity to travel. Many a modern girl aspires to greater personal freedom than would be hers with a Korean husband, for whom sexual divisions are rigidly enforced. It is still customary for a daughter to leave the parental home only for her husband's. She has, in any case, always been tightly fettered – as Isabella Bishop noted:

Korean women are very rigidly secluded, perhaps more absolutely so than the women of any other nation. In the capital a very curious arrangement prevailed. About eight o'clock the great bell tolled to signal for men to retire into their houses, and for women to come out and amuse themselves and visit their friends. The rule which clears the streets of men occasionally lapses, and then some incident occurs which causes it to be rigorously re-enforced. So it was at the time of my arrival, and the pitch dark streets presented the singular spectacle of being tenanted solely by bodies of women with servants carrying lanterns. From its operation were exempted blind men, officials, foreigners' servants, and persons carrying prescriptions to the druggists'.

The only women free from these constraints were the underclass and the *kisaeng*, the equivalent of the Japanese *geisha*, up-market hostesses skilled in social graces. For most girls, denied any formal education save that provided by missionaries, knowledge of the outside world was often restricted to peeps over the wall afforded by see-saws.[*]

---

[*] Korean see-saws consist of a plank placed across rolled-up matting or a bag of straw. A person stands on either end and is propelled into the air by the descending weight of the other.

Times have changed. In the 1970s three thousand American soldiers a year took Korean brides. The number is down to one thousand a year now. AFKN News periodically features block weddings, a score of GIs and their blushing brides making their vows at a common ceremony. The duration of these vows is cause for concern. Inter-ethnic marriages break down frequently (one in four survive), especially when repairing to the US, where either the wife cannot settle or the husband, back on his old stomping ground, eases back into bachelor ways. To ease potential problems, the US Army lays on 'Brides Schools', teaching Koreans how to cook hamburgers, open bank accounts, and, for all I know, fire a handgun. No one has yet proposed a Husbands School, helping soldiers respect Korean ways.

'You speak Korean?' I asked the stubbly storeman, not unreasonably I thought. He gave me a withering look.

'Be serious. She speaks English.'

'You must like Korea, otherwise you wouldn't stay.'

'Shit hole,' he replied, expansively.

The night I landed at Kimpo Airport I might have agreed. Since then, however, I'd found Korea opening up to me like a rosebud in spring. My dyspeptic introduction to Seoul seemed an age away. The country at large was not without charm. Pockets of Korea remained out of range of modern ravages, and I'd surely find Ullung-do* the most out of range of all.

Ullung-do had attracted a curious aura that I was determined to investigate. It was hailed as Korea's secret, mysterious island. The bustle of the ferry terminal was misleading, for few of Korea's forty-odd millions had ever set foot on Ullung-do. On my travels I seldom met anyone, Korean or otherwise, who confessed to having done so.

The reasons for its neglect were various. The most obvious was geographical. The island lies far out in the stormy East Sea, 160 miles north-east from Pohang. It is too far for a day trip, necessitating at least one night's lodgings. Not so long ago even this was impracticable. In the early 'seventies the island enjoyed no roads, no cars, no running water, no electricity, no *yogwans* – therefore no visitors. Now that technology and the first trippers had clawed their way ashore, Ullung-do's isolation was gone forever.

---

* *Hangul* categorises through the employment of suffixes, which, depending on whim, are sometimes hyphenated, sometimes not. *San*, for example, means 'mountain', as in Soraksan. *Gang* translates as 'river', as in Hangang. And *do* signifies 'island'. It is spoken with a short vowel, not unlike the 'do' in 'dot'. Strictly speaking, one should avoid the tautology of 'Soraksan Mountain' or 'Ullung-do Island'.

New hurdles duly arose. Promoting tourism to a 'secret' island has the ring of an Irish travel agency. Not to be out-Irished, those responsible for writing my guidebooks had clearly never been there either. The author of one graciously admitted as much. His information he acquired by twisting the arm of an Ullung-do worshipper reluctant to strip away the island's veil.

A rival guidebook served the same end by different means. It held out the temptation of a 'special treat ... to those who love ... exploring the unusual'. But the description of Ullung-do's two ports – Todong and Jodong – as on opposite sides of the island, when in fact they were barely a mile apart, was presumably to disorientate visitors who would never find their way back. Ullung-do's secret would die with them.

Nor did this take account of the weather. The East Sea is notorious. Boats are frequently unable to put to sea for days at a time. No airstrips grace the island. Anyone on a tight schedule runs the risk of being stranded.

Another tactic for drawing the veil around Ullung-do is to frustrate would-be visitors so that they abandon the attempt altogether. My maps informed that Ullung-do was served by three mainland ports: Pohang, Imwon and Tonghae. My guidebooks mentioned only Pohang. The latest edition of *Korea Traveller* referred only to Imwon. In Seoul, the Tourist Office had insisted that Imwon and Tonghae no longer served Ullung-do, but Hupo did. Hupo wasn't marked on my maps and no one I asked had ever heard of it.

I found Hupo eighty miles north of Pohang. The Tourist Office had been right – yet wrong. Right in the sense that a new ferry service did run to Ullung-do: wrong, because the boat had pranged a propeller some weeks earlier and was out of action indefinitely. No one bothered to tell Seoul. And so on to Pohang.

I pondered the source of Ullung-do's supposed mystique. The bare facts gave little hint. The island is broadly circular, five or six miles across and thirty in circumference. It is volcanic and heavily forested, with sheer cliffs that offer few harbour refuges and fewer beaches. It is known for its juniper trees and wood pigeons, but has no indigenous mammals. Its rats, bats and shrews are the product of successful stowaways. In the distant past the island was evidently inhabited, for its human settlements date back thousands of years. It had lapsed into a haven for pirates until seized as a Korean military outpost. Not until 1884 did the first modern settlers arrive. The present population numbers no more than twenty thousand, half of whom live in the major port, Todong. Maybe Ullung-do should have been left in peace. It sounded like a lost world that had, unfortunately, been found.

~

Rigorous security precautions operated for what was, after all, a domestic ferry. Identity cards were thumbed, passengers filed through security arches, and all baggage hand-checked on wide tables. All, that is, except mine, which was passed from hand to hand and back to me without so much as a fleeting grope inside. Once again I couldn't help think the North Koreans were missing a trick. I had never yet been searched in South Korea. Nor would I be.

I followed the queue on board Daewon Ferry No 1 and down into its bowels. There being no portholes, I sensed we were below the water-line. Red cushioned bench-seats framed the walls, but these were employed solely as luggage racks. Everyone sat on the raised floor, leaving their shoes in the aisle.

For the first and only time in Korea I forgot to remove my shoes. I stepped upon the floor and heard the room go quiet. I de-shod myself, grovelled '*Mian hamnida*' (I am sorry), and bowed sheepishly in all directions. I settled into a few square inches of floor-space and con-templated the Korean capacity for forgiveness. Within seconds a woman to my right pressed a can of OB Beer into my hands. From my left came two slices of peeled peach, and from an unknown source I received a packet of dried cuttlefish.

Most of the passengers were women, off, I assumed, on company excursions, for many were dressed in work uniforms. Never had I seen Korean women so boisterous. Opposite me a group of red-jackets performed the Korean equivalent of the Chicken Song. Further aft a gang of flower-printed smocks yelled and squealed over dice-sticks (*yut*) tossed into the air. Everyone was having a party. Pockets of song swelled and ebbed, accompanied by joyful hand-clapping. Nobody watched the video, where Ernest Borgnine was whirling around firing out of helicopters. Not that anyone could hear above the hubbub.

I spoke later to an ebullient hand-clapper. She worked for Hyundai, the heavy industry giant. She handed me her card

Miss S S Kim, Product Control Dept., Semiconductor Ass'y & Test Division, Hyundai Electronics Industries Co. Ltd.

Miss Kim willingly told me her salary – W380,000 (£300) per month. She was university educated, her English was good, and her income less than a bus driver's. Hyundai workers enjoy fringe benefits that include eating in Hyundai canteens and sleeping in dormitories.

Employees' clothes – private and working – are company issue. These benefits augment their living standards, but at a cost to their individuality. Not that individuality ranks high among Korean priorities. Hyundai's slogan is 'Diligence, Cooperation, Self-Reliance', a catch-all throwaway to be interpreted any way one pleases. Miss Kim put the Hyundai lifestyle into better perspective. In Korea, she said, a person's working loyalties are firstly to the company, secondly to the state, and only thirdly to oneself. The individual, the loner, the independent spirit could not survive.

'How much holiday do you have?' I asked.

'One week only.' (She didn't admit that many Korean companies award female workers 'menstrual holidays', twelve extra days *per annum*.) The high spirits on board were doubtless due to the prospect of vacation. To Ullung-do?

'Oh no, these are not holidays. Company is on strike. That is why we go.'

There, in the utterance of that explosive six-letter word, hung the Damocles Sword over Korea. Throughout 1987 (when I visited Ullung-do) the country had been beset by turmoil. Then-President Chun had refused calls for an election. The students took to the streets, the middle classes joined them, and workers put down their tools. It was a heady alliance that obliged Chun's nominated successor, Roh Tae Woo (the 'R' pronounced confusingly as an 'N') to back down and declare a popular ballot by the end of 1987. It was the prospect of industrial chaos that tore at the government's earlier resolve, for it threatened the continuance of Korea's economic miracle, and with it the fragile stability of the country at large. Low wages were one factor in that miracle, for they undercut foreign rivals; lack of trade union muscle was another. Larger Korean companies model themselves on those of Japan, their role that of a surrogate family, taking care of workers' needs beyond retirement and insulating them from the harsh, hostile world beyond the factory gates. Industrial relations, so far as the term applies, do not reflect the Western 'them and us' confrontations. Korean unions, by their very existence, smack of disloyalty. But all this looks set to change. Rising expectations among the workers, together with the growth of union power, promise an uncertain and turbulent future.

~

On board the ferry my little pile of gifts was continually augmented. A plastic bag appeared for my shoes. Here came more biscuits, and a swig of Captain Q Rum. The foursome at my feet sat peeling peaches with a cut-throat razor. I handed them my Swiss Army knife. With the return of the knife came the lion's share of the fruit.

I was prepared for the partying to continue till we reached Ullung-do, eight hours away. But that was not the Korean way. One moment passengers were singing, clapping and clowning, the next they all lay down and went to sleep. It was like someone had uncorked a canister of sleeping gas. There was barely enough room to sit, let alone sleep, so heads snuggled into adjacent bodies, everyone acting as another's pillow. A man tiptoed over from the far wall, settled himself down and cradled his head in the stomach of a tubby woman presumably used to instant popularity at times like this.

I had already noticed that one or two passengers displayed white plasters behind an ear. Now I could see they numbered not one or two but thirty, forty, or more. I began to feel conspicuous for want of a white spot, and wondered if some epidemic had broken out at Pohang, or on Ullung-do itself. Only later did I learn that the plasters were a folk-preservative against seasickness. They contained no medicaments: they applied pressure behind the ear. They were in any case unnecessary this trip, for the East Sea was as flat as an ice rink.

Some hours later the congregation began to stir. Bladders needed emptying, feet stretching, tongues wagging. Ernest Borgnine had met his comeuppance and been replaced by some kungfu nonsense. I was joined in my niche by a bespectacled man with rheumy eyes who announced that he was twenty-seven and would like to talk with me. His name was Mr Yun and he was a businessman – 'shoes and wear'. Armed with his Nikon and assortment of lenses he was off to Ullung-do for a short vacation. After a discreet interval I got to my feet.

'You are going to wash your hands?' he asked. Indirectly I was, and I smiled at his delicacy. So that's what Koreans learned – washing one's hands meant paying a penny. Assuming, of course, that they weren't actually dirty.

For some time I was aware of being eyed up by a well-developed woman with long curly hair swept back off her forehead. She put me in mind of a beardless Demis Roussos. She had positioned herself near the foot of the steps, and as I passed proffered biscuits and strips of dried squid, with an accompanying precocious wink. It was the wink that was joltingly out of place. It was unnatural and exaggerated. Come to think of it, I'd never before seen a Korean wink.

She's on the game.

Mr Yun thought so too, for he pursued me to the toilet, where he found me admiring a toilet roll that 'Lasts Twice as Longer'. He seemed agitated. His English was rudimentary, but it was clear he wished to protect me.

'Carefully,' he said. This made no sense, so he traced the letters C-A-R-E-F-U-L-L-Y on the palm of his hand.

'Why?' I asked.

'Business woman!' he replied. He was full of charming euphemisms, for he evidently meant prostitute. He ushered me to safety on deck. I leant upon a perilously slack safety rope, to be startled by the glint of silver flying fish. At first I took them for birds, unable to rationalise their sea-skimming, logic-defying leaps and airborne changes of direction.

It was almost dark when we docked. I could appreciate Ullung-do's appeal for pirates, for the harbour was barely visible from the open sea, squeezed between cavernous granite walls. No sloping tiled roofs in Todong. The houses were modern, square, concrete and dull, and crammed into a narrow defile that ran sharply uphill. As we disembarked a uniformed official strode towards me. He was obsequiously polite.

'Excuse me, sir. Welcome to this beautiful island. I have something to ask you. May I show you my passport?'

I knew what he meant and broke file to accompany him to his desk, in full view of a gaggle of *adjimas* clambering over one another to promote the virtues of their accommodation and press their address cards upon me. By the time I'd been processed the last passengers had disappeared, Mr Yun too, leaving me to run the gauntlet of *adjimas*. At the foot of the main street Mr Yun was waiting. He had found us lodgings in adjacent *minbaks* ('home-stays', vacant rooms in family homes). My personal swarm of *adjimas* melted away.

Ullung-do, it was clear, was a moody place. Doubtless idyllic on a good day, pretty miserable in constant drizzle, as was now the case. The weather was still ugly next morning when Mr Yun and I set out to explore. We quickly found evidence of typhoons. Typhoon Dinah had exhausted herself before reaching Ullung-do, but in May her sister had engulfed a local fishing vessel, whose crew of twenty-four perished before reaching the sanctuary of Todong. Near the harbour was a shrine, candle-lit photographs of the missing mourned by their women-folk. Theirs was a piteous vigil. Nearby we located the island's only night-club, decked out with 'sixties psychedelic wallpaper.

A sudden downpour drove us into a coffee shop. I reached over for Mr Yun's map of the island to find he'd used it as a kind of diary. Across the legend in childlike, uneven letters he had written:

'Today I met Mr Clive, from England. He stayed in home-stay house for the first time. I am tired now my friends, so I must go to sleep.'

The rain was unrelenting, so we took a bus, whose very existence on Ullung-do was cause for wonder. Todong was situated in a kind of fjord, girdled on three sides by steep forested slopes. The only obvious access was seaward, though Mr Yun's map showed metalled roads extending east and west, before petering out into the tracks that served the island's remoter communities. I remained sceptical. I could accept the possibility of a road over the col to the east, but looking up at the mountainous barrier I could conceive no westward escape from Todong.

I had failed to take account of Korean ingenuity. Shunting between forward and reverse gears the bus driver first negotiated a narrow switchback. He then tackled a double spiral loopway – a spectacular figure '8' erected on enormous concrete stilts. The road spiralled upwards through 360°, first anti-clockwise, then, for the sake of giddying parity, another 360° clockwise. Todong disappeared from view as if at the flick of a switch.

Three miles later the road stopped. It had either been washed away or was being upgraded. In any case, the sea wall had been breached and the gaps plugged with sandbags. The bus evacuated its passengers, performed a nineteen-point turn, and trundled back to Todong. We picked our way over the sandbags to the sheltered village of Tonggumi, with its tiny, natural harbour. An old man invited us inside out of the rain. He had no furniture, just doorless rooms no bigger than cupboards. The old man smoked cheerfully and told us of his three sons, five daughters and twenty grandchildren. He asked to see some British money, but I had none with me and felt guilty for the oversight. Coins were a useful keepsake.

My bachelorhood caused the old man some concern. He reflected a moment, stroked his chin, then suggested to Mr Yun that I stay awhile in the village. There were some lovely girls there; he would introduce me to some. He asked about my parents and whether I lived with them. I confessed I did not. He did not respond, his face showed no expression, but I knew his thoughts. In Korea, even in the poorest home, the best room is the sanctum of parents or grandparents. The Western practice of expecting the old to fend for themselves or be herded into old people's homes is seen as barbaric and indefensible. Nor did I seek to defend it. Not for the first time in Korea was I confronted with deficiencies in my humanity and my culture.

~

If Ullung-do wished to be my friend it had an odd way of showing it. It rained for days – solid, grey vertical sheets that obliterated the landscape from view, with no hint of any wind to shoo the gloom away. The island's physical grandeur was reduced to an unseen presence; its mountains like inverse icebergs, nine tenths out of sight, wrapped in a leaden brume.

Ullung-do boasts a central summit, Songingbong (3,200 feet) the ascent of which in this weather was out of the question. Mr Yun and I climbed only as far as a waterfall (*pokpo*) – passing a gang of elderly, sullen taxis. Their drivers were on strike, Mr Yun informed me, final confirmation that modernity had reached the island. Houses lined a walled stream. Old doors, ladders and miscellaneous planks served as footbridges, some framed with potted plants. A family hailed us.

'What did they say?' I asked Mr Yun.

'They-say-they-like-you,' he said, each syllable striking exactly the same note.

'Like me? Why?'

'Be-cause-you-are-for-eign-er, and-be-cause-you-are-grand-fath-er,' he added, pointing to my beard. Beards are uncommon in Korea, save among old men. Judging from the family's jolly waves, mine was not taken as scruffy or impertinent.

The falls themselves were fenced off, visible only through mist and spray. Mr Yun and I took damp pictures of one another. He set up his tripod, fiddled with the dials, and stepped back in line with the falls. Koreans seldom smile when being photographed, thinking it detracts from their dignity. But not even Captain Scott, posing at the South Pole in the shadow of Amundsen, conveyed a greater image of morose dejection than Mr Yun.

The island's second port, Jodong, lay over the bluff to the east of Todong, half a mile legging uphill and half a mile down again. Jodong was distinguished by a hand-shaped rock thrown up by the harbour's edge, and by a mighty zelkova tree in the middle of the road, unmarked by warning signs. A man in a golfer's hat marched over to me, shaking a long stick.

'Where you from?' he yelled. 'San Francisco?'

'No.'

'Washington DC?'

'No. London.'

'Ah, London! English gentleman,' and he went whistling on his way.

Down by the harbour mountains of squid were being off-loaded. In back yards all over town they were skewered on bamboo poles and hung up to dry, like matching pink socks. The inclement weather frustrated the drying, but alternative methods were at hand. Through an open gate we watched a girl fanning cuttlefish with a hair-drier.

We ducked again out of the rain and found ourselves in the company of two wizened old fishermen, trousers hoisted to their knees. They welcomed us with a bowl of *makkoli* poured from a copper kettle. I thought twice before accepting, for *makkoli* had a fearsome reputation. *Coping with Korea* warned:

> At its worst, it is a vile, dangerous brew that leaves an unappetising sediment in bottles, glasses and stomachs. It survives only because poverty does also, and because some people will drink anything … Makkolli [sic] consumption is still an unsavoury feature of social life there. Several times a year, newspapers carry reports of mass illness and even poisoning resulting from contaminated makkolli.

One fisherman was sixty-three, the other sixty-one. They had both been born on Ullung-do and scarcely ever visited the mainland. I stared at them as I would Martians, for no less did we inhabit different worlds. Ullung-do even now was remote enough, and I could not conceive of the hardships it must have imposed all those years ago. I wondered at the thoughts of these gentle fishermen. What stereotypes did the word 'British' conjure up in their minds? Had they ever before met an Englishman? Mr Yun asked them.

I was indeed the first, though they had sometimes met Americans. They said they liked Britain best of all because, as Mr Yun translated, she was 'civilised, kind, strong, and helped South Korea during the Korean War'. A diplomatic reply, or the echoed remembrance of a bygone British empire? I couldn't tell, though at that moment I felt an unexpected and curious empathy with the likes of Livingstone and Shackleton. This was nonsense of course, but in the days ahead the more I encountered the same answer (You are the first Englishman), the more I was troubled by images not of Dr Livingstone but the wicked witch in *Snow White*. I began to dread the response from the mirror: 'No, you are the second. I met the first half an hour ago. Come in and meet him.' Since leaving Seoul I had travelled halfway round Korea with barely a sight of a Western face, and there festered within me an irrational desire that I complete my journey without encountering any fellow countrymen, thereby preserving the fantasy of my newly perceived explorer identity.

One rainy morning Mr Yun and I took a boat-taxi round the island. Ullung-do was persisting in its perversity, guarding its soul. By confining myself to coast roads and boat rides I was denied intimacy with Ullung-do, in the same way that I couldn't judge an orange by inspecting the peel.

Around the island armadas of stationary vessels harvested squid and cuttlefish. The season was nearing its peak. These tiny boats were sometimes tilled by a single hand, and had powerful lights strung from stem to stern to attract the creatures by night. Dredgers and concrete tripods shored up stretches of seaboard for tourist or military benefit.

Each time we bobbed around a headland our boat was tossed violently by cross-currents. Seldom did we glimpse sand or beach; mostly we were confronted by precipitous cliffs. In silhouette the island resembles a submerged mountain. White-painted houses of coastal hamlets tumble one over the other. I could count roofs, for nowhere was so flat that one house might obscure its neighbour. Each settlement, no matter how small, had a church. These were not humble affairs blending with the homesteads about them. They were stark and uninviting, architecturally alien, topped with bold crosses. They favoured the higher ground, furthest from the sea, some with slit-windows in the manner of medieval castles. I half expected a longbow to appear, or boiling pitch to be hurled on to the villagefolk below.

Strangest of all were the military forts. These punctuate the perimeter of Ullung-do like spokes on a wheel. By virtue of their garish camouflage they were laughably conspicuous. Cloud-like blobs of blue and pink, against a forested backcloth, is like hiding a polar bear in mulligatawny soup. Bored soldiers, rifles slung over their shoulders, gave slow, windscreen-wiper waves, as if to a passing train.

Now I understood the stilted overpass from Todong, whose *raison d'être* – considering Ullung-do's tiny population and marginal place in Korean affairs – had earlier baffled me. Outwardly, the island shelters behind a veil of fishing, farming and embryonic tourism. But like Gibraltar, like the Golan Heights, like the Khyber Pass, strategic sites seldom lose their currency. Ullung-do was once a fortress, and a fortress it remains, for it is evidently a military outpost of some import.

Ullung-do's strategic significance is clear from the map. Three other countries frame the East Sea – North Korea, Russia, and Japan. All past or present threats to South Korea's security. The island's topography is as valuable as its location. It might be searched for years and still not divulge its innermost secrets. Its ruggedness and few harbours mean that in the event of seizure it could be defended stoutly against recapture. In another age the island refuge might have served Captain Nemo and the submarine *Nautilus*. Tomorrow it might serve Kim Il Sung no less handsomely.

Nor could I rid myself of the suspicion that Ullung-do looks to its back, towards Japan. Fifty miles east of Ullung-do a yet smaller island, Tokdo, sits shrouded in military secrecy. In 1905, in the wake of her triumphs over Korea and Russia, Japan annexed Tokdo. It has since reverted to Korea. As the geographer, Mackinder, might have put it: 'he who rules Tokdo commands Ullung-do; he who rules Ullung-do commands Korea; and he who rules Korea commands east Asia.'

Numerous craggy stacks and islets snuggle close to Ullung-do, as if suckling from their mother or craving her physical reassurance. The cliffs of the largest infant, Chokdo (Bamboo Island), drop vertiginously into the sea. On its plateau summit stands a farm, complete with corralled cattle and miniature camellia forest. Calves were transported up interminable steps on the backs of farmers, and fattened cows lowered to the jetty by basket, winch and pulley.

The demands of tourism had installed park benches upon Chokdo. Kilroy had already arrived, or his Korean cousin. Graffiti blighted the concrete steps and near-pristine picnic tables. The earliest gouged date was barely a month old. It marked a sombre dawning of the tourist age.

~

All things considered there are better places to take sick than Ullung-do. My earlier hesitation about tackling its interior had medical as well as climatic cause. One night I was violently ill. Perhaps the *makkoli* had taken its revenge. At such times one's sole requirements are peace and quiet and – most important of all – an accessible lavatory. In my case that shouldn't have been a problem. My room was next to the *minbak*'s solitary toilet, and all other rooms were unoccupied.

At least they had been, but now Sod's Law intervened and an extended family took possession of the whole floor. Their shoes lay scattered down the corridor. Raucous laughter ricocheted through the thin walls. One intruder even nicked the plastic slippers I had left neatly propped by my door. I spotted them outside another and peevishly retrieved them. Missing slippers, however, I could live with. Barred access to the loo, I could not. The newcomers filed in and out in a never-ending stream. At that rate it would be occupied all night. I had no choice but to queue-jump.

The toilet was next to the washroom, which was free. I jumped inside, locked the door, and waited. I squatted and drew up my knees to my chin as another stomach cramp racked my body. I willed the toilet door to open and resigned myself to soiled consequences if it did not. With only seconds of will-power remaining upon which to draw, I heard flushing, followed by a creaky door opening. I leapt out and vaulted past a startled old man emerging from the toilet. He had a toothbrush in hand and toothpaste round his mouth. He'd been crapping and brushing his teeth at the same time.

~

The boat to the mainland was a ro-ro car ferry – an oddity in itself considering Ullung-do had few roads and in September few visitors. The car decks were empty of cars and full of freight.

We slid sedately from the island, under a sky bereft of cloud and on a sea so calm it was like mottled navy wallpaper. Propped against the rail, the sea breeze fanning my face, I looked back at the retreating magnificence of Ullung-do and its inhospitable profile. It was a picture of nobility, wildness and pathos. For millions of years it had stood defiant, protecting its baby islets, in the path of storms and typhoons. The elements it was equipped to withstand; the ravages of man it was not.

Ullung-do deserved to be left in peace. It had brought me sickness, as if posting 'keep out' signs to all who violated its privacy. I thought wryly about the obstacles – physical, administrative, climatic – placed in the way of the visitor. I had surmounted these, only to be laid low by Ullung-do's personal vengeance. My assault on the summit it had thwarted by commanding mist and rain. Only now as I left did the sun shine. It was as if the island had engaged in a personal battle of wits, which in my puny insignificance I had no hope of winning. I could not but look back at it with affection, or think of it as a living thing. Ullung-do was fierce, wild, independent, yet would no doubt soon be subjected to the indignities of package tours, its soul engraved by a hundred thousand Kilroys.

Even on board ship, it was unlikely I could be left alone for long. I was so accustomed in Korea to being picked up, propositioned, solicited – in the most charitable sense – that it was cause for surprise if I was not. I was very much public property, a novelty, a curio, and there are few people on earth less shy of approaching strangers. I was becoming uncomfortably dependent on the goodwill of Korean people to take me under their wing, escort me hither and thither, put me straight if I looked lost, and offer unbounded hospitality if the occasion arose.

To the extent that I had no privacy, I sympathised with women in the West unable to enter a pub or restaurant on their own, or even walk the streets at night without attracting attention. The insight was partial, of course, because approaches to me in Korea were never sexual or threatening, and rarely if ever from the opposite sex. Females only instigated conversation when prompted by group bravado or 'business'.

Equally, while sure that someone sooner or later would make himself known, I also knew that his presence would deter all others. Koreans solicit foreigners on a one to one, first come first served, basis. Others may gather round out of curiosity, but in a purely spectator capacity. Mr Yun had gone below to play cards, leaving me on deck, exposed and inviting, like a hooker showing a leg.

The prize of my company was won by the ship's radio officer. I'd seen him examining me from the bridge. His immaculate white uniform seemed prissy in the context of Ullung-do's savagery. An eye-patch and cutlass would have been more appropriate.

'You are from England? Two year ago I go to Immingham and Port Talbot.' Every half-hour he disappeared indoors to tune into his weather reports, each time returning with a paper cup of coffee blown cold before it touched my lips.

He was an earnest, engaging man. He enlightened me about the squid, cuttlefish and ink-fish found in these waters. He'd once earned big money on inter-continental cargo ships, but had hated the separation from his family for up to two years at a time. In mid-trip he summoned me over the ship's tannoy.

'England-man come to bridge please.' I climbed the steps to join him. He pointed to starboard where I trained his binoculars on two dolphins keeping pace with the ship.

I went back on deck. The clear sky and stiff breeze encouraged me to air my mildewing clothes. I removed my soggy towel and socks from my backpack and spread them over winches, ventilators and anchor casings. An old crone hobbled up to assist. Her skin was wrinkled and her nose blotched and bulbous. Like many elderly

Koreans her hair was parted down the middle, tied at the back and impaled with a stick. All that remained of her teeth was a solitary usable one on her upper jaw and two mangled brown raisins on the lower.

I was plainly incompetent in drying clothes, for her aim was not to teach but to do. There was a gruffness about her, notwithstanding her kindness. *This is a woman's job* was written all over her face. With care she stretched and smoothed my towel over the anchor cable. She was laying out my socks when Mr Yun reappeared. He came up from time to time to check I was all right and not being molested by business women, or other undesirables. Noticing that my minder spoke some English the woman assailed him for information. His answers clearly failed to satisfy her, for he blinked in the sunlight and said:

'She-want-read-your-mind.'

Her clairvoyant powers she demonstrated with the assistance of Mr Yun's staccato translations.

'She-say-you-have-two-broth-ers,' he said. Good guess, but wrong. I shook my head.

Undeterred, she picked up my hand and searched it intently. She muttered something to Mr Yun.

'She-want-know-if-you-have-moth-er-and-fath-er.' Here she was on safer ground.

'Yes,' I said. 'My mother was a woman and my father was a man.'

This evidently gained something in the translation, for she began cackling and screeching, clapping her hand over her raisins.

Too late. With a surprisingly loud 'ping' one sprang from her mouth and on to the deck.

7

KYONGJU AND PUSAN
Treasures and Pleasures

I was accompanied to old Fusan by a charming English 'una,' who, speaking almost like a native, moved serenely through the market-day crowds, welcomed by all. A miserable place I thought it, but later experience showed that it was neither more or less miserable than the general run of Korean towns. Its narrow dirty streets consist of low hovels built of mud-smeared wattle without windows, straw roofs, and deep eaves, a black smoke hole in every wall 2 feet from the ground, and outside most are irregular ditches containing solid and liquid refuse. Mangy dogs and blear-eyed children, half or wholly naked, and scaly with dirt, roll in the deep dust or slime, or pant and blink in the sun, apparently unaffected by the stenches which abound.

Isabella Bishop – *Korea and Her Neighbours* – (1898)

THE TOWER of London, the Colosseum in Rome, the Alhambra in Spain. Kyongju is all these to Korea. Yet it is also much more. It marks the cradle of Korean civilisation, having spent a thousand years as the Silla Dynasty's capital. For much of that time Korea was split into three rival kingdoms, the balance of power ebbing and flowing through shifting alliances. With the seventh century collapse of Paekche in the west and Koguryo in the north, Kyongju became capital of a unified Korea – known to the Japanese and the world beyond as Chosun. Unified Silla rule lasted 270 years before falling to the Koryo succession. Korea remained unified and independent, albeit by paying tribute to China, for another thousand years, until annexed by Japan in 1910. In the current spirit of Korean cultural renaissance, the treasures of Silla – temples, palace ruins, burial mounds – have become a national preoccupation. And an international one, too. In 1979 a UNESCO report described the Kyongju valley as one of the ten major ancient-historic-city sites in the world. Since then Kyongju has become the most visited Korean city outside Seoul.

All this provided strong grounds for steering clear. Outdoor museums, fantastic or otherwise, were not the reason I'd come to Korea. And Kyongju would be crawling with tourists. Had it been anywhere else I could have missed it altogether, but it sat astride my route from Pohang to Pusan.

I sensed something amiss when a guidebook eulogised a certain Kyongju hostel ('I can't recommend this place enough') and its paragon of a proprietor. My antennae twitched when I peeped at the book's acknowledgements. Lo and behold, the same proprietor had undertaken much of the research. A *quid pro quo*, perhaps: some mutual backscratching. The hostel was worth checking out.

I stepped inside. It had been weeks since I last saw a foreigner, and now I was engulfed by them. A motley assortment of Americans, Swedes, Swiss, Canadians and Israelis jammed the corridor, kitted out in the vests and shorts of the young, independent traveller. Casual to the wearer, scruffy to the locals. The distinction has to do with practicalities, not aesthetics. The jeans culture of the West is subdued in Korea, though fast catching on. Her college students, for example, look more like young executives. What in the West passes for casual, degenerates to Koreans as 'hippie' or 'beatnik', wanton untidiness having no justification. In my brief experience, Korean hospitality was not indifferent to matters of appearance.

The hostel was running high on adrenaline and anger. Earlier that day it had been fleeced. Bags had been slashed, cameras, clocks and other necessaries gone missing.

I was as shocked as anyone else. Theft of this nature may be commonplace elsewhere, but in Korea it is rare. Hitherto I had given scant thought to locking up my meagre possessions. I was accustomed to leaving my rucksack unattended or in the safe keeping of passers-by. Curious, I thought, that a hostel so praised should furnish me with my first Korean experience of a Western disease. Fitting, in a way. He who dances with tigers shall be eaten by them.

I had no intention of staying in the hostel. I was about to leave when I was hailed by an unmistakably English voice. It belonged to a dignified, silver-haired professor who had dropped in on Kyongju on his way somewhere or other. After my experiences on Ullung-do, I had half-convinced myself there wasn't another Englishman within a hundred miles. Weeks of cultural isolation may make one crave company, especially of one's own. In my case it had underlined my sense of detachment and self-reliance. This well-meaning professor intruded into my personal odyssey. He had escaped burglary but was suffering from conjunctivitis, a condition I had once contracted in Japan. I had been lucky, the problem was quickly treated. My discomfort was principally psychological, for murky eyes suggested a murky soul, and people had averted their eyes from mine.

The professor had not escaped so lightly. He had hoped the initial attack would clear, by which time he was almost blind. Blood vessels had burst, his eyelids had shut, and he spoke no Korean to summon help. The worst had passed now. He could see, but the whites of his eyes were red and he still squinted in daylight.

He regaled me with horror tales of his brief time in Korea: of a tourist hotel with its menu in comic English, offering such exotic fare as: 'Long Fish of Roast Meat,' 'Codonopsis Lanceolate,' and 'Acorn Rolls.' None of these was available, so he resorted to toast. He had taken it to his room, found it inedible, and been woken at 3 am by the sound of rats feasting upon it.

~

I found Kyongju a characterless country town, set out on a grid and grown fat on the pickings of tourism. To brighten the place and impress visitors, houses were topped by 'traditional' tiled roofs – by order of the government. There was even a tiled roof on a gas station.

It was asking much to expect hospitality and tourism to coexist. I did not expect Kyongju's bus drivers to carry my rucksack or lead me to a connecting bus. But my directional enquiries provoked brusque replies from bus drivers and shopkeepers alike. Kyongju was adept at imposing admission charges on the trivial and inconsequential. The sums were as trivial as the sights, though there were many of them. And once you'd paid, the view was often no better than from the road. The money theoretically went on upkeep and research, but more probably on window dressing – the incidental lawns and flower beds attendant upon each site. Nor were English captions adequate. They were particularly unhelpful inside the National Museum. But by then I had greater problems to worry about.

There is a case to be made for educating children in the cultural heritage of their country. There is also a case for stringing them all up by the neck, or bringing back the Pied Piper. Korean infants are not demure and cute like those of Japan or China, but pugnacious scamps whose greatest pleasure is the torment of hapless foreigners. In their yellow plastic capes and chequered bonnets, pupils are kept in order by linked hands, a teacher's whistle, and an echoed 'ya ya' to every command. I had already been driven from one secluded Confucian institute by an army of seven-year-olds who, out of sight of their teachers, discarded their crayons and paper and badgered me with the ferocity of piranhas.

I was equally accustomed to bus-loads of school children hogging the highways. It was my misfortune that a swarm of excursioning kiddies caught up with me in the National Museum. I saw them in the distance – teachers leading their pupils in a conga round cabinets and galleries. I should have hidden myself out of sight, knowing that to the average Korean child the excitement generated by a fragment of seventh century porcelain fades in comparison with a living Caucasian colossus, sporting luxuriant facial foliage of a kind unknown in their own manhood. I couldn't have drawn more attention to myself if I'd sprouted horns and painted myself green. The conga instantly stalled and fragmented, the teachers powerless to keep control. There was bedlam. The children had not bothered to read their tickets, which warned: 'One is expected not to whistle, sing, or make loud noise.' Within moments I was reduced to an exhausted wildebeest engulfed by baying hyenas. The only solution – to the teachers' difficulties as to my own – was to leave.

I went to sit on a wall outside and a wave of mental fatigue washed over me. With hindsight I was suffering from mid-journey blues. My time in Korea was half completed and I felt somehow stranded in space and time. More immediately, I was disenchanted with Kyongju. I might have responded more charitably had I not just arrived from Ullung-do. For all the rape and pillage of that magnificent, beautiful island, it aroused the senses more than the sterility of Kyongju ever could. I had momentarily lost touch with why I had come to Korea. The invasion by the children was no problem in itself: I'd survived similar attentions a hundred times. They had simply chosen the wrong time.

Paradoxically, it took another batch to lift my spirits. My ears jangled to more juvenile squeals. I'd been spotted from another fleet of arriving buses. A high-pitched scrum poured from the doors and swarmed towards me. These were high-school girls, confident in their numbers, but lacking the individual bravado necessary for the kill. They halted at a respectful distance, uncertain what to do, tittering among themselves. Then the tallest, burdened with the role of spokesperson, stepped nervously forward.

'Please,' she said, hand poised to cover her mouth, 'we want picture with you.' I smiled a yes, the shyness evaporated, and the first clutch of pubescent lovelies flew to take up position. Two sat either side, taking my arms and snuggling close, two others hung round my neck from behind, leaving the rest to improvise. In such a bundle of warmth I was helpless against filching fingers – but that was the thought of a paranoid Westerner. When would I ever learn to trust these people?

The photo-session was conducted in shifts of half a dozen. As one group climbed off, another piled on. A teacher appeared, anxiously checking to see that I was a willing participant. When all was done and fifty or sixty girls had laughingly skipped away I felt very alone and quiet and still, as though each click of the shutter had eaten a slice of my soul. In a day or two, I knew, scores of parents would be presented with snapshots: *mummy, mummy, look what we found by the museum* … Fame comes in many guises. I stood up, dusted myself down, and strolled on just as a line of coaches in tight formation began swinging into the carpark. From each window leered a yelling, waving child. I quickened my pace.

~

I'd had enough of Kyongju and took the train to Pusan. As departure time approached, the waiting room swelled with the poor and homeless. Singly or in pairs they shambled over to sit with and importune me.

Nearing Pusan the railway line joined the coast. A rusting coaster sat impaled on rocks, its holed bow rearing out of the water like a frozen fish gaping for air. In a cove beyond the ever-present security fence white-vested soldiers went through their knee-jerks. The train swung round a headland, exposing mile upon mile of white, rectangular, apartment blocks, like cigarette packets standing end to end. It was my first glimpse of Pusan.

Pusan is South Korea's largest port and second largest city, with a population of four million. It lies at the south-east corner of the Repub-lic, diagonally opposite Seoul, and is the stepping off point for the Japanese port of Shimonoseki. Unlike Seoul, which bore the brunt of the changing fortunes of the Korean War, Pusan was never occupied by communist forces and bears none of the visible scars of war. It did, however, in the darkest days of 1950, accommodate four million refu-gees fleeing from Kim Il Sung, many of whom stayed on. Pusan's cosmopolitanism and refugee legacy saddles the city with the reputation of criminal hotspot.

It was here that Isabella Bishop first arrived from Japan, in 1894, and her first impressions of Pusan were therefore her first impressions of Korea. Her first sight had been of 'brown, bare hills of Fusan, pleasant enough in summer, but grim and forbidding on a sunless February day.'

She noted how the Japanese controlled the city. The unloading vessels, the coaling station and the quarantine hospital were all Japanese, as were the city's banking, postal and telegraph facilities. The roads, street lights, sea walls, drainage and municipal waterworks of the foreign (Japanese) quarter all bore the stamp of Japanese efficiency. At that time there were effectively two Pusans, one for the Japanese and one for the locals. Up in the hills stood the walled, ethnic, old town, whose grim description opens this chapter.

As with Inchon and Seoul, it was hard to recognise Isabella Bishop's Pusan. It was now a bustling, modern city, remarkable less for any squalid native quarter than for its peculiar shape. Seoul is no less mountainous, but has nevertheless expanded outwards, like the ripples in a pond. Pusan is long and twisted. Its major thoroughfares choke with traffic at all hours. On the map the city resembles a misshapen tree, stunted branches spilling outwards. A population equal to that of Birmingham – plus Glasgow, Liverpool, Manchester, and Sheffield – inhabits that tree.

I ensconced myself in the Aerin youth hostel, phoned a contact, and arranged to meet in a downtown restaurant.

~

I'd been in Korea several weeks and was accustomed to her eating customs and recipes. The dollops of *kimchi* I consumed morning, noon and night endowed me, I felt sure, with an ever-present garlic halo that safeguarded my slumbers from diabolic attentions. A drink at a bar would be accompanied by small side-dishes (*anju*) – raw crab's legs in chilli sauce, perhaps, or fish roe dressed in garlic.

The standard Korean meal consists of rice, soup, and up to a dozen saucerfuls of *kimchi* and other side dishes. Korean food is hot only as regards spices. It is usually tepid, except when the soup is served ice cold, and kept that way by the addition of ice cubes.

Koreans draw little distinction between breakfast, lunch and dinner, eating the same food no matter the hour. At home, leftovers from one meal are commonly served up at the next. As for restaurants, these tend to specialise. In the same way that a car showroom stocks one maker's vehicles and no other, many restaurants cater for just a few related dishes.

Korean food is not just a matter of nourishment: it is also entwined with Eastern medicine, which in turn is dependent on the forces of *um* ('yin', in Chinese) and *yang*. (The split circles and bars of the Korean national flag, the *Taekukki*, adopted in 1882, reflect this search for balance and harmony.) *Um* associates with passive, feminine qualities, or – in mathematical terms – 'minus': *yang* is masculine, assertive and 'plus'. In matters of virility, one can never have too much plus, and a healthy intake of *yang* has long been a male preoccupation.

Koreans, it seems, don't have to enjoy what they eat. They include on their evil-tasting medicinal menu all those *yang*-enriched dishes assumed in some way to increase potency and sperm-count, enhance virility, and otherwise raise the libido and encourage supercharged sexual performance. It seems to be an act of faith that the more ghastly these nostrums taste, the greater must be their aphrodisiac powers. At the more palatable end of this spectrum lie eels and other sea creatures, such as sea cucumbers, abalone, and hairy sea urchins. And dog, I was informed, is even quite tasty – though that is not the main reason it is eaten.

Dog dishes come heavily spiced, and are especially popular in summer when they allegedly counter the heat and humidity. Those species making the best dishes are popularly known as 'shit dogs'. If the thought of munching man's best friend raises Western hackles, the manner of killing raises them even more. Not for dogs the slit throat or bolt through the brain. Rather, as Isabella Bishop observed: 'twirling them in a noose until they are unconscious, after which they are bled.' Alternatively they are bundled in sacks and battered with sticks, to ensure that the meat be tender. Whatever the method, the animal must not die quickly. The more terrified it becomes, the more adrenaline it secretes – to the supposed betterment of its taste and virility enhancement. Knowing Western susceptibilities in this respect, and fearing adverse publicity during the Olympic Games, the Korean Government banned the consumption of dogmeat in areas frequented by tourists. Needless to say, the ban enjoyed little success. Among other pseudonyms, dogmeat answered to the name 'four-season stew'.

'In Britain, we say that dog is man's best friend,' I had remarked, only to be told 'In Korea, we say that dog is man's best food.'

Korea cares little for the subject of animal rights. Black bears, for example, are 'farmed' in appalling conditions, specifically for the bile from their gall bladders, which is used in traditional medicine to dissolve gallstones in humans. In recent years indoor fishing ponds have become popular, not to mention indoor pheasant-shoots. Punters hire crossbows and a couple of arrows. In the confined space birds cannot long escape even the bad shots, and are afterwards despatched for instant eating.

Other exotic Korean nostrums include powdered deer antler and any number of snake recipes. But the queen of aphrodisiacs and all-purpose body-mind conditioners is ginseng. Ask for ginseng in Korea and you receive blank stares, for it is known as *insam*. It translates as 'man root', on account of its weird resemblance to a twisted human form, complete with spindly arms, twisted tree-trunk legs, and all manner of tendrils, supernumeraries, redundant penises, and strawlike hair sprouting from lower regions. So queerly humanoid is ginseng that, top it with black conical hat and one confronts a wretchedly wrinkled witch.

You see the stuff everywhere, in cylindrical glass jars on the counters of ginseng shops or traditional medicine outlets. It comes in two types – white and red. White ginseng (*paeksam*) is the common or garden variety, grown for a mere four years. Leave it in the earth another two, then steam, dry and process it, and you have the Korean elixir of life – red ginseng (*hongsam*). Nowhere is the quality of red ginseng higher than that found in Korea, and every aspect of nurturing and marketing the root is controlled by government monopoly. Ginseng so depletes the soil's nutrients that, upon harvesting, nothing else will grow for several years.

Ginseng knows no marketing limits. Aside from buying it straight, or in one of its many guises – extract, powder, pills, and potions – one can chew ginseng chewing gum, lather in ginseng shampoo, spread ginseng jam, sip ginseng tea, wash with ginseng soap, and smoke ginseng cigarettes.

Its supposed benefits are no less extensive. Among the less extravagant are ginseng's anti-ageing, anti-cancer, anti-diabetic, and antibiotic properties, its stimulation of the central nervous system, and resulting enhancement of physical stamina and mental awareness. It even cures hangovers, it is said, not to mention functioning as an analgesic and prolonging the erection. With white ginseng, minute doses over a long period are recommended, as with any homeopathically-approved substance. The greater concentration of red ginseng encourages heavier doses. Like other oriental therapies – acupuncture, moxa combustion – ginseng has its Western devotees and its sceptics. I was now set to sample ginseng for the first time.

My contact, Mr Song, greeted me with 'Have you eaten rice yet?' The phrase equates with 'How are you?' with the added inference that anyone 'without rice' must be in need of feeding. He led me to a restaurant whose balding proprietor sat upon a hard chair by the door bowing his head to all who entered. Mr Song ordered *sam-gae-tang* for two.

Sam-gae-tang is chicken and ginseng soup. Korean soup does not correspond to the liquid 'first course' at the Western dining table. It is the main dish, and in the case of *sam-gae-tang* has more the consistency of stew. It consists of a spring chicken stuffed with rice and flavoured with chestnuts, jujubes, and slices of ginseng. It is steamed in its own broth and served in an iron or porcelain pot.

I fished around for a slice of ginseng and discovered that it resembled soggy carrot, and tasted not unlike soggy rubber. It was by no means disagreeable, but somehow left you with the feeling that it wasn't put on this earth to be eaten, and that but for its alleged magical powers no one would have thought of doing so. It provided no flash of spiritual insight, but then it wasn't supposed to.

Mr Song was sixty-ish, shy, dapper, compassionate. Like most Koreans of his vintage he spoke fluent Japanese, the result of the 'Japanesification' of this country between 1910-45. During the Second World War he had studied at high school in Japan. He visited Nagasaki in December 1945, four months after the Bomb fell.

Koreans of Mr Song's age and background encountered insuperable handicaps to career advancement. In *Korean Patterns*, Paul Crane explained:

Second in importance to family loyalty is the school tie. A schoolmate or classmate must look after his fellows when in need. To act otherwise is 'treason', against the school and the very order of things. A classmate has the right to demand help from a more fortunate classmate. This goes for the children of classmates as well. This is an obligation that cannot be easily sloughed off or forgotten. To fail one's classmate or schoolmate would cause one to lose the respect and good will of one's other school associates. One might even be exiled from the group as an 'unperson'. Security in positions in government and in business depends heavily on having fellow alumni in strong positions, where they may assist one another and eventually gain control of an office, a firm, a political party, or the nation itself. For example, the 1961 coup d'état was carried out largely by members of the Eighth Class of the Korean Military Academy. Every Eighth Class

member, whether or not he actually took part in the coup, became
a powerful person.

Through spending his childhood in Japan, Mr Song had missed out
on the Old Boy routine. He had no Korean school chums, no mates to
grow up with, grow rich with, and with whom to scratch each other's
backs.

'Here I am nobody,' he said, resigned rather than resentful. He had
founded an orphanage – orphans being considered outcasts – and a
clinic for children with cerebral palsy. Without government assistance
and whip-rounds from the 'network', funding was a constant problem.
His dream was to open a special hospital.

'Your family must be very important to you, as you have no school
friends,' I suggested. Mr Song waited while I scooped out another
ladleful of *sam-gae-tang*, then told me of his wife.

As a young man he had wanted to do so much with his life. He
treasured his independence and his freedom. Marriage was not part of
his plans. His ailing mother, however, had one wish before she died, to
see her only son settled and content with a fine woman. She talked with
him, scolded him, and finally begged him to think of his future, his
parents, his honour. Faced with these pressures Mr Song took himself
to the countryside to seek peace and quiet and have time to think. He
put these questions to himself.

How can I find the best woman in the world?

He knew he could not, for there were millions and millions of
women and he knew but a few, and none of these was the best. The
best woman in the world was probably thousands of miles away, in
another country, in another continent, and probably married already.
He could never meet her.

How, then, can I find the best wife in the world?

That too was impossible. How could he pretend to re-enact Romeo
and Juliet? Romances like that were rarer than diamonds and more
distant than the stars. He could never expect to find such love.

But if he could not find the perfect woman or the perfect wife, he
could at least try to find the perfect mother for his children. He would
try. He would not marry a city girl because she would wish to attend
college, would spend hours inspecting her make-up in the mirror,
would waste all his money on the latest fashions, and be out to work all
day ignoring their children. Instead he would find a country girl. It did
not matter whether she could read or write. It did not matter if she was

beautiful. It did not matter if her family was poor. But she must be kind and gentle and devote herself to his children.

Mr Song paused while I fiddled with a quail's egg.

In time, he continued, he found someone who fulfilled his requirements. They married and she bore him two sons and a daughter. She was, he told me, a fine mother, the best mother for his children, and they grew up as he wished, healthy, strong and respectful.

As the years passed he realised that through her kindness and gentleness he had grown to love her. More than Romeo had ever loved Juliet. He had found the best wife in the world. And one day, as he gazed upon his growing children and his devoted wife, he knew that she was, without doubt, the finest woman in the world. He had found her after all.

He looked up from his soup and held my eye.

'I am sorry she cannot be here to meet you this night. She is with cancer, and soon she will die.'

~

The Aerin youth hostel hired out function rooms for company get-togethers. Chants, recitations, and oaths of allegiance swelled from behind closed doors. They reminded me of the All Blacks' *hakka*, only wilder, more frenetic. Through one door, slightly ajar, I spied on a Lions Club social. The room could have been any public bar in Britain – wooden tables and chairs, the tables stacked with beer bottles. The men assembled in one half of the room, tipsy and worse, loud and coarse, while their women – dressed in red and yellow *hanbok* and looking like flowering tulips – sat under a veil of ennui in a group by themselves. They looked so bored it was a wonder they came. Professional entertainers and drunken revellers took turns to croon through microphones on the stage, exchanging vulgarities with the floor. I had become adept at gate-crashing Korean social events, but was not tempted to do so on this occasion.

Drunkenness is not considered anti-social in Korea and carries no social stigma.* After a hard day's work, a hard night on the razzle is both accepted and expected. Isabella Bishop noted: 'I should say that drunkenness is an outstanding feature in Korea. And it is not disreputable. If a man drinks rice wine till he loses his reason, no one regards him as a beast.' Intemperance, I presumed, enjoyed social acceptability because it promotes more kisses than kicks, as I discovered the following day.

---

* Consumption of *poktanju*, beer and whisky, invites admonishing editorials.

It was Sunday and I had been invited to lunch by a fish merchant. He brought along a school-teacher to make up a cosy threesome. By mid-afternoon, already unsteady on an ocean of beer, we left the restaurant for a beer hall. Two hours later we moved on again. My companions, reserved and strait-laced at first, had long since lost such inhibitions and were draping and drooling, giggling and gushing, fondling one another's fingers in a way likely to be misconstrued in a bar in Hackney. It was dark before my companions completed their hugged goodbyes and set off for their homes. The cold light of day evidently restored their sense of dignity, for the next morning the fish merchant was waiting for me in the youth hostel. Sober once more, he'd come to apologise for his behaviour.

~

Any charms Pusan possessed did not reveal themselves lightly. Before the Olympic Games yachtsmen complained about the polluted waters of Suyong Bay, close to a favourite tourist area. Floating garbage threatened to rip off rudders, and crews refused to enter the water to clean their hulls. This prompted an unprecedented change to Olympic rules, permission being given for the boats to be raised from the water and cleaned on land.

Nor does Pusan earn Brownie points for its official bumph, which is full of Donald Duck English – excusable, comical and even lovable elsewhere, but not in a city of Pusan's resources. 'The beloved trade mark of Pusan is among Koreans,' declared one tourist pamphlet, nonsensically.

Pusan seemed even more compressed than Seoul, its hills closer and more catastrophic, its traffic still slower. It was September now, marginally cooler and less muggy than in high summer. Some of Pusan's street scenes were common to Korea – the woman bearing concrete slabs on her head; the stack of owls huddled in cramped cages on the back of a moped; the blue traffic signs giving distances in metres to the next 'rotary'. Labourers strained under A-shaped back-frames (*chigae*), like the wooden skeletons of giant rucksacks. *Chigae*-men hung around shopping centres like taxis without wheels, seeking hire as beasts of burden. Boys marched to school in the leopard-skin uniforms of military cadets.

I joined a crowd of children gathered round a trolley, behind which a man sat in the dirt stirring golden sugar in a saucepan. He poured the gooey liquid upon an aluminium tray and deftly moulded the hardening sugar into intricate shapes and patterns – a stork on matchstick legs, a butterfly, a rabbit, a bee. When solid these were prised up and sold as candy for a few *won*.

I jumped on the subway and alighted at the northern terminus, Nopodong, where I stepped out into a silent green world. No houses, no cars, no people. In the distance an expressway disappeared behind some hills. I found a stream and followed it to a cluster of secluded hovels, each topped by curved tiled roofs that I was beginning to think I would never see again. Makeshift gangways traversed the communal ditch. The curiosity of the locals, even the dogs, was intense. A child previously engrossed with a skipping rope raced off to forewarn his family of my presence. I rounded a corner to confront a reception committee. Its members faked idle chitchat, but fell dumbly silent as I passed by. My bowed '*annyong hashimnikka*' (hello) prompted stilted bows and grunts of acknowledgment. Isabella Bishop herself couldn't have made a stronger impression.

The city's municipal cemetery was not far distant, extending over a vast acreage of juniper-avenued real estate bright with rose and azalea. Not all Pusan's dead were so fortunate. The cemetery to the north of the city was matched by a suicide-spot at the south. A finger-like island, Yongdo, was attached to the mainland by two road bridges of unequal height. The furthermost tip of Yongdo was marked by precipitous cliffs, where locals would take themselves to picnic or to throw themselves to their deaths off the lookout platform. So institutionalised was this lovers' leap that a plaque warned:

Just a moment. Stop and think.

I talked myself into visiting the 540-foot-high Pusan Tower. In the surrounding gardens two youths sat by a flower bed, spitting so effusively that an embryonic stalagmite took form between their feet. Official photographers capitalised on the ban on private cameras up the tower. There was the usual tourist paraphernalia, but also something unexpected. A Horror House. I paid my money and went inside.

Korean horror I discovered to be based on Western precepts, though with a greater tactile element. A rope-tail flicked out of the darkness and curled round your ankles; a soft skull dropped on your head; a witch sprang up to slam loudly into a wooden board. None of the disembowelings or impalings I half-expected.

The tourist literature recommended Children's Park, which offered: 'many amusement facilities and anti-communist exhibition hall. An ideal spot for both children and adults.' Having an anti-communist exhibition hall in a children's park said much about South Korea's notions of entertainment and enlightenment. Get 'em young before they can think for themselves. All countries do the same, of course, but not all quite so brazenly.

The hall was closed. The young soldier said so. He pointed to an undated sign that read: 'Close from today.' In Britain that would be the end of the matter. I would know better than to attempt a ploy like: *Oh no. I phoned yesterday to check and was told to come right along. I've flown in specially from Alaska and my return flight leaves in a couple of hours.*

But things work differently in Korea. You ignore anything that smacks of bad news. I stood my ground and tried to look sad.

'Just a moment, sir,' said the soldier, and he went to confer with another. Then, 'would you come this way, please.'

Not only was I allowed in: I had my own personal escort, pleased at this unexpected opportunity to practise his English.

'I would like to help you, sir, all I can.' He seemed so young, so fresh, so unmenacing. I couldn't imagine him, or any other ROK soldier I'd met, levelling a rifle with intent. This was dangerous non-sense, of course. I had only to read the history books or talk to United Nations POWs to know the Korean capacity for bestiality. Massacres and mutilations had barbarised a gruesome civil war. POWs had written of their treatment at North Korean hands, whose inhumanity shocked even the Chinese, into whose keeping many were gratefully transferred. To seal its affinity with the United Nations, the Seoul government later sent detachments to fight in Vietnam. They reputedly relished skinning alive Vietcong captives. Koreans did the Americans' dirty work as they had earlier that of the Japanese.

What, I wondered, was the fabric of the Korean mind that turns fresh-faced sons into brutal savages. Koreans, some claim, endured such suffering that cruelty in war comes naturally. Others maintain that those who invade relinquish their right to humane treatment: they are unpersons, especially when cowardly surrendering, and no better than animals. I thought of the fierce reputation enjoyed by Gurkhas, most recently during the Falklands War. But these were deep waters. My soldier-guide was speaking.

'I major in English literature before I do military service. My father is Baptist Minister. Before, I want to major in theology, but now not possible.'

My god-fearing escort switched on the lights and led me through the deserted corridors. The exhibits were pure guff. There were no English captions, but none was needed. I inspected statistics for this, graphs for that, all highlighting the fearless, selfless quest of the South in its conflict with the superior numbers of the barbaric North. There were standard stills of mourning mothers and screaming children – from the South, naturally – and of po-faced, goose-stepping squaddies – from the North. The most intriguing display cases contained material from Pyongyang – magazines in English I dearly wanted to read, gramophone records, tins of vegetables. They fuelled a mounting curiosity to visit 'the other side'.

Pride of place in the museum went to a replica of the North's Third Tunnel of Aggression, discovered under the DMZ in 1978, and eagerly recruited into the country's folklore. Visitors marched though *papier-mâché* 'granite' tunnels, which reminded me of Santa Claus's Christmas Grotto in the High Street stores of my childhood.

My guide was busy explaining the Book of Revelation, interlaced with insights into Hemingway. I directed the conversation back to the museum and its contents.

'North Kor-ee-ah,' he said, is a communist country. You know, South Kor-ee-ah is democratic.'

'Democratic?' I queried, sceptical of a right-wing military cabal fronting a civilian government, adept at ballot-rigging and repression.

'Yes, of course. This is democracy,' he affirmed benignly, as if I'd asked a slightly daft question. He liked words like 'democratic' and 'freedom', several times speaking of a mysterious 'Freedom China', which turned out to be Taiwan. What did he think of Kim Il Sung?

'There are three K's in the world,' he replied, enigmatically. 'Kastro, Kadaffi, and Kim Il Sung. 'I hate them all, especially Kim Il Sung. I am Republic of Kor-ee-ah soldier.' He still looked no more threatening than the Milky Bar Kid. Few Koreans are shy about offering their opinions, and few Korean opinions are grey. Theirs is a conceptual world of black and white, contemptuous of doubt, indecision, compromise, unresolved complexities. Strength, be it physical or intellectual, is admired. Certainty, one might almost say bigotry, seemed to me a hallmark of the Korean mind. And no certainty is more certain than the iniquity of Kim Il Sung. No matter how I probed my soldier-friend for a glimmer of give and take, good and bad on both sides, the reaction was always the same. South Korea and the West were good; North Korea and the communists were bad. The ending of the Cold War in the West meant nothing to South Koreans. Whatever divides them on religion or politics, they are united in their abhorrence of Kim Il Sung

He is regarded as both evil and mad, a self-glorifying tyrant intent on deifying himself in the eyes of his people and achieving the goal of forcible reunification of Korea before his death. In 1992 he turned eighty, so his moment of decisive action grows ever nearer.

~

Waiting at a bus-stop one blustery evening I was treated to the force of Pusan's stink. Korean drains are covered by paving stones with cut-away hand-holes at either end. The hand-holes permit a free view of the passing sewage and ample opportunity to inhale its stench.

A salesman boarded the bus. He stood by the driver, delivering well-practised patter before handing out his samples. He would have bypassed me had I not reached out my hand. Into it he placed a bottle of dark solution and a cotton bud. I presumed I could keep it, but then he came round again. It was buy or return.

The chap next to me also returned his sample. He was an ebullient school-teacher. Conversation opened normally.

'You are forty?' he asked incredulously, 'you look fifty, at least.' He patted me on the arm, pleased to have reassured me that I was more venerable than I looked. I thought back to those I had described as looking younger than they were, and I bit my lip in embarrassment. I should have realised that not all cultures cherish the appearance of youth.

Formalities completed, the teacher commenced his disquisition. Did I prefer Pusan to Seoul? I should, because the population of the Korean capital were 'narrow minded' and 'stingy'. They were intensely competitive. Pusan people, by contrast, considered themselves more broad-minded and international. Seoulites regarded Pusanites as provincial dogsbodies, and thought themselves so smart that they were known as 'larks'. Seoul people were 'lark people'.

He uncorked a stock of Americanisms. Reagan and Thatcher were 'bigwigs': and should North Korea invade she would be defeated 'no sweat'. Had I been to Japan? Yes? The Japanese, I should know, have 'excessive formality. They do not like so much noise when eating as Koreans like.' This was news to me. The Japanese slurp was, I recalled, no less slurpy than the Korean slurp.

What did I think of the strikes? He did not call them riots, or demonstrations, or disturbances. 'Strikes' was the word. The Korean middle classes were angry about them. 'If wages go up, then prices go up, then nobody buy from Korea.' I'd heard it all so often, for this was the political orthodoxy of South Korea.

The school-teacher got off before me, leaving my mind swirling in his wake. I was sufficiently distracted to miss my stop. I had told the driver I wanted Pusan central station. Now he was summoning me through the intercom. The entire human contents of the bus turned to stare at me. Those within prodding distance prodded; those that weren't pointed to the door.

I was seeking what the tourist blurb called 'a swinging lane called "Texas" for pleasure and shopping for foreign seamen.' 'Texas' is Korea-speak for brothel. Across the road from the station I found the broad alley that boasts Pusan's equivalent of Seoul's Itaewan. It was dark and the girls were out in force. Within the shadows I espied a costume of breathtaking impudence. Its owner stepped out before me, a siren in knee-high white boots, black skirt that stopped short of her crotch, silver cummerbund, crocheted waistcoat, and curly hair tumbling down to her waist from under a thin black headband. She moved with the tiny steps of someone going nowhere, the top half of her body swaying to a different rhythm to the lower. It was a wonder she didn't fall over.

Her pals were no less bashful. Each doorway thronged with hip-wiggling, hot-panted beauties. One had died her hair red, another blonde. Some were content to catch your eye and entice you in with a wink. Others were vocal, strolling out to intercept with lines like 'hi there,' and 'hey, where're you going?' A few adopted a physical come-on, trailing a finger along your thigh as you passed.

The customers were mostly American, and by their haircuts mostly military. The women were mostly gorgeous. I had come to take pictures, but had not realised that most girls were living secret lives. Their parents probably thought they were waitressing. 'Business women,' even hostesses, are considered unpersons by respectable Korean society. In which case, it seemed, the outcasts number millions. Nevertheless, pretences must be maintained, and parents kept unawares of the sorry truth. Consequently these girls feared exposure. The sight of my camera provoked a minor stampede: those that stayed ducked indoors or shielded their faces. My monetary desirability was instantly quashed, so that when I strolled back for a double-take I was shunned almost as a pariah.

A Kojak lookalike stumbled noisily from a bar and implored me to try 'Green Street'. I'd never heard of Green Street. He said the taxi drivers knew it by another name, but it was only 3,000 *won* to get there and enjoy some 'window shopping'.

'Fifteen girls will leap out and grab yer, and yer sure will have a good time.'

~

The next day brought with it an offer much harder to refuse. I had one more contact, one more phone number, and the promise of one more place to stay. I telephoned my contact and was invited to meet him for lunch.

He was smooth, hospitable and slick. He took me to a Japanese restaurant and into a private room where dubious acquaintances were already assembled around a low table. Where he was immaculate, they were open-necked and casual, with hedgehog haircuts that lent them the appearance of bandits.

Korean etiquette prohibits a guest from sitting at table until shown his place. These are ranked higher and lower, as with every other aspect of life. I was shown to a space to the right of Mr Slick. The table was overflowing with sushi and sashimi, and bottles of soju and beer. Dishes and glasses were stashed on the floor to make room. The guests were already half cut. They passed round empty glasses with one hand, received refills with the other, and yelled '*kombay*' (cheers!). The practice was democratic and egalitarian, mixing drinks and saliva with commendable unselfishness.

The conversation turned to sumo wrestling. Somebody mentioned Konishiki – at thirty-eight stone the heaviest wrestler in the history of sumo – and, inevitably, his sex life. How could he get on top without crushing her?

At this point a woman entered. She was Korean, and yet … She was tall and dressed in the casual jumper and jeans of a Western student or housewife. She was evidently expected, for my host rose to greet her, as did we all. Light banter was exchanged before she sat down. She could have sat anywhere, but she sat next to me.

'Say hello to Miss Kim,' said Mr Slick.

I said hello, reached over to shake her hand, and looked at her closely. Her long hair was permed, and her tight, faded blue jeans concealed well-padded legs and thighs. Her pullover sleeves were rolled up to her elbows. She did not have the tiny bone-structure of most Korean women. She was confident and relaxed in male company. So far as I could tell she spoke not a word of English.

We continued eating, all except Miss Kim, who light-heartedly parried the jests fired at her. If she wasn't hungry, what was she doing in a restaurant?

For some time no one paid me further attention. I was content to eat, drink and observe. Then Mr Slick turned to me.

'Miss Kim will kindly put you up this night.'

Really, that's very kind of you, sir. I looked at my watch. It was 1.45 pm. Mr Slick and Miss Kim started talking across me. What were they saying? Why the hell couldn't I understand? Did they look and sound conspiratorial? Not at all. It felt like a business meeting interrupted while the chairman phones his wife to tell her not to forget the cereal.

That must be it. He was telling her that Western men prefer cereal to kimchi for breakfast.

I'd eaten enough and manoeuvred back from the table. No one else had finished, but Mr Slick got to his feet and escorted Miss Kim and myself into the street. A handshake for me, a few more words with her, and he turned back to his guests.

'See you again,' he called over his shoulder. Somehow I didn't think that was likely.

Miss Kim led me to a bus-stop. She quickly tired of waiting and stopped a cab by the simple expedient of stepping out in front of one. All I could do was follow blindly. We headed westwards up one of Pusan's urban tributaries. She paid off the driver and we continued on foot through a series of narrow streets, stopping at a four-feet-high metal gate that threatened me with cranial damage in bending through it.

Our lack of communication, verbal and visual, made me uncomfortable. Beyond the metal gate stood a neat, compact house shielded from public view. She unlocked the door and led me into a small, sparsely furnished living room. There was a table, a few chairs, a cooker by the wall, and little else.

My eyes, however, had already speared to the half-open door beyond. Despite the restricted angle I could see it was a bedroom, of considerable opulence. I sat myself at the table with my back prudently to the bedroom and reached for my well-thumbed phrasebook. This particular publication was invaluable when seeking everyday items like cuticle remover or hair setting lotion. The medical sections were ideal for identifying insect bites or toothache, but travellers afflicted with vaginal discharge or testicular swelling were expected to suffer a little longer. The publishers lived in a world where unmentionables were indeed unmentionable. I thumbed through its pages looking for conversational inspiration

Miss Kim disappeared into the bedroom. I heard the rustle of clothes and involuntarily looked over my shoulder. She had left the door open and was standing with her back to me, naked except for white, voluminous panties. She was hanging her clothes on one peg and removing from another a blue silk nightdress.

All this I recorded in an instant, for I whipped back to stare at my book. What was going on? What was Miss Kim's relationship to Mr Slick? The rules of male-female courtship were alien from those I knew back home. I could not read the signs and the signals. Had I just arrived in Korea I would have jumped to the immediate and obvious conclusion that she was a prostitute and that I would soon be invited to dip into my pockets. On the other hand, I knew enough about this country to know that hospitality does not involve payment. But that raised another question. Was I a client or a guest? Mr Slick did not strike me as a pimp. No, of one thing I was reasonably sure: whatever was happening I was not expected to pay for it.

That left two possibilities. She might emerge at any moment fully clothed. Alternatively she might not.

My thoughts returned to the lovely Miss Choi, who'd stroked my arm, murmured little innuendoes, giving all the signs of seeking affection, and then fled to be with her boyfriend. That had taught me not to assume the obvious.

Keep cool, Mr Clive, and see what happens.

I turned round again. She still had her back to me and was as unclothed as before. This time I held my gaze. Her too-tight brassiere had left faint reddish marks under her arms and across her back. She turned her head and uttered a squeal of fake embarrassment, clutching her nightie over her breasts like they do in the movies. She made no effort to move outside my line of sight, far less to close the door. She held my eye, clearly expecting me to make the next move. I obliged. I turned again and busied myself with my book. Over to you, my dear.

She was swiftly by my side. She had put on her nightie, which brushed against my arm and leg. She leaned across me provocatively, like a cat arching itself around a leg, and began thumbing through my phrasebook. She would soon learn we were way beyond its utility. I had already made a desperate search of the sections entitled 'Making Friends' and 'Dating'.

What a lovely day! ... Can you come round for cocktails this evening? ... Have you got a light please? ... Are you waiting for someone? Nothing of use at all, damn it.

Miss Kim handed me the book and pointed to *Can I get you a drink?* She gestured me towards the bedroom and went to put the kettle on.

The bedroom was even more opulent than I had imagined. She evidently lived in this one room, a bed-sit with style. It had a huge firm bed, a jade telephone half-hidden under the pillow, a pink-handled mirror by its side. A hairy white rug covered the floor. An illuminated goldfish tank sat on the bedside table. Toy ornaments rested on the TV. The extensive bookcase at the foot of the bed was well stocked with leather-bound encyclopaedias and biographies. These included a nine-volume *Strategy of the World* (only the titles being in English); and a collection, still in cellophane wrappers, of biographies of major world figures, including – *Krushchev Remembers* and *Douglas MacArthur's Reminiscences*. One shelf constituted her drinks cabinet, her taste extending from Paul Masson Sweet Vermouth, to Sirop de Grenadine, to Kahlua Licor de Cafe. The top of the bookcase bore the weight of half a dozen jars of spices and candies – presumably rarely eaten, for they were too high and too heavy to be easily accessible.

The wall was cluttered with clothes stands, a freezer, a huge mirror, and shell encrusted, black laminated chests and cabinets of the kind for which Korea is renowned. On top of the wardrobe sat a pile of cuddly toys and a shiny plastic sports bag, from which protruded the handle of a tennis racquet. Around the room were several photographs of Miss Kim, always alone, on holiday in the snow, looking wistful by a fallen tree, unsmiling by a fountain. I detected no sign of permanent male presence, either in the room or in her life.

I sat on the edge of the bed feeling awkward and curious in equal measure. She returned with two mugs of coffee and placed them unsaucered on her expensive rug.

She didn't drink but suddenly leaned over, rubbing herself against me, and murmuring those 'take me, I'm yours,' whimperings that women are conditioned into believing are seductive and irresistible to men. They were the same noises heard throughout the Far East in kungfu films showing violent sex, where rape is depicted as perfectly harmless, and women only nominally resistant.

Maybe she did, after all, want 'business' rather than 'pleasure'. I reached into my pocket and fished out a handful of notes and coins. She shook her head crossly and motioned me to put them away. This confirmed my earlier instincts, for a business woman in a cosmopolitan city like Pusan would surely know harlot's English: she would at least be able to count! As if the interruption had never occurred Miss Kim began purring and whining afresh. If this was hospitality, it lent a new dimension to the word.

I had read accounts of oriental welcomes extending to pleasures of the flesh; of fathers insisting that the honoured guest take the pick of his pubescent daughters; of tribal chiefs ensuring that the visitor need not spend the night alone. Such stories assume the status of fantasy. In any case they always – assuming their veracity – happened to someone else. I'd never come close to the situation I now found myself in.

I was not deluded into thinking Miss Kim was attracted to me, or some such convenient Western explanation for instant sexual availability. Perhaps she'd been set up by our mutual friend. Perhaps he was her 'sugar daddy', as we might say; perhaps she was his 'little wife', his mistress, who catered for his public and private pleasures while leaving the child-rearing and household chores to his actual wife.

By now Miss Kim, finding no response from me, had adopted a cross-legged pose to ensure nothing escaped my eyes. I froze, all my personal values and expectations redundant. What ought to have been a simple pleasure produced nothing but cultural confusions. I did not wish to offend her, but what constituted offence in her alien, inscrutable mind? Would rejection bring relief or shame? She stretched herself on the bed and patted the pillow beside her. And then I learned she did know at least one English word.

'Sleeping?' she asked, in a small voice, straightening out the crinkles in the pillow.

Still I didn't move. The timorous, whimpering look wiped itself from her face. She reached over to the phone and picked it up. Whatever was she up to? Summon some rogues to work me over? Bring over some more women in the hope that they'd have more success? She spoke urgently, impatiently ... and then handed the phone to me.

'Hello, Mr Clive, what is your problem? It was my host in the Japanese restaurant, Mr Slick himself. I wasn't aware that I had a problem, so I asked him outright if Miss Kim was, er, offering me pleasures. It was a dumb question, for the answer was hardly in doubt.

'She is.'

'Is this your will or hers?' I wanted to know.

'Why is this a problem?' he persisted.

I fumblingly explained that I was unsure whether I was a client or a guest, while reassuring him that Miss Kim was indeed very attractive.

'Yes, she is. You are very lucky. Why is this a problem?' He sounded baffled.

'Because I thought I was here as a guest.' I was beginning to sound absurd.

'Mr Clive. You are a guest. This is Korea, not America, not England. Miss Kim is very good to you. Is she not? I think she wishes to make you comfortable. Enjoy yourself, Mr Clive. You are very lucky.'

I mumbled something and put down the phone.

8

THE DEEP SOUTH
Angel Boats and Turtle Boats

We got under weigh again, and visited a large fishing-boat which
was at anchor. The structure of these boats is very rude, and in a
high sea they are entirely unmanageable. We could not conceive
how they could hold together, as no iron, not even a nail, is used
to unite the parts. There is neither order nor cleanliness aboard;
they are as slovenly in their persons as in their boats.

Charles Gutzlaff – *Journal of Three Voyages
along the Coast of China* – (1840)

A WEEK I had spent in Pusan. This admission would provoke the
reply: 'A week? Whatever kept you so long?'

Such response was easy to appreciate. I'd walked Pusan's
streets, ridden its buses and subways, and was still no nearer to
locating the pulse of the city. Assuming it has one. In fact, I'd come to
think of the whole south-east of Korea as the country's Empty Quarter
– Pohang's shapeless, industrial flatness; Kyongju's pretentiousness;
Pusan's drab anonymity. Taegu was so short on smiles that its tourist
map featured an 'excretions treatment factory'. Taegu is an inland city,
the country's third largest. To keep it from communist hands during
the Korean War, the defensive 'Pusan perimeter' embraced Taegu at its
innermost extremity. Battle lines had enveloped the city, none more
critical than those at nearby Waegwan.*

Waegwan was the most disagreeable town I encountered in Korea.
Responsibility surely lay with the proximity of Camp Carroll, for
Korean affability rarely coexists with American military bases. The
town was dotted with sinister, windowless buildings. These were
illuminated at night with flashing red lights, and entered by means of
red padded doors without handles. The folk of Waegwan, taking me for
an iron-hat, averted their eyes. *Adjimas* lied, saying their *yogwans* were
full, thinking I had a whore in tow.

---

* Waegwan means 'small', and by extension, 'Japanese'.

Down by the Nakhtong River, near a wartime bridge blown to frustrate the communists and mothballed today in barbed wire, a couple of GIs were walking an Alsatian.

'I've heard there's a war museum round here,' I said. 'That right?'

'Sure is. It's a couple of miles up river. There's no bus. Even if there was, it would run you over.'

'Ever been on a Korean bus?'

'Nope. Don't intend to either.' With contempt like that, no wonder Waegwan looked mean. I asked about Camp Carroll.

'Why have a military base in a dead-end place like this? Is this still the mentality of the Pusan perimeter?' The GIs looked at each other and shrugged:

'To be quite honest, sir, I don't know why we're here.'

~

I was happy to escape Korea's south-east. In my mind I clung to a vision of a real, timeless Korea, as illusory perhaps as El Dorado or Atlantis. I had come close on Ullung-do, but had arrived ten years too late. Maybe I'd find my pot of gold in the deep south. I took the ferry from Pusan across to Koje-do.

Koje Island warrants no mention in guidebooks and draws few visitors. During the Korean War, however, it was a byword for violence and skulduggery. It was to Koje-do's squalid compounds that North Korean and Chinese POWs were herded in their multitudes. Chosen to police them was 'the scum of the American army, the drunks, the drug addicts, the nutters, the deadbeats'. Battalions of prostitutes took up residence. So lax was camp discipline that commissars conducted drills within the wire, and so ferocious the internees that South Korean guards lured inside disappeared without trace. The inmates built blacksmith's works to forge weapons, and sequestered petrol, food, maps and contraband from corrupt guards. The fraught bureaucracy of repatriation – separating those wishing to return to the North from those seeking asylum – provoked murderous riots. In effect, the last two years of war elevated Koje-do to a second front.

In search of the camps I took myself to the coastal village of Shinhyon. Finding little outward evidence of inglorious history, I resorted to my map-reading trick, a variation on the lady's dropped handkerchief. I selected a public place and pored quizzically over my map, knowing that assistance was but a moment away.

A young man was instantly at my side. With some difficulty he grasped my request and pointed towards the shore. I followed his finger to some wasteland and shortly wandered upon what was, for all I knew, a remnant of Roman wall. It was perhaps twenty feet high, buttressed and tapered towards the top. Its crude stones lent it deceptive vintage. I might never have learned its purpose but for the arrival of the same young man, who suddenly appeared bouncing over the rough terrain on a bicycle. In one hand he flourished a dictionary. He pulled up, thumbed through the pages, and announced:

'This quartermaster stores.'

My new friend became my guide for the day. Leaving his bicycle propped against the old wall, he hoisted my rucksack upon his back.

'I am a man,' he explained, brushing away my protests. He led me up a hill, permitting gorgeous views of islets and waterways, and unsightly exposure to reclaimed land and ugly shipyards. He brought me to a school. In its shadow stood the remains of guards' barracks – bomb-proof, arched end-walls with square window holes. A plaque said: 'Cultural Property Other than the Designated Properties Historic Site No 24.'

The prisoners-of-war camp on Koje Island was built for Communist troops taken prisoners by the United Nations Forces during the Korean War (June 25, 1950 – July 27, 1953) started by Communist north Korea.

Opened on February 1, 1951, this camp had 170,000 prisoners. Inside the camp, strife and friction often involving violence and murders between anti-Communist and pro-Communist prisoners continued. Pro-Communist POWs went so far as to kidnap and detain for three days the camp commander, US Army Brigadier General Dodd from May 7, 1952.

President Syngman Rhee of Korea ordered the release of 27,000 anti-Communist prisoners-of-war without consulting the UN Forces, to great astonishment of the world. After the cease-fire accord was signed on July 27, 1953, the camp was closed and pro-Communist POWs were returned to north Korea by way Panmunjom.

All the camp facilities except some 30 barracks used by guards had all been torn down.

Helpful charts indicated the layout of the vast camps, which extended throughout and beyond the peaceful valley below. I found some latrines, open to public use. A plaque apologised: 'This building is appointed as a cultural treasure, so it is not permitted to be refurbished. Excuse us if the toilet is difficult to use and dirty, for this is a place of real history.'

~

For real beauty I bussed across the archipelago to Chungmu. Korea was at her most beguiling. This had nothing to do with the sublime September sun, but rather my rapport with an environment no longer polluted by cars, noise, and modernity. Chungmu was so sleepy it hadn't woken for its lunch.

The town seemed to straddle a lake, but the map showed an isthmus connecting the mainland to one of the myriad islands that contrived to make Korea's southern coastline almost undrawable. To students of naval history Chungmu ranks with Trafalgar or Jutland, for in these waters were fought remarkable battles between remarkable vessels. In 1592 the Japanese warlord Toyotomi Hideyoshi rampaged through Korea to invade China. The Korean Army quickly capitulated. Not so its Navy, for Admiral Yi Sun Sin, son of a Confucian scholar, had pioneered a peculiar ship. It was reputedly an ironclad.* If so, this predated by two hundred years the construction of iron-sided vessels in the West. The prow of the *Kobukson* (Turtle Ship) was distinguished by a turtle-head-shaped iron ram, while its oarsmen were protected by a humped roof and galley sealed by spike-studded iron plates. The heavily outnumbered Turtle Ships could thereby repel projectiles and boarders alike. In the narrow waters of Hansan-do Bay, east of Chungmu, some 250 Japanese barques were crippled or sunk by the *Kobukson*, and Hideyoshi withdrew.

He tried again five years later. Admiral Yi in the meantime had fallen victim to court intrigue. He was reinstated and duly resumed his earlier tactical mastery. He died from gunfire in the final engagement, but the outcome was already decided. Korea remained free from Japanese predations for nearly three centuries. Statues to Yi and models of his Turtle Ships may be found all over Korea. He, and they, stand as potent symbols of Korean resistance to Japan and the outside world. Nor is his genius forgotten. Following the Russian naval defeat of 1905 a Japanese admiral reputedly said: 'You may wish to compare me with Lord Nelson but do not compare me with Korea's Admiral Yi Sun Sin ... he is too remarkable for anyone.'

---

* This notion is threatened by some Korean naval experts, who insist that the Turtle Ship was wooden-hulled but studded with spikes. In the current nationalistic climate, most Koreans passionately insist on 'ironclad' Turtle Ships.

Little prepares the unsuspecting visitor for the sight of Chungmu's waterside. It was worth coming to Korea just for its memory. Boats old and new (mostly old), large and small (mostly small), were tied up at the water's edge, chattering and chuntering against a backdrop of island peaks. The boats were alive with industry and improvisation. The single cylinder motors of the smallest emitted rapid 'ton-ton-ton-ton' noises, like the ticking of small tractors. This endowed them with the onomatopoeic nickname 'ton-ton' boats. On the quay a lad hammered nails into boxes, which he passed to a younger boy for varnishing. I picked my way amid coils of piping and stacks of petrol cans. One shack housed a welder, who had the good sense to hold a protective shield to his own eyes, while threatening retinal damage to everyone else.

Chungmu market extended down to the waterside. A rocking-horse trolley sat in the shade, two little girls 'riding' excitedly under the gaudy canopy, hopelessly out of sync with the music. I bought a drink and found a toilet. It was designed to frustrate anyone over five feet tall. The urinals were like small rectangular coffins clamped upright against the wall. The problem lay with the low protruding 'lid', for it blocked off the natural angle of attack. The only means of directing the flow into the proper receptacle was to improvise on the Dam Busters technique, stand well back and aim horizontally. This, of course, required a high-pressure hose and ran the risk of exhibitionism. The flat tops of the urinal supported a lidless Fanta can to act as ashtray. Noticing two smouldering butts, I performed a welcome fire-fighting service to the community.

The aesthetic impact of Chungmu halts the traveller in his tracks, insisting he linger to potter about the harbour and ride the boats. Alas, desecration is afoot. A guidebook informed: 'Chungmu has been designated for massive development into a full-scale resort, involving the construction of international-standard hotels, a marina, and numerous facilities for recreation.'

This was sacrilege. To mutilate Chungmu with all the wretchedness of one-arm bandits and video parlours, and replace the ton-ton boats with plastic-seated ferries constituted another assault on nature's sanctity. In fact, the desecration was well under way. I departed westwards by means of the much-trumpeted Hallyo Waterway, which guidebooks have us believe offers an unforgettable experience. For example:

For those who love islands, seascapes, picnics on perfect beaches, swimming, and boating, the Hallyo Waterway, a stretch of islands surrounded by the seas of the Straits of Korea, is a dream come true. Basically, this waterway is an inside protected water route from the port of Pusan westward to the traditional port city of Yosu, which lies a hundred miles west. Following this route, you pass to the north of several major islands, which provide a buffer against heavy weather from the open sea to the south for the many boats that ply the route with cargo for outlying ports. This waterway, a hundred miles long from east to west, and about fifty miles wide from top to bottom, contains 115 inhabited and 253 uninhabited islands, and these create dozens of wide sounds, protected bays and tiny coves, perfect beaches, seascapes of magnificent variety, and superb saltwater swimming.

Waiting on the wharf at Chungmu, enjoying the symphony of plops and gurgles, I was joined by an American couple. They looked at my rucksack, saw the Union Jack and came over.

The Union Jack was one of my foibles. During earlier travels in Japan I had found it irritating to be taken always for an American. In the heyday of empire it must have been equally galling for Americans to be assumed British. I had, however, been anxious to avoid falling victim to cultural stereotyping, particularly in view of the United States' high profile and critical involvement in the affairs of Japan.

But there was another reason why I had determined in future to proclaim my Britishness in the Far East. In the context of Japanese diffidence, humility and civility, American assertiveness – commendable in other circumstances – appears brash, rude. Time and again I had been received more warmly by the Japanese upon learning, firstly, that I was not American, and secondly, that I was British. For the moment, east Asia receives so few British travellers that one is still welcomed as an English Gentleman. This sentimental and archaic view will not survive the wider dissemination of Britain's unenviable yob culture, but in the meantime I was not above wrapping myself in the cloak of Britannia. Before flying to Korea I had pinned a small Union Jack to my rucksack. It had been a wise move, for the US presence in Korea is essentially military and self-serving, unlikely to foster sympathy with the host culture. There is effectively little integration. The nearest the average GI gets to the Korean soul is inside her knickers. The flag was by now tattered, but still distinct.

'Hi there. Australian?' asked the man. I corrected him.

'Oh, England. My mother grew up in Bedford,' he added, as if suggesting we were long-lost cousins. He now worked for the US Air Force at Pusan's Kimhae Airport.

I settled into a window seat of the Angel, directed by a hostess in one of those feathered triangular hats one sees at royal weddings, and sat back to enjoy a relaxing cruise through Korea's maritime paradise. The Korean passengers dozed off, but then they weren't tourists, they were using the hydrofoil as a bus. The Angel provided the quickest means between Pusan and Yosu.

I felt like dozing too. There wasn't much of a view, or if there was I couldn't see it. The weather was balmy, yet we were bottled up, denied exposure to the scents of the sea, save those afforded by an opened hatch at the front. The windows were plastic, so scratched and scarred it was like looking through spectacles scraped with sandpaper. And such was the hydrofoil's speed, anything worth looking at – a miniature desert island complete with miniature beach, a huge barge hauled by insect-like tugs – whizzed past in the blink of an eye. Too often the sights that lingered, like distant hilltop temples, were tarnished by neighbouring gasometers or industrial chimneys.

Yosu – host to a petrochemical complex – announced itself by an immense suspension bridge. The town was attached to a tiny island, Odong-do, accessible via a paved causeway. Odong-do is hailed as a place of sanctuary and refuge, and is famed for its camellias and bamboo groves. In reality, it is dominated by a barbed-wire fortress, with Keep Out signs and radio masts probing the sky like syringes. Korea, it seemed to me, provided a never-ending juxtaposition of tractors and troops, rice-fields and rifles.

Yosu's market was more agreeable. It was there I stumbled upon Korean traditional wrestling – *ssirum*. The tournament was sponsored, said the bunting, by the 'Association of Youth Cultural Celebration, Exhibition of Potted Plants'. The philosophy of *ssirum* equates with Japan's sumo. He wins who floors his opponent inside the ring, or ejects him from it. But that is the extent of the similarity. *Ssirum* lacks sumo's ritual and pageantry. Instead of a purified clay ring, under a ceremonial Shinto canopy, the *ssirum* wrestler fights outdoors, on a heap of sand. In the rain, if necessary. Instead of distinctive belt wrapped around the crutch, he wears football shorts, together with a rag that passes around his waist and thigh. At the commencement of each bout the wrestlers kneel in the sand and grasp each other's rag.

The referee, dressed in civvies, hauls them to their feet. Let battle commence.

'Copy?' asked a smiling young man, as I drifted away. Koreans have difficulty distinguishing 'f' and 'p'. They also have a delightful habit of putting an 'ee' on the end of foreign words that lack them – 'Britishy', 'languagy', 'fishy', 'shoppy'.* I was outside a shoppy marked with a green cross, which sign signifies 'medicine'. The copy was offered by a vet, whose surgery had space for two wooden chairs and a metal tray upon which to operate. Overlooking the tray was a portrait of Jesus wandering among the lambs. Posters advertised 'Common Pathogens' and 'Roundworm Infestation in pigs'. Chickens and dogs were illustrated in various stages of terminal disease. The drip-feeds by the operating tray were Japanese.

A small crowd gathered to watch a foreigner drinking 'copy'. It tasted like no coffee of my acquaintance. It was white, and turned out to be Vegimil – a soya beverage sold in little plastic shampoo bottles. The vet called it 'copy' for fear that I wouldn't know Vegimil.

He was just closing. I therefore missed out on the sight of pigs being slit open. In the privacy of his tiny surgery Vegimil gave way to soju, by which time we were discussing pig breeding. This led on to choosing the sex of human babies.

'There are two ways to make a son,' he said. 'If the man climaxes before his wife, she will have a daughter, but if she climaxes first, they will have a son!'

This was not just gobbledygook, it was sexist gobbledygook, implying that a good lover who satisfies his wife will be blessed with sons. Fathers of daughters have a second shame to bear, that of being inferior lovers.

'The second way,' continued the vet, oblivious to my scepticism, 'is the method of sex. If the man climbs on from the left or the right, this makes a daughter. To make a son he must climb on from "the middle side".'

'You mean he must drop from the ceiling,' I suggested, downing the remains of my soju and rising to my feet. The sun sets rapidly at this latitude and it was dark when I completed my goodbyes and stepped outside. I narrowly missed being mown down by an unlit bicycle. It had a crew of two, the passenger clutching a six-foot length of plate glass.

---

* This is the result of trying to express English sounds through a Korean alphabet that may not recognise them. The single-syllable word 'desk', for example, is written, and therefore articulated, by most Koreans as three syllables, not unlike 'desaka'.

Evening time, as other shops close, highlights the number of pharmacies in Korea. They may be found on every street corner, every street, and in most bus terminals. The pharmacies stay open late, dishing out packets of this and tubes of that to a hypochondriac population anxious to avoid the prohibitive fees of 'Dr Yoo's Urologic Clinic', or 'Dr Lee's Allergy Clinic'. The local druggist assumes the role of a British GP, enjoying the same kind of communal trust, as well as the power to dispense almost anything without prescription. For the moment, Korea has no drug problem, though higher wages and increased imitation of Western vices suggest a darker future.

~

A visit to a Korean cinema could no longer be delayed. It was on my list of must-do's. The only proviso was that it be a rundown provincial, not plush city-centre, cinema. The film itself was of no consequence. In a side-street near Yosu's port I stumbled upon the local flea-pit. Half a dozen films were advertised, though which was running today was impossible to tell.

I pushed some money through a tiny slit in the wall. An invisible presence withdrew it and returned the change, but no ticket. I walked inside to enquire – and was handed my ticket.

In view of a floor-sitting population I shouldn't have been surprised by uncushioned plywood seats. As a rule of thumb, the wearing of shoes equates with the street, not the home. Sure enough, the cinema's uncarpeted floor was littered with ice cream wrappers, spent matches, and cigarette packets. The uncurtained, illuminated Exits left the auditorium light enough to read by. This dispensed with the need for usherettes. My nearest neighbour was a tarted-up woman two seats to my right, who repaid my admiration by coughing up a mouthful of mucus and dribbling it between her feet. The cinema was no more than a quarter full, and, so far as I could tell, I was about the oldest person present.

I didn't notice the lights dim, so was taken by surprise by the national anthem, to which everyone stood. The soundtrack was accompanied by now-familiar film clips of Soraksan – sunrises, waterfalls, scarlet blooms of summer, golds of autumn.

I knew that, whatever the film, any naughty bits or anti-government sentiments would be excised. The 'Korea Public Performance Ethics Committee' (PEC) exerts a heavy hand. Part of the reason is moral – to protect Korea from Western values; part is pragmatic – to widen the audience by snipping the offending parts.

The main feature looked to be *Platoon*. Damn. I'd seen it before and loathed the violence. But it was merely a trailer for Arnold Schwarzenegger's latest, which looked equally unpalatable. Thankfully, that too was restricted to the odd clip. Next came some oriental nonsense, a kungfu expert who preened herself in the mirror after every dust-up. Miss Kungfu was also short-lived, and we dived into the commercials; miracle headache cures and sexy disco queens plugging soft drinks.

At last the film began. It was *Back to the Future*, starring Michael J Fox. On Korean TV, Western films are dubbed. Not so in cinemas, which employ subtitles. This was, of course, to my advantage, though subtitles encourage a noisy cinema. As the audience may follow the action with their eyes, not their ears, they are encouraged to wag their tongues. The subtitles were not always indispensable.

'12.28,' showed a clock in the film.

'12.28,' flashed up the translation.

My intention had been to pass an hour in contemplation of Korean audiences. The subtitles meant I could see the film through, numbed backside permitting. To understand the shaping of modern Korea, it seemed to me, no film could have been more enlightening. *Back to the Future* encapsulated all the Western values lapped up by Korean youth. Its premise was the generation gap, allied to the celebration of Western manliness.

'I think a man should be strong,' cooed one of Fox's female admirers. Sex before marriage was implicit. Love affairs were free from parental approval. Technology was the dream of the future, with academics portrayed as boffin-like eccentrics. Nail-biting car chases glamorised the bloody reality of Korean roads. Libyan terrorists were ritually portrayed as murderous thugs without any legitimate grievance. Violence by the good guys paid off. In short, the film preached that American youth culture was a virtuous model for its Korean counterpart. The audience around me watched enthralled. Nobody minded the sparrow that entered the auditorium and for the last hour buffeted itself against the screen.

The film ended at 11, whereupon I stepped stiffly into the street. A beggar was waiting for the exodus, like a taxi for an incoming train, confident of imminent reward. He sat on his haunches, dropping a coin noisily into an empty tobacco tin. His eyes bored into me until I was lost from sight. I waited for a bus, but none came. Somebody said: 'Bussy finishy ten and half.' I had no idea they stopped running so early. My *yoinsook* was a couple of miles away and I ran for fear of being locked out.

~

At some stage in any remote journey a feeling of familiarity and acceptance envelops the traveller. He finds himself at one with the culture through which he is travelling; is no longer surprised at what he sees, and has eased himself from those initial doubts, fears, and vulnerabilities that overshadowed the excitement of his arrival. This realisation of oneness with the host culture does not come in a flash of understanding, rather a growing inner confidence in the ability to survive and thrive. The imagined hazards presented by a strange land soon fade to the point of invisibility, even inducing self-reproach for having imagined them at all. The further west I headed the more the clock regressed. Staring over the bus driver's shoulder at two *kyong-un-ki* chugging neck and neck and blocking the road, I was aware of how much a part of Korea I had become. I no longer felt on the outside looking in.

I had enjoyed ample time for reflection. Korea's principal misfortune is to possess the least enviable of geopolitical locations, a small country surrounded by water and enemies. She dangles from the vast Asian landmass like an appendix – a conduit for Japanese ambitions in Asia, and the spread of Chinese culture to Japan. Korea is the historical battleground for east Asia's dominant continental and maritime powers. The Belgium of the Far East. As the Koreans themselves say: 'When the whales fight; the shrimp gets hurt.'

Leaving aside the coldest of Cold War frontiers with North Korea, South Korea's neighbours are superpowers of one kind or another. China's Shantung Peninsula lies just two hundred miles west of Seoul, across the West Sea. North Korea borders both China and Russia, the latter for just a dozen miles. The economic might of Japan looms from the south and east. And the United States, separated by the width of the Pacific in geographic terms, nevertheless dominates the political, military and, increasingly, cultural life of South Korea.

Disaffection with the United States exists principally among the young, among the 70% of the population born subsequent to the Korean War. They are less scarred by its memory or indebted to American assistance. In this they are at one with much of Europe's youth; a shared hostility towards perceived American militarism and neo-colonialism.

Pyongyang's propaganda pin-points the imbalance in superpower domination of Korea. The armies of the Soviet Union had pulled back from the North in 1947, and those of the Chinese following the Korean War armistice. The view of a growing number of young South Koreans is that the Republic remains little more than a client state of the United States – whose policies are dictated by American interests, not Korea's – and that the continuing US presence hinders peaceful unification. Put another way, the United States fulfils the paternal role in Korean affairs previously assumed by the Japanese, and by the Chinese beforehand. Whether through payment of tribute, outright annexation, or the junior partner in a military alliance, the people of South Korea have never breathed the invigorating air of genuine independence.

For the most part, however, South Koreans cannot countenance American withdrawal. It is part of the received wisdom of the country that Kim Il Sung is waiting for that very moment to unleash his forces. Psychological indebtedness to the United States for having 'rescued' the south still prevails, though the lamp of gratitude burns less brightly each year, each month, each week, and with each new-born child.

Koreans have a taste for parables. Americans, they will say, are like farmers and Koreans are like cows. America gives food, then takes the milk. Japan, on the other hand, gave no food but still took the milk.

Korean attitudes to Japan, for the most part, do not rise above the meanest sentiments. Words like 'evil' spill from the tongues of most Koreans pressed into giving an opinion. This reflects bitterness for the suffering inflicted over the centuries, especially during the annexation. During the 1930s, when Japan conceived her 'Great East Asia Co-Prosperity Sphere', Koreans ceased to be Koreans and became Japanese. Their culture was suppressed, their language forbidden, their young men sent to the mines or conscripted into the Emperor's army, their girls herded in their thousands to 'battlefield comfort stations', alias brothels. The athlete who won the marathon at the 1936 Berlin Olympics received his gold medal as a Japanese, under the banner of the Rising Sun. But he was Korean.

From time to time Korean hatred of Japan boils rather than simmers, as with revelations of the forced wartime prostitution of Korean schoolgirls. As with photos of past atrocities released to the press. I have before me as I write a newspaper photograph of a Korean lying on his side in a field. His hands are bound behind his back and his head is being dragged under the blade of a fodder chopper. Japanese soldiers stand about, barking orders. In the background Korean villagers stand subdued, forced to observe the 'execution'. The victims – for several heads lie like bloody turnips by the chopper – allegedly conspired with the Korean Independence Movement in the 1930s. Needless to say, the photograph is shocking, and it shocks.

In all my time in Korea I scarcely heard a good word about Japan or the Japanese, other – paradoxically – than from the old. While many elderly Koreans harbour bitter memories, others had benefited from a superior education in Japanese schools and cherished their old Japanese links. The duration of Japanese control, thirty-five years, led many Koreans to assume its permanence (consider the number of French collaborators in just four years of Nazi occupation), and with no prospect of Japanese withdrawal saw little choice but to settle into Japanese ways. Following liberation in 1945 Korea persisted in the methods of Japanese administration, conceding their efficiency and acknowledging no known alternative. Unchanged to this day is the Japanese-style running of schools, railways, banks, courts, police, the government monopoly of certain industries.*

One is tempted to say memories are short. It is no longer 1945. Modern Japan, moreover, is not even an ideological enemy. She is the economic power upon which South Korea models herself and against which she gauges her own industrial miracles. Yet few Koreans do not direct a cocktail of emotions towards Japanese prosperity – envy, fear, suspicion. Koreans will tell you that Japanese are like ducks: calm on the surface but paddling away like crazy underneath.

~

At Sunchon a chap mounted the bus to sell books. He might have had more success had his head not blocked the view of a Jack Palance and Ursula Andress video. The horizon on the westward run became progressively less serrated. From now on the gradients were less steep and the peaks less jagged. Rice-terraces commandeered the landscape. This was provincial Korea, historically the poorest area of the country. In the fields straw hatted, leathery faced old men guided oxen harnessed to ploughs. Bus terminals west of Sunchon were little more than corrugated outhouses attending rutted and pitted bus-parks.

I had grown fond of this particular driver, notwithstanding his impatience with tardy cyclists and tractors. It was a longish run between Yosu and Kangjin, long enough to build a rapport independent of words to sustain it. He made no attempt at elemental conversation, but accepted my supply of digestive biscuits with good grace. At one stop he disappeared towards the confectionery stall, returning with a box of

---

* Korea opened its cigarette market in 1988, whereupon Japanese imports, especially the 'Mild Seven', have gained popularity.

Korean cookies which he prised open on his dashboard. In one swoop he lifted half the contents between finger and thumb and released his payload into my cupped hands. From his pocket he withdrew a bottle of yoghurt, which he deposited in my lap. All without a smile or any other acknowledgment of my existence.

I changed buses at Kangjin. The small town served as a regional crossroads and its bus terminal had some claim to luxury. Its waiting room housed back-to-back park benches, and in the far corner an unlidded oil barrel served as a trash can. The toilets were marked by imaginative blue cut-outs: the Gents with Sherlock Holmes pipe and Elvis quiff.

I was headed for the southern port of Wando. The posh buses came and went. I was directed towards a dilapidated specimen that looked on the point of dissolution. Rear seats had been removed to increase luggage, or rather vegetable, space. No pretence was made at matching seats with backrests, and much of the bus seemed held together by string. It was no place for a conductress, and even the conductor wisely clung on to the door rails to prevent being flung through the windscreen.

Wando was the furthermost point of the island of the same name, connected to the mainland by a garish blue steel bridge. The coast road ran past tiny islets, which from the air looked no doubt like lilies in a pond. Wando served as the gateway to Tadohae National Seapark, which offered even upon this slight acquaintance all the beauty and none of the overkill over the Hallyo Waterway. Crab baskets and drying rice and seaweed littered the quayside. The women attending the baskets giggled at the sight of my camera, adjusting their clothes and combing their hair.

I had yet to sample Korea's much-maligned tourist hotels. Such a hotel existed in Wando, whose cuisine I was prepared to favour, if not its beds. The restaurant was otherwise empty. The menu offered Japanese, Koran [sic], and English dishes, of which there were three options: beef cutlet, pork cutlet, and hamburger steak. A pleasant-faced girl came for my order.

'Pork cutlet, please.'

'I sorry. Pork cutlet no.'

'Then I'll have beef cutlet, please.'

'I sorry. Beef cutlet no.' I began to laugh, but the girl continued unabashed:

'You like hamburger steak?'

I didn't. But the exercise had to be consummated.

'Yes please.'

The radio was playing *When a Child is Born* when the hamburger arrived. The side-dishes included boiled rice, white cabbage and yoghurt sauce, *kimchi*, cold and slimy bean-sprouts. The principal plate comprised three rings of battered ham, nineteen peas, two gherkins, and a nearly raw egg. Hiding under the egg was a minuscule hamburger.

The entire meal, hamburger aside, was Korean. This was hardly a problem for me, as I'd grown accustomed to Korean food. But I sensed the frustration of unsuspecting tourists presented with what lay before me. I looked across at the waitress, all shy smiles and willingness to please. Long may she stay that way.

The problem is the very existence of tourist hotels. They promise an acquaintance with Western notions of comfort impossible to fulfil outside the major cities, and which even then may only be enjoyed at exorbitant prices. Far better, I thought, to do away with them.

Wando Island is ten miles long. The main road runs down the east coast, but the map indicated a lesser route to the west that looked tempting. At the bus terminal I was pushed aside from the ticket window by a man whose impatience gave him right of priority. This was perfectly common, and not seen as incivility. Nor were queue-jumpers ever told to get in line.

I'm sorry sir. This English gentleman is ahead of you in the queue. Kindly wait your turn.

The offender in question addressed me in the waiting room. He wore a creamy jacket that needed a wash. The first two fingers of his right hand were so stained with nicotine they appeared dipped in dye. His opening conversational gambits were non-personal and therefore non-Korean, indicating extensive exposure to Western culture. He was, he said, born on a GI base. He talked only about fighting. England was 'good' because it was not always fighting. Unlike Korea, which had too much fighting. I asked him his job.

'Same as you,' he said.

'But you don't know me or what I do.'

'Same as you,' came the riposte. 'I don't know you: you don't know me.'

This verbal sparring set him apart. Although Korean by blood, he was a cultural half-caste, living with half his mind in an alien West. Judging from his seedy appearance and abrasive manner he had not found comfort in either world. He was not the first Korean I'd met who'd once lived or worked on the coat-tails of the American military, and the experience rarely seemed salutary. I had difficulty in understanding the man's English, which made him visibly impatient, another un-Korean trait.

'Why you can't understand me? Americans do.'

The relationship had plainly exhausted itself and happily my bus now pulled in. I climbed aboard to find it in even worse repair than its predecessor. For three miles the metalled road undulated through a benign landscape. Then, abruptly, the asphalt ended, replaced by a rutted stony track that tossed me like a cowboy on a bronco. I expected the asphalt to return at any moment, but it didn't. And as the bus pitched through ruts that caused its springs to groan and wheeze I realised that these were no temporary road works but an enclave from the onslaught of technology. The ideas of Brunel and Macadam had yet to permeate the hinterland of Wando Island. In the 1960s few of South Korea's roads were metalled: I had just stumbled upon one of the few nowadays that wasn't.

I now appreciated Wando's dilapidated buses; the necessity for running repairs, and why the windows were so caked with dirt it was pointless to clean them. I regretted thinking unkind thoughts about Wando's transport, and marvelled that buses operated at all.

Ahead of us a man struggled with a tree branch over his shoulders. The woman at his side was leading a cow by its nose-ring. She had a babe on her back and a loaded basin under her free arm. Almost instinctively I knew I had found it. This was the real Korea I had been searching for. None of the guidebooks mentioned this place. They sent you to Kyongju and the palaces of Seoul. Yet here, for the price of a bus ticket, a fortified bus and its heroic driver were chauffeuring me to Korea's past, a past all the more precious in the face of the encroaching 'progress' that would soon consume it.

The driver set me down. It was a delicious day, the temperature self-regulating as if on automatic thermostat. The sun beamed and a breeze fanned my cheeks.

The stony track made for slow walking as well as slow driving. It snaked along forested slopes, plunged down to the water's edge, then wound inland past fields of marrow and squatting women sowing garlic. Each woman was dressed in the billowing blouse and bloomer uniform of the Korean peasantry. These display no thought for aesthetically pleasing combinations. Blue flowered blouses happily topped brown striped bottoms.

In the distance, framed by islets large and small, scores of midget boats converged on some fixed point. These craft, no bigger than two-man canoes but powered by ton-ton outboards, would have been invisible except for their wakes disturbing the millpond waters. The origin of this unexpected armada, the village of Samdu, came into view round the next headland. The last dozen boats were just pulling away, each weighed down by sharpened pine stakes, twelve to fifteen feet long. These fantailed either side of the stern like Concorde wings. The stakes would soon be sunk into the sea-bed, nets attached, to harvest the abundant seaweed.

A van, kicking up a spume of stagecoach dust, stopped by me. I hadn't flagged the driver.

'Going?' he enquired. I shook my head. There was too much to savour out here in the Korean outback.

Nearby, a thumping, asthmatic machine pummelled red peppers into powder. Beyond lay a cluster of what looked like thatched cottages, circular and domed. The thatch was criss-crossed by string, like straw wigs secured by hair-nets. The 'cottages' had no doors. They were built over ditches and supported by wooden horizontal frames. Inside the thatch seaweed was being dried and matured.

Even Wando had its army camp, whose presence out here seemed almost an affront. Not far away stood a white shack. Some workers were preparing a meal. I guessed the menu, for hanging from the doorpost was a duck. Its wings were tied behind its back and its feet hooked to a nail. The bird dangled helplessly. It raised its head as I approached, and we examined each other intently. Just another bird, just another meal.

9

CHEJU-DO
'An Adventure into Paradise'

August 17, [1832] – We passed many islands of every imaginable shape, the most southern, [Quelpart], (lat. 32° 51', long. 126° 23') is a charming spot. It is well cultivated, and so conveniently situated that if a factory was established there, we might trade with the greatest ease to Japan, Corea, Mantchou, Tartary, and China. But if this is not done, could not such an island become a missionary station? Would it not be giving a fatal blow to those hateful systems of exclusion, by establishing a mission in so important a situation? I know not how far the Corean government exercises control over the island; but I should think that a missionary residing there would be less subject to dangers than those in New Zealand, and the first harbingers of the glad tidings in Labrador and Greenland. One thing is true, these islands are not inaccessible to Christianity.

Charles Gutzlaff – *Journal of Three Voyages along the Coast of China* – (1840)

NOR WERE 'these islands' inaccessible to Christianity. In time, a trickle of missionaries came and settled. In 1952, prompted by the international focus on the Korean War, a hundred Irish priests uprooted for Cheju-do, sixty miles south of mainland Korea. Their efforts have resulted today in an extensive ranch ('pasture'), whose five thousand acres cater for four thousand pigs, two thousand sheep, and almost as many cattle. The sheep's wool is hand-woven in Irish style and exported around the world, while the faith does quite nicely too.

~

Wando is one of the ports serving Cheju Island. The ferry sailed at 4 pm. A trail of unattended baggage, suitcases, plastic bags and holdalls stretched from the 'No Entry' barrier in a wiggly line across the concourse. Queuing by proxy. The 'Ticket Window for The

Disabled' was no different from the other windows other than being five inches lower. Presumably it was for people in wheelchairs, except that I hadn't seen any wheelchairs in Korea. They apparently don't exist, apart from those of disabled foreign tourists bringing their own.*

Having earlier told me to 'come back tomorrow', then 'come back later', the cheery ticket-girl now directed me through a door marked 'Police'. On the desk lay a dog-eared manual entitled *A Guide to English Conversation for Terminal Business*. Visions of a condemned cell, gallows, and a request for a last cigarette flashed before me, and I entrusted my soul to the policeman's understanding of 'terminal' as noun rather than adjective. He phoned a superior, was presumably told to clear me, and stamped my embarkation form.

This individual attention inadvertently elevated me to VIP status. An announcement that boarding might commence precipitated a stampede to locate baggage, identity cards at the ready. It would take an age to process all passengers, but an official tapped me on the shoulder and pointed to the gate. I already had my clearance and I strolled, casual as you like, past the jostling hordes and through the checkpoint, permitting myself a wicked grin over my shoulder.

The tourist blurb raved about Cheju Island – the Hawaii of the Orient. In 1975 *Newsweek* magazine promoted it as one of the ten not-yet discovered world-wide tourist attractions. It proved the kiss of death. One guidebook subtitled its chapter on Cheju-do 'An Adventure into Paradise', and eulogised the island as a 'picturesque vacationer's world of palm trees and tropical flowers, lava monuments carved by nature, tumbling clear waterfalls, a snow-capped mountain, ancient pavilions and temples, and a sparkling shoreline with broad bathing beaches – all wrapped up in a subtropical climate.'

The island is a favourite retreat for Korean honeymooners. However unspoiled Cheju-do may have been, it is now Korea's Blackpool, Palm Beach and Costa del Wotsit all rolled into one. It is popularly known as the island of three abundances (*samdado* – rocks, winds and women), and today boasts its own Hyatt Regency Hotel.

Cheju-do's relationship to Korea stands comparison to that between Crete and Greece. Each island is sufficiently remote to foster a culture and mentality distinct from that of its motherland. A distinct history,

---

* Korea does not tolerate the physically afflicted. When a blind singer performed on television, the network was swamped with complaints about viewers' distress. As a result, blind persons are now barred from the nation's television screens. Nor do taxi drivers stop for the disabled. Much responsibility for Korean attitudes in this regard is laid at the feet of Confucius, who stressed the importance of appearance and decorum.

too. Portuguese traders knew Cheju-do as 'Ilha de Ladrones' – Isle of Thieves, reflecting Korea's policy of despatching there its criminals and undesirables. Respectable folk stayed away: the name 'Cheju' translates as 'the district over there'. As recently as the Second World War, the island was designated on European charts as Quelpart (or Ouelpoert). A 'quelpart' was a Dutch sailing vessel, the ship-shaped island having been charted in the seventeenth century by vessels in the employ of the Dutch East India Company.

But the Dutch did not just bequeath the name Quelpart. They also provided the first account of it – and of the Korean mainland. And the circumstances of that episode rank among the epic tales of shipwreck, capture and escape ...

~

Being first on board I had, for the moment, the ferry to myself. Second-class was divided into two sections, to permit sitting upon the floor or upon cushioned chairs. I settled into a chair in front of the video and fetched from my pack ye olde tales of bygone mariners. The Prussian Gutzlaff had been a Protestant missionary aboard the *Lord Amhurst*, an East India Company vessel sent to exploit the opium trade with the northern ports of China, while permitting Gutzlaff to salve his conscience by distributing Chinese bibles, sowing potatoes, and generally weighing up Christian prospects. With respect to Korea, he was not overly optimistic:

'They [the Koreans] heard and read repeatedly that Jesus Christ, God over all, was also their redeemer; but their affections were never aroused. Such callousness of heart bespeaks great degree of mental apathy.'

The coast of Korea delayed the *Lord Amhurst* a month only. Gutzlaff referred occasionally to 'our hardships from the winds and weather', and entered his brief remarks about Cheju-do, quoted above, on 17 August 1832.

Nearly two centuries previously, in the early hours of 16 August 1653, the crew of the *Sparwehr* ('Sparrowhawk') endured rather greater hardships from wind and weather, as a result of which the three-masted barque was lost on Cheju's rocks. Half her crew perished in the wreck, the survivors being denied repatriation by the locals for fear of what Korean secrets they might divulge. Being Christian ('southern Barbarians'), they were lucky not to have been slaughtered outright. As it was, they were conscripted into the palace guard at Seoul, then exiled for life elsewhere on the mainland. After thirteen

years, by which time just sixteen of the original survivors were still
alive, eight – aided by the lucrative proceeds of begging – escaped by
boat to Japan and to freedom. The eight left behind, including a
Scottish gunner by the name of Alexander Bosquet, or Basket, were
freed two years later.

One of the escapees was Hendrick Hamel, the ship's secretary. His
startling tales of the Hermit Kingdom (it was only sixty-odd years since
Admiral Yi had sent the Japanese packing, whereupon Korea had
clamped the doors against foreigners) were published and placed before
the world. Korean schoolchildren today are taught about Hamel's place
in history. A plaque in his honour stands at the assumed point of the
Sparwehr's destruction near the south-west corner of Cheju Island.

In view of the typhoons that wreak their summer havoc over the
Philippines, Taiwan and southern Korea, it had taken a fearless captain
to set course from Formosa (Taiwan) across the East China Sea to the
Japanese port of Nagasaki. For twelve days intermittent storms and
calms impeded the *Sparwehr*'s progress. Then 'a south-west wind grew
up into a storm, with a heavy rain, and forced them to run north-east,
and north-east by east.'

By this time the frequent beating of the Sea had much weakened
our Vessel, and the continual Rain obstructed our making any
Observation; for which reason, we were forced to take in all our
Sails, strike the Yards, and commit ourselves to the Mercy of the
Waves ... A Wave coming over our Stern, had like to have
wash'd away all the Sea-men that were upon the Deck, and filled
the ship so full of Water, that the Master cried out, My Mates, cut
down the Mast by the Board immediately, and recommend your
selves to the Mercy of God; for if one or two such Waves return,
we are all lost.

I trusted the Wando-Cheju ferry was sturdier than the *Sparwehr*. By
now the first passengers had arrived and were rushing for the best
seats. I was aware of a blue presence fidgeting behind me, and sensed
it would not be long before it shifted to the vacant seat beside me. The
presence duly materialised, sat down, and for the moment feigned
preoccupation with his newspaper.

This was our Condition, when the second Glass ... being just
running out, he that looked out a-Head, cried, Land, Land; adding,

we were not above a Musket-shot from it; the Darkness of the Night and the Rain having obstructed our discovering it sooner. We endeavour'd to Anchor, but in vain, because we found no bottom ... Thus the Anchors having no hold, three successive Waves sprung such a Leak in the Vessel, that those who were in the Hold were drowned before they could get out. Some of those that were on the Deck leaped Overboard, and the rest were carried away by the Sea. Fifteen of us got ashore in the same place, for the most part naked, and much hurt, and thought at first none had escaped but our selves; but climbing the Rocks, we heard the Voices of some Men complaining, yet could see nothing, nor help any body, because of the darkness of the Night ... [The next day] we were touched at the loss of our Ship, and to see that of 64 Men only 36 were left in quarter of an Hour.

The ferry was well under way, the video showing routine kungfu violence. The rape scenes were repugnant. Bandits took impatient turns to leap from improbable heights on their victim, like diving off a high board into a swimming pool.

'Right, you've had enough time,' protested (in subtitles) those in line, as they heaved one another aside. Predictably, the woman did not so much scream in terror as moan in ambiguous pleasure.

I looked about me at the reaction of the passengers, unable to accept that so kindly a race could welcome such scenes. The expressions were vacant, registering neither shock nor enjoyment. The eyes just watched, while the mouths chewed cuttlefish or sucked tangerines. I sought the opinion of my blue-shirted neighbour. He looked delighted to be spoken to, being shyer than most and hesitant about breaking the ice himself. He studied the screen for a moment, then shrugged:

'Koreans like very much,' he said. 'It is humorous.'

Humorous? I looked up 'terrible' in my dictionary, and suggested that *chidokha* was a better description for what we were watching.

He was an electrical engineering student touring the country on his 90cc motor cycle, stopping off to repair televisions and radios to pay his way. Our conversation soon asphyxiated through want of common language, and I returned to Hendrick Hamel.

On the 17th [of August], as we were lamenting our deplorable Condition sometimes complaining that we saw no body, and sometimes flattering our selves with the hopes of being near Japan

CHEJU-DO

... we spyed a Man about a Cannonshot from us. We called and
made Signs to him; but as soon as ever he saw us, he fled. Soon
after Noon we spied three more, one of them with a musket, and
his Companions with Bows and Arrows. Being come within Gun-
shot of us, they halted; and perceiving we made towards them, ran
away, tho' we endeavoured by Signs to show them we desired
nothing but Fire of them. At last one of us resolved to attack
them; but they delivered up their Arms without making any
opposition, wherewith we lighted the Fire we wanted. These Men
were clad after the Chinese fashion, excepting only their Hats,
which were made of Horse-hair; and we were much afraid lest
they should be wild Chinese or Pirates.

Hamel may have supposed that he and his companions were the first
Europeans to have set foot on Korea. As it turned out, they were not
even the first Dutchmen to do so. This became clear when in due
course an interpreter was sent down from Seoul to interrogate them.
The interpreter introduced himself as John Wettevree. He had been
born at Riip in Holland and had been on his way to Japan in 1627 when
a storm drove his ship upon the coast of Korea. Desperate for water,
the crew commanded him and two others to go ashore to seek
provisions, where they were duly captured and interned by the
inhabitants.

In later years Wettevree was impressed into the wars against the
Tartars. Unlike the survivors of the *Sparwehr*, he would never return to
his homeland.

~

I had a contact in Cheju City, a twenty-seven year old clerk. Mr Park
was almost six feet tall – enormous for a Korean.* His English, he
explained, was self-taught, with the aid of his bedroom mirror to detect
misalignment of lips, teeth and tongue. He lived in a traditional Korean
house, whose courtyard was accessible via an alleyway and low door.
Rooms were arranged around a central space, like an internal courtyard, which appeared to have no practical use whatsoever. I was shown
to Mr Park's room, in which he worked, ate and slept, and in which I
too was to sleep. The toilet was outside, round the corner. The washroom was round the other corner, equipped with cold tap and buckets.

---

* Had he equalled the height of the author, 6 feet 4 inches, he would have been absolved the
necessity to perform military service, on the grounds that such a height, and therefore such a
person, was 'abnormal'.

My host was an eldest son, which bestowed duties and responsibilities unique to eldest sons. He was something like a crown prince.
Whilst his father was titular head of the household, to Mr Park befell
its day to day management. In due course the assets of the house would
be his, but equally its obligations. To look after his younger sisters, for
example. Potential wives traditionally shied away from eldest sons,
whose first loyalties were always to kin. True enough, Mr Park was
unmarried. He hadn't found the right person, he said, adding:

'I never had a girl-friend at college because I have a long head like a
horse.'

But he faced other difficulties. His parents were divorced. Custom
dictated that he abide with his father, while his mother lost her house
and custody of her only son. She lived nearby and Mr Park kept in
close touch. Divorce, he said, was easily obtained through 'family
courts'. His father had married again and had two more children, both
under ten years old, thereby increasing the duration of Mr Park's
responsibilities. His relations with his step-mother, he insisted, were
amicable.

Mr Park had a social conscience. He and his father ran a ping-pong
'salon' in a cellar large enough for three tables. Students were encouraged to attend, socialise, and practice their English.

Practice their English? Would I mind helping, to pay for my board?

~

On the map Cheju Island resembles a suppository. It measures forty-
three miles by nineteen. Cheju City lies halfway along the northern
coast. The island's geography is as distinct from the mainland's as
Hokkaido's is from the rest of Japan. Where mainland Korea is jagged
and wild, Cheju-do is exposed and grassy. All points lead inexorably
upwards towards its central volcanic summit, Mt Halla ('Hallasan') –
at 6,397 feet the highest peak in South Korea.

Cheju-do's geographical symmetry lends itself to symmetrical
roads, which circumnavigate and bisect the island. It is difficult to
avoid Cheju-do's tourist face, for that is the side most in evidence.
Take the Dragon Head Rock (*Yingduam*), a lump of basalt near the city
and hailed as a geographical wonder. One may imagine dragons, but to
me it was just a rock that wanted to be left in peace. It was a mercy
there was no admittance charge. A solitary photographer looked at me
and knew better than to ask.

It was no better at Song-up folk village, site of ancient, seven feet
high, bulging eyed, soapstone phallic sculptures known colloquially as

Grandfather *(harubang)* Rocks. Their noses are all but rubbed away, the result it is said of countless rubbings by countless hands. Noses, being phallic substitutes, symbolise fertility. It is for that reason that Westerners, having comparatively big noses, are presumed to be generically virile.

Tourism, as yet, has little defiled Cheju-do's expansive interior. Horses roam freely along the verges, long grasses rustle in the breeze, and you may be forgiven for thinking yourself on Dartmoor or Connemara in a heat-wave. The landscape was too precious to be defiled. The horizon was a series of gentle hazy curves, while the upper slopes of Hallasan hid shyly behind a modesty cloud. The open expanse of trees, pasture, and dry-stone walls screamed its beauty. Given a motorcycle at that moment, I would have been Steve McQueen roaring away in *The Great Escape*.

The bus to Sogwipo, on the southern shore, passed orchards of tangerines and oranges, and the 'Gospel Pediatric Clinic'. From a cramped store I bought a 'corn sandwich in woolli bread' in an airtight wrapper. It tasted like stale cake with a cheesy paste. A scrap-metal collector pushed his cart down the road. Koreans doing the rounds associate themselves with distinctive sounds. Mendicant Buddhists tinkle tiny bells; bean-curd peddlers clang larger hand-bells; while waste-metal dealers clatter metal-cutters the size of shears.

'Hello,' he said, so naturally that I took him to be born in Brighton. His black baseball cap was pulled down over his ears. He set down his cart, rummaged inside and unearthed what was once an executive briefcase. He shook off the surface dust, brushed away the remainder and snapped it open. It was crammed with books, pamphlets and dust. He selected one volume, hand-brushed it, and conspiratorially showed it to me. It was written in Korean with no pictures. I just grinned. He was, I thought, seeking approval rather than a sale, and I tried to look impressed. He put away the book, gave me a blackened smile, and said goodbye as fluently as his earlier hello.

~

Korea boasts many myths and legends. The people take them seriously. In places like Cheju, they take them all the more seriously now that tourists cough up to hear them. The waters of Chongbang waterfall, do you know, provide the elixir of life, and a golden dragon will emerge from the sea and dance – provided its paws are suitably greased.

Another waterfall, Chonji (Natural Monument No 27), wasn't worth the effort except for observing the honeymooners. They strolled around, took their ritual snaps, with or without hiring the professionals, and ambled away. A man carried his bride's handbag Dick Whittington-style over his shoulder. He waved away the lurking photographers and snapped her unsmiling against a rock. They seemed so joyless, but Koreans believe that should a bride smile before her husband they will be punished with a daughter.

Sogwipo did offer some pleasures, away from its abused waterfalls. An old man, hidden under a wide-brimmed straw hat, sawed patiently through a fallen sapling with a hacksaw. He looked up and the lines of his face dissolved into a toothless happy smile. I paused by a trader's cart, stacked with apples, black grapes, persimmons, chestnuts and cuttlefish. In the midst of the food, almost as if space had been scooped out, lay a child, wrapped in a green quilt, fast asleep. Nearby houses had roofs of corrugated iron, weighed down against storms by rocks at each corner. With the assistance of coloured clothes pegs, a woman fastened to her washing line a dozen squid.

One morning I took an early bus east from Cheju City. We passed a factory producing fake Grandfather Rocks. These are a lucrative industry. Grandfathers and Grandmothers, large and small, to suit any occasion. They stand outside public buildings with placards round their necks saying: 'In Korea we are here to help – American Express.'

Manjanggul cave was billed as the longest known lava tube in the world. The carpark was empty, apart from a few contract coaches serving the big hotels. Their drivers chatted and smoked. The adjoining tourist complex, modelled to my mind on a typical motorway service station, bode ill for the coming experience. So did the obtrusively jolly music. At a hut marked 'Police Information – Checking,' I handed over my ticket and descended into the darkness. I was welcomed at the foot of the steps by a 'Wellcome' sign, with the second 'l' semi-erased, and the helpful instruction: 'When the electricity goes off don't be perplexed.'

Lava caves, considered purely as a tourist attraction, are somewhat dull. They offer none of the grotesque shapes and mysterious shadows of imaginatively lit limestone caves. Walking through Manjanggul was like taking a stroll through a half-finished Dartford Tunnel. It was dark, it was damp, it was cold. The walls were bare and black, the lights few.

To ease the tedium, visitors pause at a dollop of lava, where they are asked to imagine a stone tortoise. It bore more resemblance to a blancmange. No one else bothered to go further; they turned on their heels. They missed the Wedded Couple Rock. Barbra Streisand cooed *The Way We Were* from hidden speakers, and I was invited to perceive a man and woman in coitus. Either that, or they were bathing in blancmange.

Outside in the breezy warmth I chanced upon a German. From Stuttgart. Mid-twenties, longish hair, canvas shoes, just passing the time. To an earlier generation he would have presented a hippie, but he was content to appear 'cool'. He was aggrieved at Korea's obsession with filching tourists as a means of demonstrating her modernity. He examined my entrance ticket and remarked upon its expense. Not the expense of buying it, but of making it – glossy paper with colour pictures. They were always like this in Korea. Bus tickets would have sufficed, at a fraction of the cost, except that in Korea appearances are everything.

We bussed together to Ilchul volcano, which was linked to the island by a thread-like causeway. The tourist eaters were out in force, constituting a sizable base-camp. Tethered ponies attracted rent-a-rides to the top.

The view was worth the hassle and the innumerable steps to the summit. The sun beat down and god was in his heaven. Koreans are wont to show off when on holiday or socialising. A man held a can of beer as a pretend microphone and wailed a frightful melody to ecstatic applause. Newly-weds posed for routine snaps, the yellow-armbanded paparazzi forced to stand idly by.

Stuttgart and I clambered round the back of the volcano. Far below white dots bobbed about in the water. These were the foam floats of Cheju-do's famous diving women (*haenyo*), and we slipped and slithered down for a closer look. The 'beach' on this, the leeward side of Ilchul, was black volcanic ash pitted with scarred boulders. Cliff walls were honeycombed with caves. The scene was as grim as death. No tourists here. No buckets and spades. No deck-chairs. No life at all, apart from scurrying, centipede-like creatures which fled over the pockmarked surface, up slabs of lava, and across tidal rivulets at improbable speeds. A dozen wicker baskets stuffed with divers' clothes lay strewn on the rocks.

Cheju-do's fast-fading matriarchal dominance is epitomised by the *haenyo*. Those we had seen from on high were between thirty and sixty yards out to sea. They surfaced from time to time, then flipped over backwards and remained submerged for several minutes. As we watched, two wet-suited flippered women waded out of the water towards the baskets. Ursula Andresses they were not. The myth tells of bathing beauties in cotton swimwear. Souvenir dining plates depict them as bare-legged, bare-shouldered lovelies: approaching Ilchul I had passed a billboard showing a 'diver' with an hour-glass figure pointing at a phone number.

The reality was harsher and more heroic. The women were middle aged, with grizzly, weather-beaten faces. Theirs was no easy life and it showed.

The reality was harsher in another sense, too. One diver contrived a smile, thinking we wished to buy a still-quivering squid or an aphrodisiac hairy sea-urchin. The smile vanished when I brought out my camera. Camera-shy, perhaps? Not quite. The woman rubbed her fingers together: money-money. Another convert to the worship of mammon. If I wanted her picture I'd have to pay. Even ten years ago this would not have been the case, and I did not love Cheju for the change.

It was late afternoon and the heat was intense. Stuttgart and I wandered far from the well-trodden path, through clifftop fields, and stumbled into an army camp shielded by camouflaged haystacks. Not an inch of South Korea, it seemed, was unprotected by hidden guns.

~

It was wise to avoid outdoor pursuits on a Sunday. Otherwise one ran the risk of ten million Koreans sharing your footpath. But I was determined to climb Mt Halla while the weather held. It was necessary to reach the summit by midday, after which Hallasan is daily veiled by its personal shroud. Hendrick Hamel had noted 'in this island there is a mountain of a vast height, covered with woods'. Not so vast, perhaps, but the ascent is assisted by cross-island buses serving well-marked trails to the summit.

The mass of bodies at Cheju bus station should have deterred me outright. I fought my way aboard, accompanied by hikers, hampers, pick-axes, scythes with naked blades.

I followed the crowd to the start of the forested trail and, for safety's sake, pencilled in my downward route. I had proceeded barely half a mile when I was overtaken. It was Mr Soe, the 'blue' TV repair man from the ferry. He seemed overjoyed to meet me again. Small world: small Cheju.

The track meandered through conifer forests and up through craggy open land. Mr Soe wished to talk. With few exceptions, any conversations reported in this narrative were not conversations at all, but precious word-nuggets mined out of a wall of incomprehension. Many Koreans know a few English words, though it is often hard work making sense of them. The extent of the latent English vocabulary, however, never ceased to amaze. Mr Soe's exchanges with me on the ferry had been monosyllabic. Now, warming to the practice, he asked the most unexpected questions. Like did I do the tango? To be precise, he uttered the two words 'you ... tango?' followed by an impromptu little dance on the mountainside. Then, learning I lived in Scotland, he wanted to know about 'Mary Scotland Queen'. Here I was, on the slopes of Hallasan, being quizzed about Mary Queen of Scots. Recollecting my own school days, I had learned nothing about Queen Min of Korea, nor anything about Korea, nor, come to think of it, much international history at all.

Nine tenths of the climb was little more than a steady hike. The final tenth was by means of steep, artificial steps, no less exhausting for their convenience. The climb had taken three hours. Hallasan's tributary pathways had been largely empty. Now that they converged, a steady line of hikers filed their way up.

The view from the summit justified the attempt. I had beaten the clouds and could inspect the entire island simply by turning my head. To the south, Sogwipo, with its dog-leg harbour wall, looked no bigger than a hamlet. An Orion's Belt of rocky islets, rudely visible as tiny blots against the shimmering sea, stood guard over Sogwipo's approaches. To the north, Cheju City sprawled untidily along the coast. Planes taking off from the airport looked like silver kites hoisted by invisible strings. They remained below my line of sight until almost lost from view.

Mt Halla's crater had lain undisturbed for a thousand years, and I trusted it to remain quiet till I got back down. One guidebook warned: 'there is snow on the mountain year-round, so first-rate hiking boots and cold-weather clothing are a must.' As I threw back my head to sunbathe my face and contemplated my battered trainers I wondered weather the guidebook had got the wrong mountain.

It was triumphal to stand on the summit of Korea. Not for the climb, which all but the aged and infirm could manage, but for the peace and serenity instilled by gazing out upon three hundred square miles. Mr Soe settled into the lotus position and closed his eyes, the breeze ruffling his hair and a fly settling on his uncomplaining cheek. He was unusual for a Korean in travelling alone. Other climbers we had passed had been in pairs or small groups, the ascent of Hallasan being for them not the end but the means. Koreans climbed as much for the company as for the mountain.

Neither of us was in a hurry to descend. For all its touristy excesses, Cheju Island was truly a natural paradise. No gaming tables or escalators disfigured the summit of Hallasan, though doubtless they would come. Far below me a horse galloped freely, tail erect, a symbol of Cheju-do's spirit.

Not everyone made use of the litter bins, for Hallasan was scattered with ring-pulls, bottle tops and broken glass. Four boisterous US servicemen arrived just as Mr Soe stirred from his meditation.

Nearby picnickers hailed us to join them. We tucked into wooden trays of sushi (dice-shaped segments of raw fish and rice, wrapped in seaweed), followed by the crispiest apples. My waterbag was passed from person to person, mouth to mouth, spittle to spittle, without so much as a cursory wipe. The food preceded the inevitable photo call. I fear it was improper of me to sit the youngest woman on my knee, and I instantly regretted doing so.

We were a quarter of the way down, other hikers having dispersed among the various descents. The trail passed through a narrow stepped gully flanked by camellia. There we came upon an old man, clinging unsteadily to the arm of his wife. With his straw hat, Gortex grey zip-jacket, dark striped trousers, white sports socks and dainty running shoes he looked like a townie who fancied a shot at Everest.

Without warning he pitched sideways into the undergrowth and lay still. We clambered over to him and felt his rapid, weak pulse. His skin was clammy and cold and flecks of saliva bubbled from his mouth. We removed his glasses and loosened his belt. This was not the ideal place to take ill. It was mid-afternoon and he was several hours from medical help.

Mr Soe and I parlayed among ourselves – that is to say our eyes met – and agreed that we should carry him. It was typical of my companion that he should seek to do most of the carrying. But he was slightly built and – he told me later – had broken a leg as a youth. Its latent weakness manifested itself with every burdened step he took. In fits and starts we took turns to piggy-back the semi-conscious old man. He could not stand the jolting for long, and we would gently lower him to the ground, where he flopped with arms wide, eyes half open with only the whites showing.

Two teenagers skipping down the mountain were – unbeknown to me – despatched to send help. The man was not heavy, but it was hard to keep balance on such uneven terrain. Several times I feared I would stumble.

For an hour or more we continued in this fashion. The dipping sun caressed the landscape as if with a golden brush, though we were hardly in a position to stop and admire. I feared the approach of sunset here on Mt Halla no less than I would in Transylvania. Dracula's teeth carried less threat to the old man than the exposed chill of an autumn evening at altitude.

We had gone no more than half a mile when two mountain-rescue soldiers came upon us. They administered smelling salts and intimated that they would take over. Mr Soe and I were free to go.

The old man revived sufficiently to effuse thanks, reinforced by his wife and translated adequately by Mr Soe. A soldier added: 'we thank you for your kindness.' I told him that in Korea many people had been kind to me. The soldier asked me my country, and upon my answer the sound of '*yong-guk*' echoed around the little gathering. The old couple lived in the city of Kwangju, and pressed me to call them if I passed through. The wife gave me their number and I said I'd ring.

A shared drama binds people no matter the linguistic gulf. I had already come to respect Mr Soe with his kind eyes and quiet intelligence, and now we stepped lightly down the mountain, resting at intervals to enthral at the lengthening shadows and humbling view over Cheju-do's evening golds and browns.

His 90cc motorcycle looked fit for the scrap yard. He insisted I wear his crash helmet. I hadn't been on a motorbike for twenty years and could find nothing to hang on to. He reached back and pulled my arms around him. We buzzed across Cheju Island, passing ranks of swallows on power lines and taxi drivers snapping stiffly posed newly-weds against a sinking sun.

Cheju-do's reputation for honeymooners had not been overstated. They descend on the island for reasons of tradition, climate, finance and government restriction. Couples could find accommodation in any number of honeymoon hotels, all well-practised in catering for the big moment. Cheju-do's weather is benign, lacking Seoul's summer humidity and icy winter. The Korean work ethic restricts honeymoons to just two or three days, deterring any search for alternative destinations. South Koreans are, in any case, barred from visiting neighbouring countries on political grounds, Japan apart, where the barrier is financial. Few Koreans can afford honeymoons further afield. Nor does the government encourage them to do so. Passports were until recently hard to obtain, the reasons being hedged with double-talk, such as insisting that military service be completed beforehand.

~

It was my last night with Mr Park, the ping-pong man. Each evening we sat with students – English majors at Cheju National University. They would interrupt their games on my arrival and rush to arrange their chairs around me, as if around a guru.

Just to sit with them was to confront the distinction between the Korean and the Western student. Times may be a-changing for Korea, the values of filial piety rapidly being supplanted by more material ideals. But if so, they were slow to affect these students. Confucius had taught that a student must not even tread on the shadow of a teacher, and their politeness verged on the obsequious. Their first concern was how to address me. My natural preference for Clive, or Mr Clive, would have been misconstrued as lacking self-esteem. They sought a grander title – professor, doctor – even amongst our casual exchanges.

'You are very brave, Dr Clive,' said one student. 'You must be very brave to live near the North Pole.'

She thought latitude reflected temperature. She was unaware that Seoul's mid-winter temperatures plummet far below Britain's, despite the Korean capital sharing a common latitude with Athens and San Francisco. She seemed only half-convinced by my denial.

'Living near the North Pole I think you are very pungent!' She was not referring to halitosis, but meant 'patient', which word resembles the Chinese character for pungent. Another student had voluminous black tresses piled on one side, requiring a compensatory tilt of the head. She wanted to know what British students talked about.

'We talk about democracy,' she said, her face a picture of lop-sided earnestness. I did not disillusion her by confiding the more earthy, not to say lascivious preoccupations of her British counterparts, and changed the subject to North Korea.

I was more likely to find apologists for Kim Il Sung in present company, young and idealistic, than anywhere else in South Korea. In the event, I was to be disappointed. Either these students kept their heads down when talking politics with foreigners, or, which was more probable, their hatred and contempt for the man was sincere. I confessed that the more I learned about South Korea the more curious I became about the North, and the more determined to visit Pyongyang.

Consternation greeted this admission. It was as if my wish to see North Korea conferred respectability upon Kim Il Sung and his regime.

I searched the crescent of keen faces, admiring the students' discipline and courtesy. They never spoke above one another or sought to impose their views. They would have been lost amid the cut and thrust of Western debate, where the heckler sharpens the speaker's wit. I feared for the long-term survival of *kibun* and other Confucian attributes. Public diffidence and self-restraint may enhance social harmony, but they obstruct the new morality – the drive to excel, the ruthlessly individualistic and competitive ethic shaping Korean business and, increasingly, higher education.

The students lived with their parents and would, they said, do so until they married. So how did they find boy- and girlfriends? Even today, I was told, it was customary to be introduced by a third party. A boy does not casually walk up to a girl and ask her out. An intermediary makes preliminary soundings. The old ways of parents selecting a spouse are not yet extinct, and though nowadays increasing numbers of earmarked brides and grooms have some say in their future, few would go so far as to defy their parents' strongest wishes. Professional matchmakers are still big business in the cities, earning fat fees for their abilities to match a suitable couple.

'We call this marital harmony – *gung-hap*,' said Mr Park. 'In your country, marital harmony develops after marriage. In ours, it is decided beforehand. A fortune-teller considers all the aspects, and whether two persons are right for each other. Marital harmony is a matter of mathematics, not love. The man should meet the woman on the second, or third, or seventh floor of a building. But if he meets her on the first floor this is very unlucky. A husband should be exactly three years older than his bride.'

'Supposing someone of my age wanted to marry one of yours, would that be possible?'

'It is possible, but unlikely. We call that kind of relationship a "romance grey". I do not think this is wise, because it does not respect marital harmony. If marital harmony brings great love we say the couple are like two cockroaches. If you kill one the other one will die too.'

I wanted to know about the obsession for virgin wives? How could this be reconciled with Korea's abundance of prostitutes and hostesses, and the wider invasion of Western sexual norms? The students looked bashful and took time to weigh their words. Ideally, the boys concurred, they would prefer virgins. But unless they were virgins themselves, how did they square the circle? Catering for male oat-getting implied a great number of prostitutes in Korea. I was treading on stony ground now, and the flow of information dried to a trickle. But one boy, heavy-set with thick eyebrows, was not so bashful.

'I know,' he said, 'that one fifth of male students go to prostitutes.' We did not pursue his statistical sources, but let the conversation drift naturally to palmistry. Did I know, asked the eyebrows man, that Napoleon Bonaparte's 'fame' line was so long that it went all the way up one finger and down the other side?

'Anyway', he continued. 'To make money these days is much more important than girlfriends or fortune-telling. I try to make a dream each night.'

I could not see the connection. 'To dream of what?' I asked.

'To dream of pigs. We Koreans believe that to dream of pigs means we will wake up rich. It is the way to find our fortune. Maybe we will win the state lottery. I think of pigs when I go to bed every night, but I always dream of other things. If anybody finds the secret of pig-dreaming, he will be very popular.'

~

After the students dispersed, my host took me out On The Town. Cheju City is small by Korean standards, with a population of half a million, but apart from its fake grandfather rocks and tourist excesses it is otherwise unnoteworthy.

Down by the sea wall Cheju's lovers congregated in the still of the evening air. They sat perched two by two as if on some latter-day Noah's ark. Mobile eating tents did brisk business. It was 10 pm and a ladies hairdressers was still open. One street offered Wild West-type saloons, with electronic shooting ranges and dummy targets.

Further on the atmosphere grew sleazier. Women loitered in the shadows. One approached Mr Park and they exchanged words. She was old and hard and coarse. I asked him what she wanted.

'She says she has nice house with six nice girls.'

I hadn't seen any nice girls, apart from a woman sitting on a bollard across the road. She looked innocent enough to me, but not to Mr Park. Emboldened by my presence he marched over, and back.

'She wants 30,000 *won* for one night.'

Thirty thousand *won*? I did some hasty mental arithmetic. That was about £23. I took a longer look at her. She was forty-ish and looked from a different planet to the hookers of Itaewon and Texas St. She sat round-shouldered on her bollard leaning forward with her hands on her knees. Her costume was maroon cardigan and acrylic trousers. She exhibited no precociousness or nous. Her lips weren't pouting and her eyes were like concrete.

She was proof that GIs seeking fun did not descend in droves on Cheju. The skimpily dressed hostesses of Pusan were not just on the game; they were playing the game. The woman in front of me was a victim, the classic proletarian labourer hiring out the only thing she possessed. More than likely her clients were Japanese, plying the skies between Cheju and Osaka to hunt for cheap pleasures. From her down-at-heel demeanour it was doubtful they treated her well. I wondered if she closed her eyes and dreamed of pigs.

10

THE WILD WEST
The Taxidermist and the Thug

The west coast of Korea is hedged in by a fringe of islands so
thickly clustered together that a glimpse of the mainland can be
obtained only at rare intervals ... The sea ... is so shallow that
thousands of square miles of mud-flats are left bare by the fall of
the tide [which] is abnormally high, averaging close upon 30 feet,
thus necessitating the utmost caution in navigating [the] strong
tidal current. The flood-tide rushes in like a mill-race, and the ebb
flows out with scarcely less velocity, exceeding three knots an
hour ... In spring and autumn there is much mirage, in the summer months dense fogs prevail; in winter a sheet of ice forms
along the coast. It seems probable that these natural conditions ...
have had a large share in predetermining the exclusive policy of
the Corean people.

J C Hall – *A Visit to Corea* – (1883)

I WAS leaving Cheju Island with thoughts warmer than when I
arrived. It was 7 am and the ferry terminal was packed. Queues
doubled over and back like snakes in a basket. It was with difficulty that I located the queue for the mainland port of Mokpo.

A Western couple lounged by the window, she with Latin looks, he
with spiky blond hair and a proboscis of a nose. I wandered over. The
moment he opened his mouth he exposed his Englishness. Not just
English, but *English*, with the too-hearty-by-far accent of a million
middle class males from Maidstone to Middlesex.

He was only the second British person (after the professor in
Kyongju) I'd met on my journey, though I'd had reports of several
sightings on Cheju Island. In this alien Korean world he stood before
me exposed in all his psychological nakedness. It was like meeting a
twin in the jungle. Every gesture, every nuance, was part of a shared
Britishness. His battery of insecurities was written in his eyes. I joked
about my disappointment in meeting another Briton. A moment later,

when his Spanish girlfriend had popped to the confectionery stall, he asked:

'You're not really upset that I'm English are you?' To carry such sensitivities to the other side of the world was asking for trouble.

His confidence was not even wafer-thin. Just to look into his eyes was enough to know he had been distressed with, preoccupied by, and ashamed of his nose from the moment pubescence demanded that first close, self-critical look in the mirror. I sensed he would shortly make allusion to his nose. It came almost at once.

'I usually wear a wide sunhat because, as you can see, my nose is rather large ...'

His name was Peter, he was thirty and he had been teaching English in Spain. Now he and Estelle were off to see the world. We three were shortly joined in the concourse by a German with biscuit crumbs glued to the corners of his mouth, and a younger Swede with golden blond locks tumbling over his shoulders. Knowing the Korean contempt for anything effeminate or hippyish, I feared he was having a hard time.

The boat, if such she could be described, was of antiquated appearance. Maybe she had been designed when Humphrey Bogart's *African Queen* was the height of luxury. Either that or she was a converted coastal freighter serving out her days. Unbeknown to me, there were three classes of ticket. Mine was pink: third class. Those of my companions were green, denoting second class. It made not the slightest difference. We wandered where we chose without hindrance.

Third class was a hovel in the bowels of the ship, near the engine room. Second class was a hovel one deck up, with dirty green tiles decorating the walls and ceiling. The rear wall was lined with empty green chests, above which hung Titanic-vintage photographs showing 'How to Wear the Life Jacket'. Rusting oil barrels served as litter bins.

The ship's engines lay exposed, with metal plate-covers removed. Watching the valves clattering and hissing in their risings and fallings was like watching open-heart surgery. No squeaks or rhythmic irregularities to indicate a nervy ride in prospect. The toilets had fractured pipes that spewed their contents upon the deck. A snack bar filled an alcove, offering Pepsis, milk, yoghurts, raw eggs. The salesgirl was squashed behind the trolley, from where she had little chance of swift escape. If the ship went down, so would she.

The ship's galley prepared hot meals and takeaway noodle soup (*ramyon*). The sight of the galley was enough to induce an instant fast. Swill splashed across the floor and slopped into gaping drains.

Eight hours was a long time on such a boat. I could walk faster than it could steam. It's wash was so puny I could make bigger waves in the bath. But the weather had smiled for a week. I had no need for a sweater, even out at sea, and on deck the air was crisp and clean. You could snap your teeth and bite it.

Peter joined me staring over the bow. Back in Pusan he and Estelle had discovered how to effect a free return trip to Japan. The trick was to exploit heavy Japanese import duties on spirits. They had bought several bottles of duty free whisky on board the ferry to the Japanese port of Shimonoseki. There, in the car park, an old hag had waddled up with a large bag hidden under her coat. She offered to pay more for the whisky than its cost and that of the boat tickets combined. Travellers undertaking the reverse trip could buy a celebrated Scottish whisky at Shimonoseki. This could then be sold at a handsome profit to waiting couriers in Pusan.

Bananas were also big business. These could be procured after clearing passport control in Shimonoseki. The 'goods', wrapped and stamped by quarantine officers, were duly declared at Korea's customs. There was no need for secrecy. Everyone knew the score: the crew made monkey gestures, and port police as likely as not guided you to waiting delivery points.

~

A family of islands loomed. They were inhabited it seemed, for we were heading towards them. The map named them as Chuja-do and Hoenggan-do. There was nowhere to put in, so we were met by a launch that tied up alongside. Mail and baggage were tossed upon its cabin roof, and a man more courageous than I vaulted after them. Passengers were exchanged less acrobatically.

We bobbed among the islands, some boasting a semblance of a road, others being no bigger than a roost for a pair of squawking gulls. A lighthouse protruded from the depths, as if from the midst of an oceanic Venice. The scene was captivating.

It was, perhaps, disadvantageous to visit Korea after having known Japan, for Japan presents most Western visitors with a shattering dose of culture shock. Korea is subtler, more restrained, offering little to compete with Japan's sheer spectacle – for example, Japan's sumo wrestlers, her tea ceremony, lava baths, awesome Mt Fuji, love hotels, bullet trains, pachinko parlours, street bunting, dragon dances, A-bomb museums in Hiroshima and Nagasaki, the dawn calls of her sweet-potato sellers.

Korea's culture has absorbed so much from China, Japan and America, and lost so much through erosion, banishment, and subjugation, that, to her detractors, little remains that can be called truly Korean, other than her *ondol* underfloor heating, her *hangul* language, and her *kimchi*. Korea, I felt, is enjoyed not by seeing but by being. The name 'Chosun' (Land of Morning Calm) hints at the softness of her real charm. A night out in provincial Korea is to wander the market-place or stroll the waterside in some tiny fishing port.

~

Mokpo is Korea's principal south-western port. It is so sheltered by offshore islands that the second half of our journey was a maritime slalom through straits and channels. I reproached myself for writing so disparagingly about the vessel now bearing us sedately on our way. No other craft could have played its part so well. It was like drifting up the Nile through a timeless landscape in a timeless boat, water and craft equally protected from the present. I thought back to the Hallyo Waterway, to its transformation into a tourist slough, the islands flashing by through the scarred, Perspex prison windows of the Angel hydrofoil.

We chugged gently past Chindo Island, home of the furry Chindo dog, Korea's only indigenous species. The dogs are considered a national asset, and are permitted neither to leave the island nor mate with other, lesser breeds. Each spring thousands of visitors descend on Chindo-do to witness the parting of the waves. For a few hours each year the waters separating Modo from Chindo Island are pulled apart by a combination of lunar forces and the West Sea's extreme tidal range, exposing a causeway eagerly tramped by sightseers.

Far ahead I glimpsed the first intrusion of Korea's technological miracle, the Chindodaegyo suspension bridge. It was miles away, yet already I could see traffic flowing over a metallic blue arc, flanked either side by huge, rust-red 'tuning forks'. Passing underneath seemed to me no less unreal than a Viking galley passing under Tower Bridge. Thereafter the timeless journey resumed. Protected from the open sea the waters were as still as a pond, apart for occasional eddies and whirlpools from warring channels and currents.

Like many Korean ports, Mokpo sits cramped against a fringe of mountains. Our little European party had passed the time exchanging anecdotes and travel hints. But the relationships formed were shallow and functional. There was no exchanging of addresses or vague suggestions of meeting again. Even the goodbyes were reduced to a cursory 'Good Luck', or dispensed with altogether. Peter and Estelle, the German and the Swede were off into the unknown, to places without a name and a time with no end. Perpetual travellers. I felt tame knowing I had a plane to catch home.

The Swede for some reason stayed the night with me. We shared a *yoinsook* and spent the evening wandering Mokpo's streets. He was a baby-faced college graduate. With his flowing yellow mane and androgynous physique, he appeared even more startling to Korean eyes than were my height and my beard. I walked in a welcome slumber of anonymity. When he went to buy an ice cream the woman stared at him, then suddenly reached out and tweaked his nipple. Just to make sure. Was he tempted, I asked, to get his hair cut. Just to make life easier for himself. No chance.

He had no maps with him, save a couple of pages torn from a school atlas. He had no idea where Mokpo was for the simple reason that it was too small to appear on the 'East Asia' page. But he was resource-ful. He had come to Korea via the Trans-Siberian Railway and Japan, where a Japanese helicopter pilot had taken pity on his poverty and gifted him 10,000 *yen* (£40).

Our time together in Mokpo was short but eventful. A travel agency appeared to be enjoying a binge. Counters were stacked with apples and pears, bean-curd cakes, oval platters of sliced chicken, crates of beer.

'Are you open?' I asked.

'Welcome. What is you want?' said the manager, looking half cut. He waved his hand towards the refreshments.

'Are you open?' I repeated.

'Yes, open. This Open Day,' and again the gesture towards the food.

It was already 10 pm, but the Open day was still in full swing. The beer flowed, the chicken was succulent, and the conversation warmed. The manager poured the Swede another Crown.

'You look like woman,' he said, without warning, causing me to choke momentarily on an octopus sucker which had stuck stubbornly to the roof of my mouth. The Swede smiled weakly.

In the next block, near the railway station and opposite a 'Bar-Resto-Hof', we found a coffee shop. Coffee shops (the words always displayed in English) are the ideal place to pass an hour or a day. The coffees are cheap and you are never required to refill. One may pass an evening on a single cup without so much as an irritated glance from the tarted-up females who run the joints. Coffee shops and tea houses (*tabang*) occupy basements or first floors. All offer cosy chairs, soft lights, television.

Sometimes they are sumptuously plush. The Heidelberg in Taejon boasted leather armchairs, wall plants, a gargantuan aquarium, and one whole wall lined with statuettes and figurines. Another wall was decorated with murals of historic Heidelberg, flanked by magenta curtains. From behind a glass partition a DJ whispered into a microphone. As elsewhere in Korea, the music was cosmopolitan, local love songs, Viennese strings, African percussion, Dire Straits.

Mokpo's Pyol ('Star') coffee shop was not quite so grand. Butterfly pictures adorned the room, together with black and white portraits of Claudio Abbado and Herbert von Karajan. A dozen girl customers occupied tables pulled together. Some lads sat on the fringes, but never the twain did mix. What the Star lacked in social interaction, it made up for in music. A DJ busied himself among a mountain of albums. Request slips were on hand. The unspoken boast was: 'you name it, we've got it.'

This was silly. It would be easy to catch them out. An hour later I had failed to do so, and I prepared to administer the *coup de grace*. I wrote down Wishbone Ash's *The King has Come*. A frown invaded the proprietor's eyes. Did I detect fear? Was his honour so threatened that he was about to commit hara-kiri, Japanese-style, before my eyes? He walked unsteadily to consult the DJ. I felt unaccountably nervous. He came back looking if anything even more troubled.

'Wishbone Ashy. *The King has Come*, wrong! It is *The King WILL Come*.'

~

The province of South Cholla is the butt of many an Irish-type joke. Its people are like mud-flats, goes the jibe, whose footprints quickly fade. But tensions between Chollanamdo and the rest of the country are barbed. The buffoons of South Cholla are dangerous buffoons, the legacy of mistrust stemming from Seoul's long habit of despatching subversives and ne'er-do-wells into exile in south-western Korea.

Bolshy bastards, was the common opinion. Certainly the bus drivers in Mokpo did not welcome me with a smile. And refused to hand out change, too. Ditto in Kwangju, the South Cholla capital, where the surly, crew-cutted driver hid behind dark glasses on an overcast day, and who was wooed with my digestives only with difficulty. Was it personal, I wondered? Something I'd done, or been responsible for? In a way it was.

TO DREAM OF PIGS

In 1980 there occurred in Kwangju a catastrophe. In the wake of the then President Park's assassination, political meetings were banned across the country and all universities closed. Suspected agitators at Kwangju's Chonnam University were rounded up, which act promptly touched off a popular rising. For some days the city snubbed Seoul's dictates. And so the troops moved in. Not any old troops, but front line specials, unleashed on Kwangju's insurgents. The city's student rebels fought back with improvised and stolen weapons and with machine guns mounted on university roofs. The cost of retaking the city was measured in hundreds, perhaps thousands of lives. The massacre of civilians, the tortures, the mutilations have made the name 'Kwangju' echo in the manner of Sharpesville or Amritsar.

And the grounds for my responsibility? Because I was presumed American, and because American HQ in Seoul (and hence Washington) was presumed to have permitted (and hence approved) the despatch of Korea's toughest troops from the DMZ to engage in a little domestic butchery. The modern wave of anti-Americanism had been set in train by the Kwangju massacre. Her disclaimers brushed aside, the United States was found guilty of complicity, if nothing worse, in the most sanguine peacetime atrocity in South Korea's brief, turbulent history.

~

I arrived in Kwangju during Autumn Full-Moon Festival (*Chusok*). This year it followed on the heels of 'Armed Forces Day'. National flags flew in abundance and for a couple of days the country donned its Sunday Best and rushed about visiting relatives or the tombs of ancestors. Bus terminals were choked, street-barging worse than ever. The atmosphere was excitable and frenetic, as if the nation was high on oceans of Royal Jelly gulped down at pharmacy counters. It was customary to bear gifts at this time, and shops were stocked high with colourfully wrapped coffee jars, toiletries, confectionery.

I had come to Kwangju at the invitation of Mr Kim, the old man who had collapsed on Mt Halla. Mr Kim was very different from last I saw him. He was up and about, dapper and sprightly, and slightly owlish in his thick-framed spectacles. His collapse had been caused by his stomach, and he awaited surgery.* Meanwhile he was forbidden to eat solids. He could not enjoy the pre-wrapped gift I had bought at the corner shop, which on opening I discovered contained an assortment of candies.

---

* Stomach ailments, notably cancer, are more common in Korea than in the West. The incidence of other forms of cancer, together with arthritis and cardio-vascular disease, is lower.

Repaying imagined personal debts, I learned, is not lightly undertaken in Korea. His wife fetched a brick-sized bar of soap and rubbed together the insides of her fists in the action of scrubbing clothes. I emptied my rucksack at her feet. By the time I left she had darned my socks and laundered my trousers. These she dried in one metal bucket that rested inside another lined with glowing coals.

On the evening of my arrival my hosts performed a *chusok* food-blessing ceremony. They donned traditional costume. Fruit and bean-curd cakes were decorously arranged upon a low table, while various inscriptions were stuck to the wall with a dab of bean-curd. With as much bowing as his infirmity would permit, Mr Kim rendered blessings, then cleared and replenished the dishes several times. Each layout required a fresh set of inscriptions. At length he gathered them off the wall, took them to the door and set them on fire.

In my honour his wife prepared a banquet of *kalbi* (marinated beef ribs sliced up with giant scissors). The rules were simple. The three of us sat round a table and I ate. He couldn't and she wouldn't. His gratitude would only be assuaged once I'd cleared his house of a month's food. On a stomach shrunk from hand-to-mouth living, my needs were more modest, whatever the cost to his self-esteem. He pointed to the various dishes, made chop-chop noises, and offered mumbling commentaries ('Number One, Number One') on their deliciousness and health value.

Mr Kim was not the smiling sort. His stern eyes never left me, and he inspected everything I did with solemn intensity. I began to peel an apple. Incorrectly, for Mr Kim snatched apple and knife in order to demonstrate. The peel ought to come away in one continuous spiral. *Like this, Englishman. Got it?* It was a relief to get to bed.

He banged on my door at dawn. He was fully dressed and impatiently beckoned me to follow. I didn't have time to buckle my sandals, so with straps flapping, stumbled after him down the street, like a roller skater without wheels.

Operation Gratitude 'Phase One' had been to fill me to bursting point. Phase Two was to wash me. He was taking me to a bath house (*mogyoktang*), which I recognised by the distinctive red sign outside. As many homes until recently lacked hot water, bathhouses are an established neighbourhood institution. Most Koreans nowadays no longer need to leave their own homes in pursuit of cleanliness. But the bathhouse's luxuriant allure is undiminished. Mr Kim ushered me into a steaming sauna and mimed humourless and incomprehensible instructions through the fog. The instructions were brief, for the simple reason that I could not breathe, and I staggered outside to stare at the steamed-up dial. The needle was in the red zone.

We moved to one of the pools, where I was shown how to soap myself by the approved means. In my ignorance I picked up a slab of yellow soap. Mr Kim shook his head crossly. *Don't they teach you anything in England?* He lathered a pocket-sized white towel, transforming it into a soggy, frothy flannel. He lifted up my right leg and began to scrub it as if planing a length of timber. There was no knowing the limits to this planing, and I edged away.

Elderly Koreans, I had noticed, maintain a formal exterior. It adds to their sense of dignity. At first I feared Mr Kim was embarrassed to be seen in the company of such an incompetent, and when I heard him barking sternly at our naked audience I was sure it was to my discredit. But then I made out the words '*yong-guk*' and 'Hallasan'. I looked up and saw him stooping low, miming a piggy-back sequence and pointing round at his back. He was singing my praises after all.

Boiled and frozen in sequence to the point where pain gave way to rapture, and cleansed to the point of godliness, I tip-toed to the locker room to clean my teeth. The attendant unwrapped a disposable toothbrush and with the flourish of a master craftsman upon it squeezed a dab of toothpaste. I fully expected him to sit me in a chair and say 'open wide'.

Breakfast was the remains of the *kalbi* I'd left the night before. On saying goodbye I was presented with a bagful of yoghurts and 'woolli' sandwiches. At the gate Mr Kim unsmilingly pressed a piece of paper into my hand. In a childlike scrawl he had written – evidently with help from somewhere – 'Thank You'.

~

Iri is a university town which swings to its own rhythm. I arrived by train on a Sunday morning. The station concourse was jammed with guitar strumming, hand clapping, foot stomping Christians, who distributed leaflets on behalf of a presbyterian church. Iri's Super Disco Night Club was packed in mid-afternoon and deserted by 8, by which time youthful bouncers were patrolling the door. A nearby piano school had crammed four pianos into a tiny studio: it was impossible to concentrate on one for the noise of the others. Iri's university – Wanguang – was reputed to possess a fine museum. I never saw it, for a mile short of the campus police buses with wire-covered windows blocked the road. The buses were empty so I walked on by, and in the distance perceived shapes last seen in Chunchon – the rubbery brown uniforms of riot police. In Chunchon the 'action' had finished; in Iri it was in full swing. Darts of fire flashed through the air. Molotov cocktails. At a crossroads ranks of riot police crouched behind shields. They were evidently well out of range of rocks and flaming bottles lobbed by distant masked students, for they had removed their helmets and were smoking, stretching, yawning, waiting to repel the next concerted assault. Dangling from adjacent buildings red and yellow streamers screamed: *Let's club to death the ruling party and the conspiracy to renew the Cabinet; Today marks the uprising of 16,000 students to defeat the government of Roe Tae Woo.*

I was excited at having stumbled upon an ongoing riot. I was, however, hugely conspicuous. Other than the combatants I was the only person abroad. I had no wish to act suspiciously, thereby drawing even greater attention to myself. Rather than attempt to conceal myself in a doorway while taking pictures, I pulled out my camera in full view and began pressing the shutter. An officer materialised in seconds, hand raised. He was polite. Where did I come from? What was I doing? Where was I staying? All these questions I evaded. I didn't want him examining my passport or visiting my *yogwan*. Besides, I was perfectly entitled to be here and to do as I pleased. I smiled and moved to the kerb to take yet more pictures. He raised his arm to stop me.

'We will take to you your hotel,' he said. I didn't want to go to my hotel.

'I would like to stay and take pictures. What is happening out there?'

'This is Korean comedy,' said the officer, gesturing towards the distant students. 'They make protest for North Korea, for unification, for democracy. It is our kind of comedy.'

I was by now concerned for my camera film, and rather than risk its confiscation, resigned myself to retreat. I backed away from the drama.

'We will take you to your hotel,' repeated the policeman.

'No thank you,' I said, trying to appear resolute. He did not persist, but later, from the sanctuary of my *yogwan,* I became irritated by my feeble compliance. I had every right to take pictures, and I wished I had held my ground.

~

I don't know what made me head inland to Muju. Maybe it was because it was easy to read and easy to say. It wasn't mentioned in any of the books. That was another point in its favour. It just stared out from the map and said 'Come here Mr Clive'.

The bus ride was justification in itself, along twisting winding roads that threatened to pitch us into a lake far below. I tried to decipher the sign language that bus drivers used to warn one another of speed traps or police cars. When actually meeting a police vehicle, drivers gave military salutes through the windscreen. Snakes snoozed on the tarmac, playing chicken and slithering away only at the last moment. This was rice country: a hundred years ago the British vice-consul, Carles, painted a patronising picture:

Fond as the Koreans are of society, they never seem happier than when in the early summer, gangs of men stamp in the rice roots, keeping time and line with their leader. With feet high poised, they wait the next note of the chant, whose echoes will soon be sung back to them from the hills, or returned to them from the other gangs working in the distance. Studiously decent, even at such work they do not lay aside their clothes; and women who help their husbands in planting and weeding the rice fields, are reproached by their betters for their impropriety in tucking up their trousers to the knee.

Here in western Korea a new sight alerted my eye, what I took to be rude crosses upon lines of rude graves. The 'graves' were ginseng shelters, row upon row of low, wooden-framed thatched hutches, open only to the north, for ginseng cannot abide sunlight.

I found a self-appointed escort in Muju. As I stepped down from the bus, a Mr Ha came running from his shop to greet me. I didn't know him from Batman. Mr Ha immediately fixed me up with a *yogwan*.

'*Man won*' (W10,000), said the *adjima*.

'*O chon won*' (W5,000) said Mr Ha, clinching the deal.

He ran a wedding studio. Above his shop was his own personal church, complete with pulpit, organ, and wooden pews to seat a hundred. No priests ever came here. No hymns of praise were ever rendered upwards. The church was not for worship. It had no other purpose than to provide photographs of devout newly-weds. I sat among the deserted pews as Mr Ha pressed a switch, and the studio reverberated to the ghostly, automated strains of 'Here comes the bride'.

A sluggish river ran through Muju, and that evening I came upon a woman shampooing her hair in the water. The trees flanking the river were decorated with straw skirts halfway up their trunks. The skirts were secured by plastic strips and signified the approach of autumn, for they trapped bugs, caterpillars and other parasites. They would be removed in spring and tossed to the flames.

Then I saw the army. Huge transporters rolled through the dark streets. Soldiers were out in force. A loudspeaker crackled from a roving vehicle, like someone campaigning in an election. The Korean army had caught a 'bad man', said Mr Ha the next day, and the people should know and rejoice.

It was nearly midnight. The air was still. On the outskirts of town a light still shone. Through a bare window, so grimy and greasy that I had to search for a space through which to peer, the local taxidermist was hard at work. He allowed me in, and I sat upon a wooden stool, like a pupil before his master. He had lost a finger. On a shelf sat canaries, owls, *taramjis* and hedgehogs, each mounted on wooden frames. The bare floor was buried in wood shavings, sticky tape, string, buds of cotton wool, and lengths of scrap wire. He might know where things were, but to me all was confusion.

For an hour not a word passed between us. He worked, content that I was observing: I observed, content that he was working. On a blood-stained sheet of newspaper on the table was a blob. It was pink and tacky and the size of a tennis ball. But it appeared to have a head.

The blob was a hedgehog. Inside out. The innards had thankfully been discarded. The eyes too. He poked the leg bones through the skin, threaded wire through them, and secured them with powdered resin, cotton wool and sticky tape. When all four legs were in place he turned the animal the right way out.

The nine-fingered taxidermist scooped a fistful of wood shavings from the floor and wound them expertly into a miniature rugby ball. This was the hedgehog's body. The 'ball' was fitted inside the skin and knotted to the head. It was then shaped and padded with cotton wool. When filled, the body cavity was sewn up. The hedgehog was now a hedgehog. Minus eyes. These emerged from a yellow plastic bag containing 'eyes' of every size and colour. In went two buttons on stalks, like tiny golf tees, and the stuffed animal was finished. The taxidermist did not pause to admire, but spilled more newspaper bundles on the bench, like so much mincemeat from the butcher. He unravelled one to reveal a frog. Inside out.

~

Autumn was in the air. Korean seasons are sharp and distinct. Winters long, dry and bitter; spring fresh and invigorating; summers steamy, monsoonal and insufferable; and autumn the time of riotous colours, balmy skies and occasional fog. It was time to retrieve my sweater from the foot of my rucksack, where it had lain undisturbed.

The bus to Taejon was half empty, so I seated my rucksack beside me. A plump man said: 'Excuse me sir,' and pointed to the rucksack, which was a roundabout way of saying *You're foreign. I'm going to talk to you. Please move your bag.*

It took him a few minutes to get going, but that was common enough. He wanted to rehearse his lines. Not that there was any doubt about his questions, merely the order in which to ask them. Would it be age, country, name, marital status; or marital status, name, country, age? I allowed myself the silly game of trying to guess.

He was a Baptist pastor. His grandfather had been killed by North Koreans in Seoul – on 2 May 1951. He liked Margaret Thatcher and Ronald Reagan, which didn't surprise me. I'd met few Koreans who did not. He likened Mrs Thatcher to Corazon Aquino of the Philippines, a comparison I doubted would have pleased the Iron Lady.

'Both strong women,' he opined, and clenched his fist approvingly.

At Nonsan bus terminal I came across an argument. Not a ten-second squabble but a full-blooded screaming row. Neither he nor she could plead drunkenness or insanity. The strangeness of the spectacle, for I'd rarely seen any public venting of anger in Korea, was such that I sat on a bench to watch. He yelled, poked his finger at her, then she retaliated and he was forced to backpedal.

Naturally, nobody intervened. You took it for granted in Korea that no one would lift a finger, not even against daylight robbery. Yet rather than give the combatants wide berth for fear of flying fists or broken bottles, passers-by refused to deviate from their path. It was as if the brawl was invisible, which psychologically it was.

~

I had gone to Muju on impulse. I was going to Puyo because the guidebooks said I should.

Puyo was the capital of the ancient Paekche Kingdom, destroyed in the seventh century. Puyo was to Paekche what Kyongju was to Silla, though smaller and less flashy. Puyo exploited one particular myth, milked for all its worth. Beyond a rifle range with revolving targets and a museum scarred by a grotesque serrated roof, a wooded path led up to a cliff-top known as *Nakhwaam* (Falling Flower Rock). Two hundred feet below, the Kumgang River meandered among golden sandbanks. Tourist rafts plied back and forth. From the bluff upon which I stood the last Paekche king had perished against the combined forces of Silla and Tang China. And from here, too, three thousand ladies of the Paekche court, their colourful dresses billowing like 'flower petals', had leaped to their deaths rather than surrender their honour to the invaders. Or so the story goes.

I was sceptical. But at least Korean tourists entered into the spirit. They were dressed to the nines, voluble and excited, each seeking to outshout the crowd. I reminded myself how quietly spoken is the sober Korean. Strangely, only at their most high-spirited did they ever leave me in peace. I wandered as if in a personal fog amongst the parties posing and re-posing for their ritual snaps.

I stayed in Puyo's youth hostel. It boasted a swimming pool (dry), a souvenir shop, a restaurant that added a 10% service charge, and a stripe-trousered porter who offered to carry my backpack. The hostel had been built as a tourist hotel, and only downgraded when it failed to balance the books.

I found a rack of newspapers. Korea's first bilingual newspaper, the *Independent* (with a masthead similar to the British paper of the same name) had started up in 1896. Now there were two English dailies, the *Korea Times* and the *Korean Herald*. The *Herald* is reputed to be the more official, the *Times* the more independent, but to the casual eye they are indistinguishable. They are bland and featureless, heavily indebted to American-slanted news and sport drawn mainly from the wire services. British soccer results are provided only on a quiet day for baseball and American football.

Both papers have a 'fifties feel to them. You open them expecting features on James Dean or Buddy Holly. The syndicated agony aunts – 'Dear Abby' in the *Times*, and her real-life sister 'Ann Landers' in the *Herald* – exhibit to the European mind a puritanical streak. As for the humour:

Dear Abby, I am 27 and getting married. We are both nudists. Everybody will come except my mother. (signed: Bobby in Nashville).
Dear Bobby, do not give a fig(leaf) about whether she attends or not. But where will the best man carry the ring?

Dear Ann Landers, two years ago I met a man at work. I was an exotic dancer. I discovered that he was involved in making copies of hard-core porno films and selling them to guys at work.

(signed: Hung Up My Dancing Shoes in Conn.).

Dear Conn, sounds as if Ben's character is really flawed. His only hope is counselling. If he refuses to go … give this guy the gate.

The papers also act as a forum for educated Koreans who know which side their bread is buttered. They like to scorn Korean behaviour they consider reprehensible. Declared a Korean professor at Inchon University:

We happen to see some people who jump ahead in line when we wait for a bus or a taxi. Some pedestrians spit saliva on the street: others spit chewing-gum instead of disposing of it properly and dirtying our streets. Many city dwellers go to amusement parks and leave their rubbish behind, contaminating streams, creeks, and valleys. They are contemptible, and they deserve our contempt.

I put down the papers and retired to bed. All other bunks in my dorm were taken, though one still awaited its occupant. At 2.30 in the morning the door flew open, light seared into my brain and I squinted across at a plump, crew-cutted man with round glasses, like a grown-up Piggy in *Lord of the Flies*. He wore denims and furry beige waist-coat. A cigarette hung from his lip and a personal stereo vibrated about his ears. He flung the machine to his bunk, still playing, and shouted over at my bunk. I propped myself on an elbow in an effort to clear my head.

'I'm sorry,' I mumbled. 'I'm English. I don't understand you.'

'Oh, I say. English are we?' The mocking tone was razor edged. 'Shakes-pe-are, Lord By-ron and all that. Then you'd better learn Korean hadn't you!' He switched off the light, slid under his sheet fully clothed and continued smoking.

Sometime later I awoke needing a pee. I slipped on my trousers, clambered down my squeaky ladder and opened the door.

'Where are you going without a shirt?' came an unfriendly voice behind me. I took no notice.

He was up at 7, waking the whole dormitory in the process. He barked abuse in all directions and squeezed himself into a grey three-piece suit that ill-matched his puffy skin and skinhead haircut. As I threw back the covers and reached for my clothes he addressed me again.

'May I speak with you?'

I pulled on my socks and ignored him.

'May I speak with you!' louder and more insistent. I glared at him, puzzled at what I might have done to provoke his ire.

'Yes, you may speak with me. What do you want?'

'How long in Korea?'

'Two months.'

'Then why you not speak Korean? You come to Korea. You must speak Korean.'

This had no answer, at least not one that would satisfy him.

'Are you Korean?' I asked.

'I am from Japan,' he replied. I felt relieved that my image of ultra-courteous Koreans had not been besmirched. But then I had rarely encountered Japanese pig-heads either.

'Are you always so ****** rude?' The thug made no reply, nor when I borrowed his tactics and repeated myself, louder. He continued to adjust his tie in the mirror. Finally, he looked round at me, his eyes ablaze.

'I do not hear what you say. We are in Korea. If you wish to speak with me you speak Korean.'

Someone else might have banged his head against the wall. I settled for a contemptuous stare and went down to the reception desk to insist on a change of dormitory. At the desk I noticed a 'terms and conditions' notice. This stated that guests should not parade in the lobby or in the corridors in a 'state of semi-nudity'. My shirtless visit to the bathroom constituted such an offence, though its admission made me no fonder of my disagreeable tormentor.

~

Puyo and I were not destined to be friends. Escape beckoned in the shape of Anmyon-do, a pencil-thin island tucked away off the west coast. The ferry left from Taechon, a vibrant town throbbing with life and energy. I got up one morning bleary-eyed to catch the ferry and found the station square blocked with tanks and personnel carriers. No personnel were abroad, which only intensified the menace of the ghostly vehicles in the grey morning light.

The port had not yet woken. A platoon of soldiers in day-glow jackets chopped wood on the quayside. The port was a dormitory for sleeping craft, their wooden bones creaking, their water-beds slurping and gurgling. I half-expected a reveille, engines firing into coughing, spluttering life. The scene made for a perfect jigsaw, oil-stained wharf, piles of black tyres, melon-shaped light-bulbs strung along fishing craft, the pinky-grey streaked light of dawn.

The other passengers comprised two suspicious looking men in business suits, a woman with high heels and purple lipstick, and a Bohemian, wispy bearded figure in anorak sketching in the stern.

The morning mist clung to the water like a heat-haze. We pottered from isle to isle, bay to bay, until I'd quite lost sense of direction. Not that I cared. It was a journey I had no wish to shorten. I was back in the Korea of my fantasy. Ullung-do, Chungmu, Wando, the islands off Mokpo, and now Anmyon-do – these and the vessels that served them were the source of Korea's magic. Islands, islands, none too small for a white church, with white cross poking defiantly upwards.

I was deposited on a slippery jetty, dotted with yellow crates over-flowing with anchovies. A dog tied to a pole on the muddy beach yapped furiously. A yawl, stacked with nets, floats and baskets, dozed high and dry, patiently awaiting the inrushing flood tide to breathe life into her beams. A path wound upwards to a waiting bus. The bus was empty, apart from the driver, who shook my hand warmly. The bus would leave in half an hour. There was time to drink 'copy' in the 'copy shoppy'. When I went to pay, the bill had been settled. I turned to see my rucksack hoisted upon the driver's back and on its way to the bus. Gestures like these told, without my having to ask, how few foreigners came hereabouts.

Anmyon-do represents Scotland's Kintyre in its geographical loca-tion. Even the topography is Scottish, gentler, less robust than the uplands to the east. The rain clouds frowned, and before we'd gone ten miles the roads were awash. To entertain me, the only passenger, the driver unearthed a Sounds of the Sixties cassette. Looking out on a monsoonal landscape, Skeeter Davis's *The End of the World* struck the mood exactly.

Why does my heart go on beating, why do these eyes of mine cry?
Don't they know it's the end of the world, it ended when you said
goodbye.

The driver was thirty-three. He drove over four hundred kilometres a day, which on roads like these was hard going. He didn't ask if I was married, which could only mean he was not. Why not? No money, he said. He was a rarity, a contented Korean bachelor. He exuded an air of world-weary dignity. Let others fret themselves with their stressful lives. He was happy driving buses. He spoke better English than any other bus driver I'd met. Strange. Perhaps he was a spy-catcher.

Tell Laura I love her. Tell Laura I need her. Tell Laura not to cry. My love for her will never die.

Anmyon-do was named after its largest town. Anywhere else, Anmyon would have been called a village. It was so remote I expected at any moment to see veterans of the Korean War surrendering from the countryside. The rain had unearthed the frogs. Armies of them splashed among the puddles like mini hand-grenades. The road had all but dissolved, and the bus waded through swamps and mud, nose to tail with carts. A tractor slid sideways through the slime, ever nearer a gully.

Bye bye love chorused the Everly Brothers with ill-timed tactless-ness. The threatened tractor halted on the brink and slithered to safety. Now it was our turn. The churning effects of previous vehicles had increased the risk to those behind. We were not going to make it. We teetered on the edge. The driver couldn't ask me to disembark because the door overhung the drop, and there was no more purchase for feet than for wheels. Better to be on the bus than to have it topple on you.

Workmen nearby saw the peril and came running with shovels and spades. They dug troughs for both front wheels and only then, inch by inch, did we manoeuvre away. The driver was unruffled throughout, and I extended a congratulatory digestive biscuit. It was received with the oddest question.

'How can daughter of major marry a prince?'

'I beg your pardon?'

'In Korea we have hundreds of generals.'

'Really?'

'In Korea we have thousands of colonels.'

'What are you getting at?'

'In Korea we have a million majors. Are there a million majors in Britain?'

'I don't know.'

'In Korea a major is nobody. He is like bus driver. He is like shop-girl. He is no better than corporal. How can daughter of nobody marry a prince?'

'Who are you talking about?'

'Princess Fergie.'

11

PANMUNJOM
Where North meets South

The road [north from Seoul through Panmunjom] is that which
has for centuries been taken by missions from and to Peking, and
along its course the Koreans have fought many bloody battles
against the invading armies of China and Japan ... It was therefore with eager expectation of discovering some opening for
British trade that I undertook the journey, and the disappointment
was very bitter. From Soul to Kai-söng the road passes across
numerous valleys at the foot of low hills of disintegrated granite.
These, as a rule, have been robbed by fuel seekers of all grass and
undergrowth, and give a white or reddish background to the village at their feet. On the hill-sides are numerous tombs, planted
on greenswards, surrounded by a horseshoe bank of earth and protected by groves of fir.

W R Carles – *Recent Journeys in Korea* – (1886)

TRAVELLING in Korea was like journeying through time. The
visitor crosses centuries in a matter of miles – relics from a
previous millennium, ox-drawn ploughs, semiconductors and
holograms. After the unspoiled delights of Anmyon-do I did
not welcome being back in the capital.

I took the train into Seoul. I knew the carriages would be thriving
with sub-cultures – musical newspaper boys, musical beggars, sales-
folk of every description, mop-wielding cleaners. Now I added another
species to the list. Bible-thumpers. And goodness, how he thumped. He
was soberly dressed in brown suit, bespectacled, and with greased hair
so drastically parted you could drive a toy car through the exposed
valley of scalp. He stood in the aisle, countering the train's motion
with one hand on a back-rest. This left the other to brandish a bible. I
am bound to say that, understanding not a word he said, nor seeing any
inscription on the book, I could but guess at his evangelism. But
weighing the alternatives, I could think of no other profession or calling

which could induce such a frenzy. He obviously wasn't selling – at least nothing that could be won by *won*, so to speak. Nor did Buddhists harangue the public in the name of their belief. The preacher reminded me of certain American TV evangelists I had seen: I would not have been surprised had he commenced foaming at the mouth at any moment. Indeed, to receive so little feedback from one's exertions might easily provoke such a response, for no one paid his tirades the slightest heed.

A Seoul journalist, Mr Shin, had invited me to spend my last nights with his family. I located his apartment somewhere in the jungly maze of residential blocks that constitutes suburban Seoul. It was Sunday morning and a man yelled up the stairs for all the little children to come to church.

Seoul's apartments are unremarkable, except in respect of their heating. The *ondol* is so much a part of Korea that it survives the ravages of modernisation. Mr Shin showed me the boiler that in winter warmed the floor. So long as the *ondol* survives, so does the floor as the focus of family life. Although his two sons slept in beds, he and his ravishing wife ('Miss Korea Yoghurt 1986') were not so revolutionary. They could willingly accept Western toilets ('more hygienic!'), but beds? Never.

The television stayed on continuously. Sunday mornings were for educational quizzes. The Korean child passes through six years elementary school, three years middle school, another three years high school, and if lucky four years at university. This particular quiz was for children at middle school (aged thirteen to fifteen). Last week's champion returned to play this week's, the contestants shaking hands beforehand with a gravity fit for an impending duel. The first question flashed up. Which was correct: 1) two milks; 2) two glass of milk; 3) two glasses of milks; 4) two glasses of milk?

Pretty difficult, I thought, at that age and under that pressure. The fastest on the buzzer answered correctly and concealed his delight. Not so his parents in the audience. The camera zoomed in on them, uncontrollable in their pride and excitement. With encouragement like that, what child dared quit the educational treadmill? But these questions were kids' play. We soon came to the heavy stuff. The first question made me gape. Surely the children would not know the answer. But they did. What British fourteen year old, I wondered, had his grey matter stuffed with the life and works of the German philosopher Schopenhauer?

A junior talent competition followed the quiz, parading such skills as coin piling, peach-seed splitting, performing handstands, and needle threading.

~

I huddled expectantly in a doorway. One day each month is designated 'air-raid warning day', and I had taken the bus downtown to observe. On the stroke of 11, sirens that in wartime London would have cleared the streets in seconds barely disturbed the people of Seoul. Like fire-drills, like all rehearsals, the sirens generated more sloth than adrenaline. Traffic was supposed to 'freeze', but it took several minutes for the flow to subside. I peered out at marshals directing pedestrians into subways. A chap phoning from a kiosk was left undisturbed. A quarter of an hour later the all-clear sounded, and like a rusty gramophone the city began to whirr again.

My return to Seoul had coincided with momentous developments in North-South rapprochement. The two Koreas had consented to play each other at soccer, the first match televised live from the Northern capital, Pyongyang. In the same way that inhabitants of Belfast insist they can tell a Catholic from a Protestant, just by the face, I wondered if both Koreas claim comparable powers of perception regarding themselves. I peered at the screen as the camera panned rows of obedient spectators, their fixed, glazed smiles, choreographed applause, dull clothes and strange bonnet-like caps seeming to belong to an alien species. As for the players, the contrast was stark. While the North's had regimental short hair, those of the South appeared altogether more flamboyant. One or two sported shoulder-length locks.

The games were window-dressing, the public relations accompanying unprecedented North-South contacts. High level delegations from Pyongyang were here in Seoul. For days beforehand check-shirted police loitered around subway entrances, nervously fingering their batons, demanding the identity cards of those they judged suspicious. As the North Korean motorcades swept through the city, photo-journalists hung from car windows, doubtless nonplussed by the size, wealth and vibrancy of the South Korean capital. The journalists were informed that to impress their northern visitors every car in South Korea had been temporarily requisitioned and despatched to Seoul for the duration.

Mr Shin was my source for this, as for much else. As his guest I was, for example, able to observe the day-to-day management of this seemingly typical Korean household. It was patriarchal to the extent that ultimate responsibility rested with Mr Shin. Without consulting his wife he instructed her to do my washing (the washing machine was ignored in favour of soap and elbow grease.). Not that she appeared resentful. It was she who insisted I take the master bedroom, while the whole family crammed into the children's room. I was not left quite to myself, for the eldest child could not resist stealing in to snuggle up to this strange hairy being.

Mr Shin performed no labour about the house. It was he who asked what I wished to eat, and he, curiously, who took credit for the cooking. When I requested that he convey my thanks to the 'chef' – she always ate separately with the children – he declined but said 'thank you', as if deserving of the compliment himself. *You don't thank the skivvy; you thank the boss.*

'In Korea,' he warned, 'boys are taught that if they enter the kitchen their "organ" will fall off. I have never even peeled an apple or a melon. I would not know how.'

His words did not surprise, for I had already come to view Korea as among the most chauvinistic of nations. Rape trials, for example, are rare, criminal proceedings generally arising only if the victim's husband is so shamed that he subsequently deserts her. While breaking up a family constitutes an offence, rape itself goes largely unpunished. Burglars are said to consider raping the wife as a matter of policy, knowing she is more likely to keep quiet. If she squeals, her husband is likely to abandon her. Her silence thereby encourages both robbery and rape. I was astonished to read an unwelcome statistic, that South Korea harbours the third highest incidence of rape among European and Asian countries prepared to publish their records.

It was while staying with Mr Shin that I received a phone call from an English girl studying Korean at a Seoul university. In the middle of the night a Korean intruder had entered her room, tried to assault her, and been scared away only by her desperate screams. The incident was now a month old. In the meantime, both the university and the police had appeared perversely inactive. She had, she admitted, not been in the habit of locking her door. That was enough for the authorities to assume her complicity. She was a floosie who got what she was asking for. Good luck to the chap who tried. The British Embassy intervened on her behalf, but generated no response. She was now abandoning her studies and returning home.

'Don't get raped in Korea and expect sympathy or justice.' she said. She might have added don't be black either. That Korean racism flourishes was spectacularly reinforced in 1992 in the aftermath of the 'Rodney King case' in Los Angeles, when a black American was shown on video being beaten senseless by four baton-wielding police-men. The not-guilty verdict (of the first trial) sparked riots across LA, the local Korean community being prominent among the victims.

The government and press in Seoul reacted hysterically, demanding mandatory US assistance for their Korean brethren and sparking indignant correspondence in the English-language dailies. An American residing in Seoul wrote:

'Traditional predatory economics practiced by Korean entrepreneurs [in America] invites the ire and mistrust of those they are taking advantage of. Is it any wonder that there is friction among the cliquish Koreans and their American born neighbours?' Another American claimed:

'Fanatic Korean neo-Confucianism looks at society as an absolutely vertical system with Koreans at the apex. They view every commercial transaction as a zero-sum game where the Korean must come out on top.'

Anti-Korean sentiments in this vein provoked an outburst from a Mr 'Chris' Choi.

Everybody knows that Koreans are the most intelligent people in the world. Asians have superior intelligence and IQ scores. And we all know that in Asia, the Koreans are the cream of the crop. Why are Koreans so astute? Certainly, 5,000 years of history and a homogenous people and culture help. Also, the fact that Korea has four seasons has forced Koreans to be ever diligent. Being the most diligent people in the world has caused rampant jealousy by those of less fortunate ethnic background.

Extreme as these sentiments appear to the Western mind, I discerned among most Koreans pressed into giving an opinion an ingrained sense of national superiority. This is couched in terms of long history, pure blood, and native intelligence. Some two thousand years BC the nation merited a mythical creator (Tangun – the human offspring of a bear-woman), belief in whom appears to be an article of faith. Likewise the assurance that reunification is merely a prelude to a great and prosperous future. Paying a return visit to Mr Shin in 1992 I asked him about the looting of LA's Korean community and the scandals attached at that time to prominent black American sportsmen.

'I hate black men.' he said, without emotion.

'But not all blacks took part in the looting and arson.'

'That does not matter. I hate them all for what they have done.'

'Hitler used to speak like that. He hated particular races.'

'I don't like Hitler. But I like his attitudes. He would have punished Magic Johnson severely!' (He was speaking of the heterosexual basketball star afflicted with AIDS.)

'But Magic Johnson has committed no crime. I could understand strong feelings against Mike Tyson.'

'Mike Tyson only raped a woman, but Magic Johnson is disgusting.'

'But he says he only went with women.'

'AIDS is a disease for despicable persons.'

'Who do you despise most, Tyson or Johnson'

'Johnson, that is natural.'

'I take it you wouldn't let any black man marry your daughter,' I jested.

'Certainly not.'

'What about an American or European. Would you let them marry her?'

'Certainly not.'

'A Chinese.'

'No.'

'A North Korean?'

'Of course. He is Korean.'

~

Deep in the countryside south of Seoul lies the 'education centre' of Lucky Goldstar, one of the biggest of Korea's multinational conglomerates. These industrial giants – they include Samsung, Hyundai, Daewoo – are known colloquially as the *chaebol*. They provoke bittersweet sentiments in Korea. In the dark years after the Korean War the government poured low-interest funds in the direction of entrepreneurs and business leaders in the hope of building up the country as speedily and efficiently as possible. That goal was spectacularly achieved, but at the cost of creating industrial Frankensteins, so rich and powerful that they almost constitute a state within a state. They own vast areas of land, and are – to their critics – immune from the powers of government to clip their wings.

The *chaebol*, aping the Japanese, adhere to the 'old school' of business practice – conservative, nationalistic, disciplinarian, inflexible, militaristic, strong on oaths of allegiance. It seemed to me peculiarly

Korean to attempt to turn out high-flying executives by cosseting them for months in the countryside. I attended an induction meeting at Lucky Goldstar's education centre. Resident staff wore blue zip-up tunics; incoming managers and trainees beige. Officers and men. The setting reminded me of Patrick McGoohan's cult TV series, *The Prisoner*. As the centre's president entered the auditorium the congregation stood and roared '*Char-yot*' (attention!). Two anthems were sung with gusto, the nation's and the company's. The latter was commissioned some years ago, and is translated with difficulty on account of its poetic style.

> We are vigorous young workers of our nation
> Hopeful members march forward for prosperity.
> We are comrades combined with love
> to build paradise by ourselves.
>
> We are industrial workers leading this century
> We have new and steady creativity and research ability.
> There will be happiness in our nation and mankind
> When we accomplish our great mission
> Lucky Goldstar is the pride of our nation
> Lucky Goldstar will be globally famous.

At first sight the education centre resembles a well-appointed university campus nestling on a hillside amongst rural smallholdings. Its red-brick buildings, tended lawns and gardens, conference rooms, sports arenas and swimming pool speak of uncommon resources. But the gymnasium is almost permanently locked, and the swimming pool open for just a few weeks each summer. Local villagers, barred admission to the sumptuous enclaves for the rest of the year, are invited to step inside, strip off and taste the chlorine.

The centre's *pièce de résistance* is the company museum. At a cost I feared to contemplate, Lucky Goldstar have constructed a hi-tech, sci-fi dungeon of holograms, space-age gadgets, electronic 'workers' toiling at benches – all to celebrate the toothpastes, vacuum cleaners, microwave ovens and other consumer durables that have turned LG into an international colossus. But this is a museum with a difference. It charges no entrance fee, but – the centre being miles from anywhere – there are no curious queues at the gate. The museum is invariably shut. A state-of-the-art treasury under lock and key. Its few visitors are big noises from Seoul or abroad whom Lucky Goldstar wish to impress.

Otherwise, it's dummy workers stay idle. Tigers may be extinct, but white elephants are big business in South Korea as well as North.

~

I had left Panmunjom till last. The flash point between East and West, capitalism and communism, is no longer the Berlin Wall but the four-kilometre-wide, 250-kilometre-long DMZ separating the armies of North and South Korea. That line runs barely thirty-five miles north of Seoul. Stuck in the middle of this no-man's land is a collection of buildings and huts, sited on the old road north from Seoul. This place is called Panmunjom – the truce village. It was here that in 1953 the armistice was signed that suspended hostilities in the Korean War, initially for just ninety days, and where both sides have eyeballed and stonewalled ever since.

Panmunjom is so pregnant with drama and history it was inevitable someone would have the jolly wheeze to invite tourists. The precedent had been established by Checkpoint Charlie in Berlin, with its observation towers and on-site museum.

I had delayed my visit till the last moment, for to have gone on arrival in Korea would, I felt, have quickened the senses but dulled the judgment. Having travelled around the country and burrowed into its soul I had a greater appreciation of what to expect.

I almost delayed too long. It is not possible to visit Panmunjom independently, and one must sign up with a tour organised either by the American military or the Korean Travel Bureau. The KTB price was four times that of the Americans'. The GI on the end of the phone was polite but firm:

'I'm really sorry sir, but we are fully booked for the next month.'

'But I'm writing this book on Korea and I'm going home in a couple of days.'

'I'm sorry sir, but we are ...'

The woman on the line at the KTB seemed equally unbending. Booked up solid. I fed her the same line.

'When are you flying to England?'

'Wednesday night.'

'We have one spare seat that day.'

'But you just said you were booked for a month.'

'We have just had a group cancellation. The bus leaves here at 10.30 in the morning.' Click. In Korea, never take no for an answer.

The KTB office was on the third floor of the all-dominating Lotte building. I was in good time. Porters saluted me as I entered, as if I was a five-star general. *Doesn't it ever occur to people that not everyone likes being saluted?*

I recognised her by her voice. She was wearing a sober grey business suit and her lapel badge said 'Miss Song'. She didn't suffer fools gladly.

'Naturally. What did you expect?' she replied, smiling through clenched teeth, when I enquired if the tour guide would be speaking in English. Seldom outside Seoul had they done so, and I wondered if I knew her country better than she did.

She handed me the terms and conditions – no casual clothing, no shaggy hair – and my coupon. 'Royal service is our Motto,' it said, but it was not above royal printing errors like 'plae' and 'piace' instead of 'place'. I put the brochure away and went for a wee. A man with the same intent gobbed copiously in the corridor, the sound of its impact deadened by the thick carpet. Spitting in the Lotte! But then corridors are simply indoor streets, and streets are for spitting.

'No one is allowed to park outside.' The guide was speaking about the Blue House, official residence of the Korean President, which lies in the northern suburbs. The guide said he'd point it out. This surprised me, because I thought he'd deny its very existence. Unlike Washington's White House, Seoul's Blue House is not a magnet for tourists, and like much else is omitted from city maps. What price, I wondered, a map of 'alternative' Seoul, showing all the places one shouldn't visit, or even know about. In the event, the guide 'forgot' to show us.

He had begun with pleasantries. Seoul station was built in Japanese style; Independence Gate, built in 1896, was recently moved from its original site to make way for a road; every ten years the average height of South Koreans increases by one inch. But he soon warmed to his brief. He was too young to have lived through many of the events he described, too well trained in the techniques of fake sentiment. He was doing this for money, not from conviction, his dramatics altogether too glib. 'Do you know about the fourteen schoolchildren killed when North Korean planes bombed a bus?'

I sat at the back with an Aussie couple. We formed a commonwealth enclave against the rows of American and Japanese trippers (the Japanese had their own guide). Bruce was in local government, Sheila a hairdresser. She was like something out of the 'fifties. Her hair was piled up like candy floss, and her cheeks were crusted with face powder. She confessed to spending two hours in front of the mirror each morning, and she'd never heard of the Ayatollah Khomeini. They were good company, but full of grumbles about Korean rip-offs. Ten per cent extra for this, ten per cent for that. The guide rambled on.

'Do you know there is no civilian contact between the two Koreas? All families uprooted by the war are still separated. No mail service may cross the DMZ. Unlike Berlin, there are no day trips across the frontier. We envy German people very much.'

We stopped at the Philippines War Memorial, erected in memory of that country's assistance in the war. A farmer drying rice on the road, spreading it with the aid of a wide broom, attracted more cameras than the memorial.

'After the Korean War,' said the guide, 'the government gave land to the farmers, so with the price of land rising they are all rich. They have no money, but they are all rich.'

The words 'democratic' and 'freedom' formed the keynotes of his spiel, and were bandied about as self-evident truths. Patriotism ran amok in his mind, or at least in his performance.

To the extent that South Korea is democratically oriented, she seems an improbable and immature recruit to the ideals of ancient Athens. The Korean mind does not lend itself to conceptual subtleties, prefer- ring the comfort of absolutes – right and wrong, black and white, good and bad. In the absence of middle ground, these extremes inevitably provoke passions. The Loyal Opposition on the Westminster model has no counterpart in South Korea. Should the incumbent president be displaced, his successor would consider himself free to dismantle the apparatus of state and reconstruct it to his own ends. Besides, for a so- called democracy, South Korea has known few elections, and fewer still whose results were not invalidated by being preordained.

Equally, to speak of freedom in a state dominated by the military and which ruthlessly suppresses dissent is to employ the word in a highly politicised fashion. Korean political orthodoxy lies to the right of Right. High military spending, minimal or non-existent welfare concerns, a fiercely competitive social ethic, low wages, largely inef- fective trades unions, a highly nationalistic and patriotic public profile, virulent anti-communism, progress measured purely in materialistic terms, and the growing influence of a fundamentalist, born-again Christian church all point to an interpretation of 'freedom' that wins favour with hawkish Republican or Thatcherite persuasion.

As for Kim Il Sung, so vilified is he that charges are easy to make and difficult to refute. They do little to mitigate the feeling that, economic miracle notwithstanding, South Korea endures a political dark age. Never mind the North's, her own propaganda is so crude one wonders who could possibly be taken in. One begins to suspect that ideals of Korean unification weigh lightly among Seoul's military and industrial hierarchy, other than those achieved strictly on their terms.

South Korea, for instance, needs no lessons in paranoia. The northern branch of the Han River, thoughtlessly perhaps, spans the DMZ. It rises in North Korea, crosses into the South north of Chunchon, then flows through Seoul on its way to the West Sea. Kim Il Sung had allegedly engaged in building a mighty dam to trap the waters of the upper Han. Its purpose – to the South – was not to produce electricity but, should an 'accident' befall the dam, to drown Seoul. To counter this hypothesis, taken seriously by no one outside the South Korean military, an even larger dam was constructed down river. It is called, inevitably, the Peace Dam. It makes some pretence at serving economic ends, but no one disputes that its prime purpose is to catch the waters unleashed by the blowing of the North's dam. As Kim Il Sung could not be trusted to play fair and delay implementation of the 'accident', construction of the Peace Dam proceeded at an astonishing rate, engineers and site workers chasing huge bonuses by working round the clock. I visited it when writing this book. It doesn't look much, as dams go, but has become a favourite tourist destination. Coaches roll up in convoy, permitting time to pay a penny, buy souvenirs and a snack, and take a seat while guides point at maps and gesticulate into space.

~

If the Korean War had been a football match it would have ended in a 2-2 draw – all the goals scored in the first half. Since 1945 the two Koreas had been separated along the 38th Parallel. North Korea took the lead from the kick-off on 25 June 1950 with a sudden strike that drove southwards, penning the forces of the South and their hastily returning American allies[*] into a perimeter around Pusan. Under the banner of the United Nations (the Soviet Union being absent from the Security Council and therefore unable to use her veto), General MacArthur's amphibious landings at Inchon produced a spectacular equaliser. The UN then took the lead, 2-1, capitalising on their momentum to force the North Koreans back towards the Yalu River, the border with China. At that point Kim Il Sung introduced his substitutes – the Chinese Red Army – who piled on the pressure, driving the

---

[*] A year or so before the outbreak of the Korean War, superpower forces on both sides had pulled out of the peninsula.

armies of the UN back to the starting line. 2-2, and we were only nine months into a three year war. The second half got bogged down in a midfield stalemate, the front lines settling into trench warfare on the World War I model, horrendous casualties sustained for a few yards of temporary advantage. Like the battle for Pork Chop Hill. Like the bloody campaigns across the Imjin River.

Today the Imjin marks South Korea's effective northern boundary for all but the military and approved tourist buses. 'Imjin,' with its resonance of 'Injun', conjures up images of war, death and valour, whether involving Geronimo or the 'Glorious Glosters'. Somewhere up river, in April 1951, 773 men of the Gloucestershire Regiment (regimental badge front and rear in memory of fighting 'front and rear' against the French in Egypt in 1801) fought a famed holding action on Hill 235 against waves of Chinese assaults. Just before the hill fell – to answer the discordant but triumphant Chinese bugles – Drum Major Bass sent out a defiant 'reveille', followed by 'Come to the cookhouse door, boys', and every other known call except 'retreat'. Most of the Glosters that survived saw out the war in wretched POW camps on the Yalu River.*

The only way across the Imjin is via 'Freedom Bridge', across which 13,000 United Nations POWs had been repatriated in 1953. They had walked or been carried down 'Liberty Lane', across 'Freedom Bridge', and temporarily housed and processed in the tents of 'Freedom Village'. The narrow bridge once carried the railway to Pyongyang and beyond. The tracks had long gone and the bridge itself looked in a state of semi-collapse.

The bus rattled across, squeezed between walls of wire. Eight miles to Panmunjom. No photos till we arrive, said the guide. The landscape was lush and green and fertile, quite unthreatening. Unlike the weaponry. Lines of tanks slept under nets and tarpaulins. I'd noticed earlier, at Camp Page in Chunchon, how enormous these weapons looked, how still, how quiet, how colourless. I searched for a snatch of battle-green or brown, but each time a black and white shutter seemed to snap into place. Pathé newsreels controlling my optic nerve. Maybe blood was grey in this surreal world.

The signs hereabouts were all American. *This is Currahee County; Camp Greaves.* Maybe I expected a stronger Korean identity. But the

---

* I visited 'Gloster Valley' when writing this book. I trudged up a small bluff, with no idea that upon its crest the land fell away to a broad valley plain. The Imjin River slithered from right to left two or three miles in the distance. The sight of that plain swamped with ant-like advancing Chinese must still haunt the survivors of Hill 235.

pre-eminence of the US has its logic, and casts no aspersions on the expertise of the ROK Army. In 1950 South Korea and the United States had taken a sucker punch that was almost fatal. How to prevent a repetition? Shove the best and the biggest American troops up to the DMZ, so the thinking goes, and therein lies the most effective defence for Seoul and the clearest warning to Pyongyang. Should North Korea cross the line it would be tantamount to bombing Pearl Harbour – a head-on assault against the mightiest power on earth, bringing in its wake all the weight at Washington's disposal upon the head of Kim Il Sung. An explosive cocktail of defence and deterrence provided the rationale for Currahee County and Camp Greaves. Reading between the lines, Washington calls the shots.

We lunched at the officers' mess at Camp Liberty Bell. I knew what to expect from earlier exposure to Camp Hialeah in Pusan. One quickly gets used to thinking small in Korea: small country, small people, small houses. Hialeah was so big it had made me giddy. So much open space, so much grass, so little noise. It was so big that inside nobody walked, everyone jumped in a jeep. I listened to the buzz of the angry, congested city beyond, and doubted that the vacuum-like camp could long withstand that massive implosive force upon its perimeter.

I was joined at table by a posse of middle aged Belgians, veterans of the Korean War returning to refuel their memories. (The Belgian battalion had engaged the Chinese close by the Glorious Glosters, but had staged a successful retreat.) One of the Belgians didn't like Brits or Yanks.

'They are like Arabs: they steal our women.'

The mess provided a juke-box and a dance floor, but no dancing partners. No wives, no girlfriends, no women at all, except the wait-resses, mature and matronly, whose lapel badges proclaimed *Soldier Service is Job No 1 – We care.*

Americans have a taste for official days for this and official weeks for that. I'd grown used to them from those occasions when I could tune into AFKN. 'Native American Day', for example, sought to celebrate the Indians' contribution to American culture. 'Korean Augmentation to United States Army (KATUSA) Week' included a passing-out parade for young Koreans inducted into the US Army. The scheme dates back to the early days of the Korean War, when several thousand raw Koreans were recruited to make up numbers. Nowadays graduation is a big event, proud young men wearing million-dollar smiles.

'We must not forget the vital role KATUSAs perform,' spoke the sergeant newscaster – which, by his having to say so, meant everyone did. Now, looking around the billboards of Camp Liberty Bell, I noticed it was 'Fire Prevention Week'.

Ever since arriving in Korea I had conducted a private campaign for 'Raise the height of the urinal week'. Camp Liberty Bell had the perfect solution. Two urinals, one at Korean height, one at mine. Side by side.

Stomachs full and intellectual resistance at its weakest we filed into a briefing room. In a voice that would wake the dead in Pyongyang a trooper bellowed the approved line about Kim Il Sung's 'unique and dangerous communist regime'. Photographs of Panmunjom dramas lined the walls. These included the Major Henderson Incident of 1975 (when a North Korean journalist stamped upon the throat of the said major); the Soviet Defector Incident of 1984 (when a Russian fled across to the 'free world' leaving behind one American and three North Korean soldiers dead in his slipstream); and, most prominent of all, the Axe Murders of 1978.

A tree was to blame. Its foliage had obscured the view between allied observation towers. The UN wanted it trimmed. The North Koreans protested, claiming it was a sacred tree and not to be violated. Their objections were brushed aside. Under armed escort the tree-trimmers climbed their ladders, fighting erupted between escorts and North Korean guards, and two GIs were hacked to death. (One, Captain Bonifas, was honoured by having Camp Kitty Hawk – nearest to the DMZ – renamed after him.) The fracas was clearly captured by American cameras.

An uncooperative American tourist, tubby on excessive hamburgers and with hair bordering on the forbidden 'shaggy' (forbidden less from its implied disrespect than from providing the North with photo opportunities of the decadent West), demanded an explanation.

'You keep talking about North Korean spy cameras,' he interjected, 'but how come you have all this detailed film, from so many angles?' The trooper's mouth said 'I'm afraid I am not in a position to answer that, sir.' His eyes said 'keep your bloody mouth shut'.

He ended on a joke: 'When President Reagan came to Korea in 1983 it was considered too dangerous for him to visit the border. When Vice-President Dan Quayle came it was considered safe enough!'

'Any more questions?' asked the trooper. In the same breath: 'Right, the tour will proceed. Do not speak with, make any gesture towards, or in any way approach or respond to personnel from the other side.

Everything is being photographed from the other side, and could be used out of context for propaganda purposes.'

We had become immersed in a world of bewildering three-letter initials. Inside the DMZ is the JSA (Joint Security Area), in the centre of which is the MDL (Military Demarcation Line). The whole area is managed by the UNC (United Nations Command). The confronting armies represent the ROK (Republic of Korea) and the KPA (Korean People's Army.) The American military hierarchy is called the JCS (Joint Chiefs of Staff). One building houses the headquarters of the MAC (Military Armistice Commission). Briefing rooms are furnished with PVC chairs.

Here in the Joint Security Area, close quarter combat skills are demanded. Black belt South Korean troops spend thirty months here. The GIs are big, tough, and deprived, volunteering for a year-long, womanless stint. A door-sign reads: *Monastery. Home of the Merry Red Monks of the DMZ.*

Back to the bus with the trooper acting as guide. More checkpoints: inspections of our special visitors badge 'to be worn over your outer-most garment, on the left side'. It read: *Guest UNCMAC.* As the final badge-checker stepped down from the bus he yelled over his shoulder 'in front of them all'. It was a war cry, like 'banzai', or 'up and at 'em'. The words were even engraved on the dance floor. It is down to these troops to hold the line, for if breached Seoul is impossible to defend. (The natural barrier provided by the Han River is on the wrong, southern, side of the city.)

The landscape on this, the old route from Seoul to China, looked innocuous. Grey hills framed the horizon. The propaganda was inces-sant. Each side boasted a flagpole and a village. The South's flagpole was a modest 100 metres high. The North's in the distance, like a skinny Eiffel Tower, was sixty metres higher. Its flag measured thirty metres – 'probably the longest in the world'. It weighed half a ton and needed a lot of wind to lift it. It had the lumbering air of all giants, not so much flapping crisply as fighting to remain airborne. Fluttering horizontal was beyond its capability, and it settled at best for semi-erection, 45° below the horizontal, like some giant penis excited by another flagpole, struggling for lift-off but unable to overcome the dead-weight of its sheer mass.

The villages were called Taesong-dong (literally 'successful attain-ment village', but jargoned into 'Freedom Village') and Gijong-dong ('Propaganda Village'). Freedom Village actually had villagers, eking

out their lives in this woebegone world. They identified themselves by
yellow hats. The villagers paid no taxes but obeyed a nightly 11 pm
curfew. Propaganda Village – a motley assortment of walls and towers
in the distance – was supposedly erected in days and stands empty. It
was a ghost-town, a village purely for show. Its 'workers' commuted
each day, returning to their real homes at night. But what Propaganda
Village lacked in night-life it made up for in noise. Proclamations,
alternately beguiling and strident, and martial music drifted across the
ether. The breeze shifted to the north and a crackly voice spoke on the
wind. I hoped in vain they would broadcast in English, and felt
aggrieved at my ignorance of Kim Il Sung's earthly paradise.

The bus pulled up and we dismounted. So this was Panmunjom. We
conjure up in our minds extraordinary theatres for life's extraordinary
dramas. Kim Il Sung commanded three thousand tanks, primed and
ready for action somewhere over the horizon. Units of his million-
strong army, the fifth largest in the world, were presumably nearby,
bristling with fire-power and ready for the order to charge. At least,
that was the American line. Washington is compelled to demonise
North Korea, for reunification of the two Koreas would create by the
end of the century the spectre of an economic and military giant.
Added to which, the United States habitually magnifies the threat to
global security posed by small 'renegade' states. This helps to justify
US military expenditure and, if necessary, military intervention – as in
Grenada, as in Iraq. I thought wryly of one of AFKN's little homilies.
One GI to another: 'Try to listen to both sides of an argument: it broad-
ens the mind.'

Panmunjom – at least the southern side – has been transformed into
a garden. It was like pulling up in the grounds of a country house.
Artificial lakes, arched bridges, manicured gardens, flower beds. Park
benches, even. A workman pruned a tree, wheelbarrow at his side. I
wondered who was entitled to stroll among the blooms or rest on the
benches. A Keep Out garden, perhaps. We tourists were herded away.
But we could photograph it, and show family and friends how much
prettier the South was than the North.

An octagonal pavilion, mounted by a spiral staircase, functions as a
tourist observation platform. It is called 'Freedom House'. From its
elevated viewing platform we stared beyond a line of prefabricated
huts towards the North Korean equivalent. It looked like an office
block in need of a spring clean, and was, we were told, just thirteen
feet wide. A puff of wind might topple it to the ground.

From its steps two North Korean guards played peekaboo through binoculars. They were the first North Koreans I'd seen. They wore the olive green uniforms and wide-brimmed hats standard to communist forces. The hats suit the large and plump rather than the short and slim, for they seem top-heavy and forever likely to flop over the wearers' eyes. My first sight of North Korean guards did not set the adrenaline flowing.

I would have been more impressed had they taken their job seriously. Perhaps I was disappointed that they seemed unimpressed with me. They didn't rush inside and emerge running their fingers down check-lists to see if anyone answering my description was marked for special attention. They didn't jabber agitatedly and wave Kalashnikovs at me. On the contrary, mostly they were just fooling around and giving one another playful kicks up the backside. I hoped for their sake Kim Il Sung did not appear unannounced, and I wondered if I would be doing them a favour if I did something out of the ordinary, or better still broke one of the 'Don't' rules in my brochure. What would the Yanks do if I yelled out, I wondered? What would they do if I sprinted across the Military Demarcation Line?

Into the centremost blue hut. This was what most of the tourists had come to see. The nerve centre of the armistice, where the eyeballing and stonewalling had gone on since 1953, where jaw-jaw had somehow staved off more war-war. These and neighbouring huts straddled the MDL, one half in South Korea and one half in the North.

The guide milked the drama of the long room. Astride the centre, like a tennis net, was a table covered with green baize. One set of chairs was in South Korea, the other in North Korea. Microphone cables stretched the length of the table. The microphones were switched on '24-7', said the trooper, (twenty four hours a day, seven days a week), 'so everything you or I say now is being picked up at this moment in Pyongyang.' His remarks provoked a nervous titter.

Mounted flags faced each other across the table. One-upmanship extended to these, as to the villages and their giant flagpoles. The North Koreans' table-flag was taller. It topped that of the United Nations by one inch.

'But as you can see,' said the trooper, 'the arrowhead on top of our flag is broader than theirs.' He offered the predictable jocular advice:

'If you want to pass safely into North Korea and come out alive, I suggest you do so now,' he said, motioning us round to the northern side of the table. Tourists gave routine giggles, giving in to their moment of ideological treachery. Would the air be different, more chilly, perhaps? Would this smiling young soldier look even more reassuring from the edge of darkness? An elderly American put her hand to her throat and gave a little cough. The Japanese lined up for their group photograph in North Korea.

'Ladies and gentlemen. At this time we will be boarding the transportation.' It was time to go. No malingering. We bussed past the scene of the Axe Murders, past the stump of the offending tree, past the overgrown Bridge of No Return (closed since the Axe attack), back to the safe side of the DMZ. The trooper departed the bus with applause warming his ears. And so to the souvenir shop.

Inside were collection boxes for the Peace Dam. Certificates were on sale, recording your visit to the North Korean section of the Joint Security Area. You could sign the visitors book for free, and inscribe comments like: 'Emotional;' 'God Bless You, America;' 'A constant reminder to be vigilant;' and 'In Christ there is no East/West, North/ South – Fight!' Many signatures belonged to overseas Koreans with American addresses. A soldier sat drinking a soft drink at the bar. I went over and he got politely to his feet. He stood 6 feet 8, weighed 250 pounds, and had a wife waiting in Tennessee. He had volunteered for the DMZ.

'Life here's kinda depressing,' he said.

The final stop on the tour: the famous Third Tunnel of Aggression, whose imitations were to be found in freedom halls and anti-communist museums. (It was discovered in 1978, three years after the first, two years after the second.) Again the hard-sell build-up. Another briefing room with wall map and automated sermon directed against the 'uneducated' Kim Il Sung and his 'Messiah complex'. Again the fat, fair-haired American asked the awkward questions.

'How do you know there are just three tunnels? You suspect there are a dozen? Hold on a minute. You've told us about their tunnels: how many have you guys built under the North?'

And then on foot, wearing hard hats, we stepped gingerly down the steep 'interception tunnel', keeping our balance with the assistance of rubber mats and metal handrails. The invasion tunnel was seventy-three metres below the surface and was designed to permit passage to 30,000 North Korean troops per hour, three abreast, on their way to seize Seoul. Like adolescents impatient for a glimpse of What the Butler Saw, visitors queued for a two-second peep into a subterranean North Korean guard post.

'Even underground,' said the guide, 'we do not violate the rules.'

The Third Tunnel was a Disney-esque parody. For all its former threat, it was worth its weight in extracted granite as a propaganda tool. If she hadn't found any tunnels, South Korea would have had to invent them. Danger spells tourists, and tourists spell profit.[*]

~

'A mere shuttlecock of certain great powers,' Isabella Bishop had written of Korea almost a century ago. The powers may have changed, but the game has not.

---

[*] There is now a Fourth Tunnel. In April 1992 the author became the first Western civilian to gain access to it, being taken by the captain in command on a rail tour of the tunnel and shown North Korean graffiti decorating the walls.

12

A DREAM OF *JUCHE*
The Mind of Kim Il Sung

At least two buccaneering expeditions were started against the country, and one of them ended in tragedy. In 1866 an American schooner, the *General Sherman*, left Tientsin for Korea. She was loaded with guns, powder, and contraband articles, and was said to be despatched for the purpose of plundering the royal tombs at Ping-yang. The ship entered the Tai Tong river ... The Regent of Korea sent orders that the foreigners were not to be allowed to land, and that they were either to be driven back or killed ... Being ignorant of the navigation of the river, Captain Preston ran his ship on the banks and was unable to float it off ... Then came the ... burning boats, and this set the *General Sherman* on fire.

F A McKenzie – *The Tragedy of Korea* – (1908)

GAZING into North Korea from Panmunjom whetted an appetite that was already becoming insatiable. What kind of people would erect such an enormous flagpole, or would build a showpiece border village where nobody lived? What kind of being could be addressed by his people as the 'Great Leader', or his son and dynastic heir as the 'Dear Leader?' I had been exposed for so long to the Korea of the South that I now yearned to peep inside the Korea of the North. I had been subjected to so many tirades against the ruinous practices of Kim Il Sung – in power since 1945 and the world's longest serving ruler – that, far from being deterred, I became increasingly desperate to see for myself. So little was known about this paradise manqué. So little was known about Kim Il Sung, or at least his past. North Korea insists that he waged guerrilla campaigns against the Japanese, single-handedly liberating his people from their oppression. His detractors in the United States and South Korea either deflate his warrior status or disclaim it altogether. Kim Il Sung, they say, stole the name of another anti-Japanese crusader, and, in any case, he would never have come to power except as the puppet of Stalin. They would have us believe that a team of one thousand scientists works round the clock in a Pyongyang 'Longevity Institute' in an effort to keep the Great Leader alive forever.

Mind you, the outpourings of Radio Pyongyang are no less fanciful. From time to time I would borrow a radio and tune into its ravings. Over the air waves I learned, for example, of a frenzy of badge-production – the people clamouring to sport idolatrous badges of the President. His gifts are evidently supernatural, for unnamed plants are said to blossom twice a year in his honour, nourished solely by the love and affection that he beams upon them, as upon all his subjects.

For the most part Radio Pyongyang is more prosaic. The solemn national anthem heralds the News, which daily features no other subject than devotions to the President, his life, thought and policies:

A letter to the Great Leader Marshal Kim Il Sung was adopted at the ... central committee ... to congratulate Him on his re-election as President of the Democratic People's Republic of Korea. The letter reverentially extended the highest glory and warmest con-gratulations to the respected Leader, Marshal Kim Il Sung on his re-election as President of the Democratic People's Republic of Korea – in token of boundless reverence for and loyalty to Him. The letter stressed: respected Marshal Kim Il Sung admirably pioneered the modern history of our country, and opened up a new era of national prosperity, by founding the immortal *juche* idea, and wisely leading our people in their struggle for independ-ence, sovereignty and socialism with his outstanding and tested leadership. It continued: The great turns in our country and all the glories of our people are all associated with the Great Leader's august name.

The accent of Radio Pyongyang's presenters was unnerving. Their English was unlike that heard in Seoul, or anywhere else for that matter. Denied access to Western media and materials, North Koreans are taught by instructors similarly deprived, in a closeted medium of pirated tapes and politically purified textbooks. Take the word 'people'. The Korean confusion between 'b' and 'p' could not account for the presenters' laboured 'bee-porl'. 'Him' was uttered with aspi-rated emphasis, serving to deify the subject. Nowadays I cannot read anything emanating from North Korea without reawakening in my mind those chilling consonants. On one occasion I was startled to hear

Radio Pyongyang discussing daleks, and had to cock an ear before translating it as 'dialogues':

> It is entirely up to the attitude of the South Korean side whether or not the north-south dialogues become dialogues making practical progress in the settlement of the reunification problem ... The south-side delegations at the north-south talks should make due efforts to resume the suspended various dialogues.

Nor does 'Pyongyang' reflect the spoken sound of the capital city. Far from rhyming with 'wrong', the first syllable zings like a ricocheting bullet, better encapsulated in the 'Ping-yang' of earlier transliterations.

Kim Il Sung is the founder of the *juche* (pronounced 'jew-cheh') philosophy of self-reliance. To assist those seeking enlightenment in this arcane subject, Radio Pyongyang provides distance-learning tutorials. These are preceded by a shrill soprano lead-in, gentle strings, topped by the vibrant proclamation: 'Idea is the beacon of revolution! Today we'll bring you the 101st instalment of the book "The Immortal *Juche* Idea". This time we'll present the third part of What is Ideological Consciousness?'

What is it, indeed? I was keen to know. I lent an ear, and this is what I learned.

> Knowledge of natural science, which is consciousness reflecting the essence and law of movement of objective things, does not assume a class nature. There is no mathematics of one kind for the people and another kind for the exploiting classes. The addition that 1 and 2 make 3 is the same for the people and for the exploiting classes. Knowledge of natural science, being this kind of consciousness, natural science itself has no class nature, but this does not hold good with social science. Indeed we can say that social science has given knowledge by clarifying the objective law of development of society in the sense that it reflects the essence and law of movement of the objective world. But because social science deals with social movement, of which the main agency is man, it directly reflects the interests of people, so dependent on the provisions of people, their views on social phenomena differ. Therefore in social science, unlike natural science, there are

philosophy and economics for the working class, and those for capitalists separately. Then what kind of consciousness is thought? The readers should pay special attention to this question. Unlike knowledge, which is consciousness reflecting the essence and law of movement of objective things, thought is consciousness reflecting man's needs and interests ... For example, the consciousness that nuclear fission produces an enormous amount of energy, is knowledge reflecting the attribute of the thing itself called 'atom', whereas thinking if it is useful to employ the atomic energy for the production of electricity or bombs is not knowledge reflecting the attributes of the atom itself, but a thought which reflects man's needs and interests ... One and the same thing and phenomenon is often regarded by some people as useful and by others as harmful. Take one or two instances: in capitalist society a good crop pleases the farmers who have raised it. But it displeases capitalists, wanting agricultural produce stocked up in their storehouses in anticipation of higher prices. People do not want war, but war-industrialists who make money by producing arms and other war supplies want war. This shows that thought, which is a consciousness reflecting people's needs and interests, is not a simple reflection of the material world. Here is another point which must be clarified before proceeding farther. It is that thought is not a simple reflection of the material world, and therefore does not always fall behind the reality. If thought is regarded as a simple reflection of the material world it naturally follows that thought always falls behind the reality, because if thought is a simple reflection of reality, its change is conditional on the latter's change. But since thought is not a simple reflection of the reality, it can either fall behind or precede the reality. There are quite a few people who are anachronistic in their thought. Those who fail to see the developing reality may entertain backward ideas. Ideas that lag behind the reality will stand in the way of historical progress.

More wailing violins concluded the reading. I pondered the excess of clichés and slogans. Whole phrases had been repeated *ad nauseam*, yet were no clearer on the n'th hearing than on the first. Most Western listeners no doubt would respond with boredom and derision. I, however, found myself strangely hooked by this circuitous gobbledygook, though not to the extent of wishing to endure the previous one hundred episodes. It seemed to me remarkable that such an intellectual charade could be sustained. In a rapidly changing world it surely could not long continue to do so. North Korea had always been an uncomfortable ally for the Soviet Union, if only because Kim Il Sung offered no recompense for Moscow's aid. No Soviet military or naval bases were permitted in North Korea. Like other instances in pre-colonial Asia, Kim Il Sung's socialism is heavily nationalistic. *Juche* is, perhaps, the ultimate expression of their ideological combination. With the rapid collapse, first of the Soviet economy, then of the Soviet system, North Korea finds herself in dire straits. Moscow provides oil only in return for hard currency which Pyongyang can ill-afford. The socialist market for North Korean exports no longer exists. She has barely a friend left in the new world order. Her GNP, estimated at no more than 10% of South Korea's, is spiralling downwards. *Juche*, always a fiction, is now transparently unattainable. How to refurbish her coffers has become for North Korea a matter of national survival. She can contemplate reunification with the rich South. But on what terms? She can go the way of China, and experiment with joint-venture economic zones in far corners of the country, hoping to quarantine the influx of infectious ideas.* But who would be prepared to invest against an unpredictable regime with a legacy of bad debts? Alternatively, North Korea can tread the line of nuclear brinkmanship, peddling missiles and rattling sabres as a means of demanding attention. Added to which, Kim Il Sung is now in his eighties. His death is sure to herald climactic change, if not the complete collapse of his country. Few outside observers are convinced that his son, Kim Jong Il, can long cling to power. For all these reasons I sensed I had to see North Korea sooner rather than later. How to achieve this aim became for me a minor obsession.

Roaming independently, as in the South, was out of the question. Unchaperoned travel in the Democratic People's Republic of Korea (DPRK) does not exist. Specialist agencies offer tours at prohibitive cost, but I was averse both to the outlay and the packaged company. I wished to see the DPRK as independently as possible. My plans were hindered by there being no official communications between South and North Korea, nor between South Korea and China. Though, from Panmunjom, I could actually peer into North Korea, safe passage around the DMZ would direct me via a mighty detour, first from Seoul

---

* The first such capitalist zone is under consideration in the Tumen River basin, in the far north-east, by the border with China and Russia.

to Hong Kong, then from Hong Kong to China, and finally from Beijing to Panmunjom – a trip of several thousand miles.

I flew to Hong Kong, where I directed polite telexes to Pyongyang's state tourist administration, *Ryohaengnsa* (the equivalent of the Russian *Intourist*). Each went unanswered. I phoned the North Korean Embassy in Beijing, waited an age for anyone who could speak English, and was brusquely informed that North Korea was for the moment closed to visitors. Frustrated and disbelieving, I took a plane to Beijing. I would present myself at the embassy in person.

In the absence of diplomatic relations between China and South Korea,* it was Beijing's 'Korean Embassy' that I sought. The diplomatic quarter lies east of Tiananmen Square, which the previous year had reverberated to the rumble of tanks and the chatter of machine guns. These days it had reverted to being a public playground. The sky overhead was thick with kites.

The taxi driver was incredulous: 'You want go Korea Embassy? Why? Korea is bad, socialist country.'

'What is China?' I asked.

'China is capitalist country.' He grinned at me in the mirror and rubbed his fingers together.

We sped down the broad Changan Avenue and turned into the leafy boulevards that host the diplomatic quarter. The Korean Embassy, like the pariah it represents, is quarantined away from its diplomatic brethren, opposite a public park. I nodded hello at the Chinese soldier at the gate and entered. The consulate section was deserted. A plywood counter sagged alarmingly when I leant on it. Tourist itineraries and charts decorated the walls. A rack housed the latest editions – English and French – of glossy tourist magazines.

An unsmiling Korean suddenly appeared. He was not endowed with social graces and our conversation was brief.

'I would like to visit Korea,' I said.

'Your country?'

I pulled out my passport: '*Yong-guk.*'

'No visa!' The unsmiling man sneered and waved me away, as if my presence was contaminating the consulate. He disappeared down the corridor. I seemed to have been gunned down at the first hurdle, but was not unduly surprised. Such tourism as North Korea permits is heavily restricted to those of her few allies, together with Western delegations of proven socialist sympathy. I fitted neither category.

---

* These were established in 1993

I could not bring myself to concede defeat and sat down to await inspiration. I picked up a couple of tourist mags and read about the visits to Pyongyang of Yasser Arafat (revolver at hip) and Egyptian President Hosni Mubarak (awarded the title of North Korean Hero, and a gold-star medal, and the National Flag Order First Class). Cuban military delegations posed alongside the Great Leader. I stared at pictures of alleged US atrocities during the Korean War, and of hard-hatted steel workers 'beaming with joy at overflowing their daily quota'.

Kim Il Sung peered out at me in fedora hat and mustard suit. He was fingering a sheaf of wheat. The caption explained he was 'giving personal guidance at a cooperative, inspiring scientific farming along *juche* lines'.

And what was this? – a feature written by one Peter Johnson, described as a 'British scholar'. He wrote:

I looked around ... many places in Pyongyang and the provinces. I was deeply impressed. Here I would like to say briefly about my impressions of the Changgwang Kindergarten I have inspected. All facilities for children were very fine ... all the children were healthy and cheerful. This fact alone is enough to realise that the state pays deep attention to children and to their education.

I wished to know how this Peter Johnson had succeeded in entering North Korea. The magazine's *pièce de résistance* featured The Great Leader's son and designated successor, Kim Jong Il. The dauphin has been groomed for power despite apparently never having met a for-eigner or delivered a public speech in his life. He is caricatured in the West as a permed and debauched dwarf. The magazine shows him standing with four peasants to whom he directs 'personal guidance'. Although short in stature, by standing closest to the cameraman – who is bending or kneeling to frame the shot – he appears to tower over his subjects. He wears a revolutionary suit with breast pockets and high-buttoned collar, and his shiny leather shoes highlight the peasants' bare feet. His hands are clasped behind his back and he stands in half-profile pontificating towards the horizon. The peasants look ill at ease. Only one is smiling, but it is a smile by command. Kim Jong Il himself appears, as Americans would say, distinctly flakey. The accompanying article takes the form of a panegyric, simplistic and poetic, and deserves reprinting. It is called 'Brilliant Guidance'.

Dear Comrade Kim Jong Il would often work through the night till the early morning. Even though officials begged him to take a rest for a few moments he refused and got into his car, saying that he would like to have a walk.

How does he spend the early morning? None of the officials knew and it wasn't until long afterwards that they got to know about it.

Comrade Kim Jong Il told the officials who were working close to him that he would take a rest as had been requested, and he drove to the suburbs. The car halted at the edge of a paddy field in Chongsan-ri. A thick mist was hovering over the wide fields. It was still impossible to find the roads and fields. The village was quiet. Occasionally there was the sound of voices of some people in the paddy field.

Comrade Kim Jong Il looked to where the voices were coming from. He discovered an old man who was mending the gate of a rice field.

'Are you mending the gate?'

'Yes.'

'Have you finished the ploughing?'

'Yes, we have. We're now levelling the fields.'

'What depth of land have you ploughed?'

'35 cm deep.'

'5 cm deeper than you did last year. How much manure have you spread?'

'We planned to apply 20 tons in each hectare. But we have spread 15 tons.'

'That is a larger amount than you spread last year. You must have had lots of trouble.'

'No. Is it trouble when we have not carried out the President's instructions?'

Who is it? The old man wondered. Perhaps he may be some official from a county or a provincial seat. How can he be so familiar with the situation in our village.

'Have you grown healthy rice seedlings?'

'Of course. After we caused worries to the President because we raised seedlings so weak, we have corrected our mistake.'

'How many leaves does a rice stalk bear?'

'Five or six leaves.'

'That will do.'

How knowledgeable he is, the old man still wondered.

'When are you going to start the rice transplanting?'

'We are going to start in a few days. We are busy enough now.'

Their conversation continued for a long time. As the mist cleared, Comrade Kim Jong Il left the place and inspected every field in the village, despite the dew that soaked his trousers and shoes.

After he studied what progress was made in farming preparations for the spring, he returned and called for the senior officials of art and culture. He told them to take the artists to the Chongsan village and conduct political work accompanied by mass cultural activities, while giving a helping hand to the farmers.

On that early morning, the officials who had sent the dear leader off on his drive thought that he had enjoyed a walk ... The time for morning walks is good for the people's health, but to Comrade Kim Jong Il it is set aside for the good of the people.

I felt intrigued by this fairy tale drivel. Surely I would not be denied a glimpse of this never-never land. I put down the magazine as a second man appeared behind the counter. He was younger than the first and with a countenance – though not exactly amiable – less malign. Noticing that my magazine was in English he asked: 'Can I help you?'

A surge of optimism flooded through me. Here was my chance. I stood up and approached the counter.

'Yes. I am interested in your country and wish to see it. Is that possible?'

'Where are you from?'

'England.'

'I am sorry. You cannot have a visa.'

I had to think quickly or all was lost. On impulse I tried to impress him with my knowledge of the *General Sherman*, the US schooner named after William Tecumseh Sherman (Union commander in the American Civil War). In 1866 the ship had sought to plunder Pyongyang and her crew had been slaughtered for their pains. Those on board included the Scottish Protestant missionary, Robert Thomas.

'I would like to visit the site of the running-dogs' death!'

The man was momentarily silent. He had not, I suspected, met many foreigners *au fait* with the *General Sherman*. First blood to me. I next indulged in a bit of trivia, exploiting the Koreans' fanaticism for football. Each of us knows someone who can reel off the names of interminable Welsh railway stations, or list the moons of Jupiter, or chronicle every American president, or whatever. For myself, I could run through the North Korean football team of 1966.

'Exactly one hundred years after the *General Sherman* your country was very famous in England. Your football team was a shining light during the World Cup. Every player was a star. Do you remember Pak Seung Jin, who scored the first goal against Portugal in the quarter-final; or Li Dong Woon who scored the second? When your outside-left Yang Sung Kook netted a third everybody thought England would play Korea in the semi-finals. Such a pity Portugal recovered. For me, though, your best player was Pak Doo Ik.'

Orientals may be inscrutable, but I vouch that the man standing between me and my visa was stunned. I held my breath.

'Pak Doo Ik is now the coach of our national team,' he said. I had struck a chord. A moment later he asked:

'Where would you like to go?'

Eureka!

'Normally,' said the man, his face suddenly stern, 'persons should send me names and passport numbers. Then we send them information.'

Arse over head, I thought. It is natural to know the tours available before committing oneself.

'Where can I go?'

He pulled from under the counter a scrappy, plastic-covered file which he placed before me. Heart pounding I flipped through the loose-leaf pages, each detailing a different itinerary.

'You must be quick. You cannot take so long.'

'What? But I don't know which one to choose!'

'You are not allowed to read the book,' he insisted, and reached out as if to take it from me. Perhaps he thought I was making mental notes for later dissemination. Espionage undertaken while touring North Korea was, for all I knew, a capital offence for those granting the visa.

My triumph was about to be snatched from me. The file fell open at a trip taking in Pyongyang and Kaesong. Kaesong is the southernmost city in North Korea, just five miles north of Panmunjom. I fancied the idea of staring at my ghost across the green table. Maybe North Korean guards would invite me to walk around the other side, as the only means of passing safely into South Korea and coming out alive.

'I'll go there,' I said, turning the book round to show him the itinerary and the price.

'We must telex Pyongyang to make arrangements. That will take ten days. First you must buy aeroplane tickets. International travel is not included.'

'I want to see as much of China and Korea as I can. I'll make my own way across China and pick up the train at the border.'

'You must leave from Beijing,' he said, in a way that could not be gainsaid. 'We will give you your visa on the same day. Come here that morning.'

His manner was one of granting a reluctant favour, rather than seeking hard currency for his country's coffers. He asked abruptly for my passport. My spirits sank. Though no visa was required for British visitors to South Korea, the date and point of entry had been stamped in Korean script. The man would see I had come from the South. Maybe visiting both Koreas was prohibited, as some Arab states deny entry to those having set foot in Israel.

Fortunately my passport was full and decorated with the paraphernalia of international bureaucracy. If the offending stamp was noticed no comment was made. The passport was wordlessly handed back. I thanked the man and left. No papers had been signed, no notes taken, no money paid. He could, if he chose, deny all knowledge of me.

Hardly daring to believe my good fortune, I presented myself at the China International Travel Service. Boards slung above the counter proclaimed the destinations of the Trans-Siberian Railway – Ulan Bator, Moscow, Budapest. A lonely looking sign said 'Piengyang'. The crowds of Western backpackers with their cagoules and money pouches had eyes only for the Trans-Siberian. I was almost afraid to speak my destination, for fear of provoking a stampede to join me. How could a week stuck on a train clogged with foreigners compete with an invitation to North Korea?

My request for a ticket sparked a spate of phone calls. The wait seemed interminable. When the desk clerk finally put down the phone he filled in a pink cardboard ticket. It was in Russian and German, reflecting the preponderance of arrivals from the former Soviet Union and East Germany. There was no call to print it in English. The train departed at 16:48 hours, ten days hence.

To celebrate I took myself to Beijing's Jesuit Observatory, whose walls dated back half a millennium. The gateman seemed only marginally less ancient. In my hand I clutched a folded North Korean magazine. Its cover showed a portrait of Kim Il Sung. Gesticulating at the picture the gateman launched into pantomime, thrusting out his chest and strutting around in small circles. He jabbed again at the picture and his features convulsed with loathing. The gateman left no doubt about the disdain felt by Chinese for their Great Neighbour.

~

On the appointed morning I returned to the Korean Consulate. In the interval nagging doubts had surfaced. The official may have had second thoughts, or forgotten me, or Pyongyang may have vetoed my trip. The consulate was busy processing a party of Chinese Koreans, thousands of whom populate the lower reaches of Manchuria, north of the Yalu River, and who retain as far as possible their Korean way of life.

I asked for the man who had seen me. He was out. No one claimed any knowledge of my visa. Only the sight of my railway ticket, departure time looming, prompted any degree of urgency. Someone phoned the man's wife. She was at home. For all I knew, she lived on the other side of the city.

An hour later she arrived. Like her husband she spoke English. She could find no record of me, but satisfied by my train ticket wrote out my visa and slipped it loose inside my passport. It would be reclaimed upon leaving North Korea, denying me a collector's item. The trip itself was to be paid for in Pyongyang, for which purpose I was handed a scribbled voucher, like a supermarket check-out tab. I asked for an itinerary, maps, and miscellaneous handouts.

'I do not know where my husband keeps them,' said the wife.

Beijing railway station was stuffed with humanity. The vast concourse functioned as waiting room cum refugee camp. Amongst mountains of baggage, would-be passengers sat about on newspapers, sleeping, laughing, playing cards, women with their legs wide exposing their knickers.

Just four trains a week run between Beijing and Pyongyang, of which a single 'soft'-sleeper carriage at the rear is reserved for non-Koreans. It was divided into twelve four-berth compartments. Forty-eight places four times a week, a weekly maximum of 192 persons. Two further rail lines link Pyongyang with Moscow, one through eastern China, one through Khabarovsk. There being just one international sea route to North Korea (via Japan), the only alternative to rail is by plane. Air China listed one weekly scheduled flight to Pyongyang. Korean Airways offered infrequent links with Beijing, Moscow and Khabarovsk. This was the sum of international traffic with surely the most hermetic state on earth. I became more excited by the minute.

My carriage was Korean, not Chinese. It bore the state seal of the DPRK on its sides, a bas-relief of wheat sheaves, electricity pylon, and radiating red star. The ticket inspector sported a red lapel badge of Kim Il Sung. The inspector ticked off my name and ordered the loading boys to stand clear while I boarded.

The carriage was filled with Russians, Koreans, and Chinese on official business. I shared a compartment with a United Nations worker, an Ethiopian returning from home leave with her two young sons and six large suitcases. The suitcases occupied two berths, the family a third. The woman, I imagined, had worn the same strap-sandals all her life, for the African sun had imprinted zebra stripes across her instep and toes. Fearing that she was a 'plant', my conversation was polite and guarded.

'You will like the Democratic People's Republic of Korea,' she said, inviting me to drink tea, for which a flask of hot water was provided. 'It is very clean and everybody is polite.'

The journey time was twenty-one hours, with just one toilet to serve forty-eight. The washroom tap produced barely a dribble and the door to the forward carriages was locked. We steamed noisily eastwards across the great plain of China, through Tangshan, site of the 1976 earthquake reckoned the world's costliest in human lives. It grew dark, there was nothing to see, and I turned in. The next day I would enter North Korea.

~

I awoke and raised myself on an elbow to peer out of the window. We were pulling into Dandong, the Chinese terminus. Half a mile ahead lay the border, the Yalu River, across which American planes had 'accidentally' strafed Dandong's airstrip during the Korean War. The engine and forward carriages decoupled and choo-chooed away, leaving the two sleeping cars – one soft, one hard class – marooned for hours. All remaining passengers, those bound for North Korea, decamped to the platform and the street market beyond to stock up with bread rolls, fizzy pop, and sackfuls of vegetables. It was clearly a well-worked routine.

'Everything is cheaper here than in Korea,' said the Ethiopian, putting on her sandals and getting up. 'Don't you want anything?'

'I'm going as a tourist. I expect my meals are provided.'

Two hours later our stranded carriages were hooked up to a belching loco and hauled at a dawdle across the Yalu. To the right of the new railway bridge reared the stunted remains of the old. The rusty steel superstructure, peppered with shot, terminated in mid-channel. The Koreans had dismantled their half of the bridge. I visualised hordes of Chinese infantry swarming like ants along its length during the winter of 1950-51. Clad in yellowy winter garb and dragging primitive weapons, thousands had been spattered by American anti-personnel bombs.

The Korean shore inched closer. Sculptured parks and promenades crept into view, but no sooner were we out of sight of China than a different reality supervened. We halted at the riverside town of Shinuiju to await a connecting train to Pyongyang. Customs men invited me to 'take a rest' on the platform. They took no interest in my rucksack, which concealed undeclared binoculars and radio. Korean passengers had their bags minutely inspected.

It was a strange sensation, a lone Westerner wandering the precincts of Shinuiju station. I felt instantly transported to a country at war. This was partly the result of three persons in every four being in uniform, (either the military's baggy, olive green or the railway workers' slate grey); partly the 1940s and 'fifties ambience of bare concrete walls and chipped and fractured paving; partly the sense of being imprisoned within the station confines while townsfolk were equally imprisoned without. It was impossible to saunter into or out of the station. Thick concrete barriers, backed by metal railings, turned Shinuiju station into a mini-Colditz. I peered out at the town square, featureless facades and trees that looked no less grey than the station walls. A couple strolled by under a parasol. I even espied a bicycle or two. This was unexpected, as bicycles were supposedly condemned by Kim Il Sung as bourgeois inventions, an unwelcome aid to social mobility, a drain on household expenses, and unnecessary in a land of perfect public transportation. They were, I had been told, outlawed, or required a permit. Perhaps here on the border enforcement was slack: nowhere else in North Korea would a two-wheeled vehicle catch my eye.

I felt like an escaped POW, expecting at any time a tap on the shoulder and a demand for 'papers please'. The station gates were framed by revolutionary posters – flat-capped workers, clenched fists, red flags – of the kind associated with China a generation earlier. 'Everybody march forward,' shouted one poster. The in-vogue campaign was the 'thousand-mile horse', who by covering that distance without resting encouraged the populace to yet greater labours. Two workers were praised for exceeding their quotas. Their 150% output bettered even the Herculean 110% effort customarily demanded by

British football coaches. North Korea, one sensed, was exuding the revolutionary zeal that – the old guard excepted – had all but expired in China. In the march of world socialism, it was now China that was reactionary.

A platoon of baby conscripts marched stiffly down the platform. They looked faintly ridiculous with their flapping, jodhpur-like trousers and oversized peaked hats. They carried canvas knapsacks over their shoulders and paid me less attention than was my due. No doubt I was taken for an East European. Either way, no one took any notice of me: at least, not until I drew my camera.

It was one thing to be free to take pictures, it was another to expect anyone to sit still and be framed. Though my person drew no reaction, my camera had the effect of pulling a gun. Figures quickened their pace, turned their backs, hid behind doorways, crouched behind pillars. On the next platform a squatting soldier, cigarette in hand, waddled duck-like behind a post, leaving his sub-machine gun standing erect and unattended upon its butt.

This being a rail terminus, rows of idle green carriages sat inert as if waiting to be kick-started into life. I peered through windows at peeling paint and upright, uncushioned seats. The carriages looked like converted pig-pens, so different from those of South Korea, or even China. Beyond the station, industrial chimneys poked rudely into the sky, though they too seemed idle, for they exhaled no smoke. The only belching came from ancient, coal-black, steam engines. In China they still manufacture locomotives. Perhaps they off-loaded geriatric locos on to North Korea, for their emphysematous wheezing had the ring of death. One chugged slowly by, a red flag waved desultorily by a railman perched on the cow-catcher.

~

We were off again. I hugged the window as if it was a private video, each mundane feature of North Korea being to me a revelation. This, the north-west corner of the country, was flattish, green, and secretive. Few dwellings exposed themselves, the exceptions partially dwarfed by grasses and sunflowers, restricting me to glimpses of sloping tiled roofs. The road that paralleled the railway was little more than a country lane, the sort Ealing Studios have etched into British consciousness. Wooden telegraph poles kept sentry. I became fixated by this artery for the simple reason that it had no blood. I played bets with myself over the likelihood of seeing a single car. At length we overtook an ox-cart and later a tractor, but no buses, no cars, no trucks. Just the occasional pedestrian and clusters of uniformed school-children marching towards invisible schools in invisible villages. Agricultural workers bent under the weight of A-frames.

The door to our compartment opened and I was handed a menu with brightly coloured pictures of the fare on offer. Lunch would be served in forty-five minutes. The restaurant car welcomed me with a wax flower on the table and a beaming portrait of Kim Il Sung. I ordered 'Pongkak Beer', 13% proof, and a bowl of rice, for which I was invited to pay in American dollars.

In due course we pulled into Pyongyang Station. I had no papers, no instructions, no directions, no money. Just a scrap of paper that served as a voucher. It seemed an odd way to run a travel business. I stepped down into the unknown.

13

PYONGYANG
Inside the Land of Fantasy

Of Phyöng-yang it is difficult to speak briefly. It is by far the most interesting and perhaps the most beautifully situated town that I have seen in Korea. What Shakespeare is to Stratford, and King Alfred was to England, Ki-tze was to Korea and is to Phyöng-yang. Though he lived 3,000 years ago, his memory is fresh in the name of every part of the city. His grave is kept in good repair, his portrait hangs in a shrine dedicated to his memory ... Phyöng-yang has a population of over 20,000, and is the only city which impressed me favourably regarding capabilities of trade. It is only 36 miles from the sea, to which it has access by the Tai-dong river. The visit of the Gen. Sherman seems to settle the question of its navigability up to the city by light vessels.

W R Carles – *Recent Journeys in Korea* – (1886)

I LOOKED about me on the fast emptying platform.
'Mr Clive?' The voice belonged to a man, thirtyish, with the aggrieved manner of someone dragged from a banquet to pick up a parcel. Though raven-haired his complexion was pale, lending him an unfamiliar, almost Gothic mien. He was smartly dressed in fawn, pleated trousers and open-necked check shirt, and he spoke with the cool insolence of someone used to being obeyed. He had with him an accomplice, darker skinned with shy eyes, who trod a cigarette underfoot as I stepped towards them. Neither introduced himself, and it was not till the following day that they handed me their business cards. Mr Hong was the boss: he was showing the ropes to an apprentice, Mr Chung. Their cards described them not as 'guides' but as 'officers'. Their official status had been evident from the first; when leading me from the station no one demanded my ticket.

Pyongyang Station is a junior replica of Beijing's, Russian style, all lines, rectangles and columns. It is topped by an octagonal turret, from where a portrait of beneficent Kim Il Sung beamed down across the forecourt. Slogans to left and right proclaimed: 'Glorious Comrade Kim Il Sung Gives Life,' and 'Glorious North Korean Workers Party.' Unlike Beijing, Pyongyang has few trains and therefore few passengers. A group of cleaning women, bedecked in red headscarves and aquamarine smocks, hung around looking lost.

With no time to take stock I was hustled to a waiting minibus marked 'Korea International Travel Company'. This was to be my personal chariot, its driver my chauffeur. Three men and a bus for one solitary tourist. My situation was preposterous. I had no idea where I was going, what I was paying for, or how freely I could move about.

'Your hotel is one of the best in Pyongyang,' said Hong. It was only a few minutes away, and was unsurprising to anyone familiar with hostelry in Romania or Bulgaria. High ceilings, vast foyers, unsmiling cleaners, short on clients. The maid bringing fresh towels to my room refused eye contact, as if I was the embodiment of capitalist filth. I tried the shower. The water was cold and stayed cold. I went downstairs to reception.

'You must wait ten minutes for hot water,' I was informed. Three hours later it was still cold. Three days later, ditto.

My very presence, I sensed, disconcerted my hosts. North Korea's persistent dilemma is how to balance two incompatible needs, that for hard currency against the hermetic commands of *juche*. I sensed that every minute was begrudged pandering to degenerate Westerners, and that the country would be happier admitting no tourists at all. Those whom she welcomes – from her few allies – bring no income. Hence the likes of me. I handed over my voucher.

'You must pay in US dollars,' said Hong.

'If you hate America why do you insist on her money?' I asked. 'Switzerland's neutral. Why not take Swiss francs, or even my own British money?' The question seemed logical to me but my minders didn't take the point.

'Kim Il Sung is magnanimous,' explained Hong piously. 'The United States begs us for forgiveness for her crimes. It is justice that we help her economic plight.' Hypocritical hatred of America extends to barring American tourists, but not her currency. Watered-down class enemies, like the British and French, who had nevertheless fought against Kim Il Sung, constitute the acceptable face of capitalism.

~

So excited was I at simply being in North Korea that I hoped to be a polite and pliable visitor. My escorts had their instructions and I had no wish to make waves. My good intentions did not last long, for trouble brewed almost at once. No sooner had I handed over my travellers cheques than Hong said:

'Tomorrow we go to Mount Myohyang.'

Mount Myohyang? Who said anything about Mount Myohyang? I've booked for Pyongyang and Kaesong, down by the DMZ. My voucher lay on the desk. I picked it up.

'See? I am going to the border, to Kaesong and Panmunjom.'

'Impossible,' retorted Hong. 'You are going to Myohyangsan instead. It is the same price, so you are very lucky.'

'But I don't want to go to Myohyang. I don't know anything about it. Why can't I go to Kaesong?'

'The floods. The railway line to the south is damaged.'

I had set myself on peeping into South Korea from the northern side and did not take kindly to the change.

'Can't we go by bus?'

'No. The road is also flooded.'

The only other place to peer over the DMZ is from the Diamond Mountains to the east. I said:

'Then I would rather go to Kumgangsan. Let's go there.'

'Everything is arranged to take you to Myohyang. The train leaves at 7 tomorrow morning.'

I had known beforehand that the schedules of anyone entering North Korea are liable to be mucked about and even disregarded. I could have tried demanding my money back, but doubted my escorts were familiar with Western consumer values. Even Seoul suspends its tours to Panmunjom on those occasions when the truce village is employed for North-South negotiations. Nevertheless, surely Pyongyang could have telexed their Beijing Consulate to warn me beforehand.

Come the morning I performed a half-hearted strike. Chung came to my room to collect me.

'I'm not going. I'll spend the day exploring Pyongyang on my own.'

Chung was mild and sensitive, and did not emulate his partner's blunt detachment. Rather, he grew fidgety and nervous.

'But we already have your train tickets,' he said. 'Your meal has been arranged in Myohyang. You cannot eat in this hotel today. If you do not come …' he hesitated to find the right words, 'there will be much trouble.'

I looked him in the eye, seeking confirmation of his discomfort. What did he mean by trouble: trouble for me, or for my guides, for being unaccommodating and creating a bad impression of their country? In such an improbable land it was impossible to say.

'Please come,' he begged. 'You will enjoy it. You like history. It is history!'

I liked Chung, and for no other reason than to spare him unspecified consequences followed him downstairs.

From reception I picked up an 'Information Map for Tourists'. It measured three feet by two, covered the entire Korean peninsula, and said absolutely nothing. It was impossible to imagine an emptier map. It showed a few towns, a couple of mountains, and that was all.

The railway to Myohyang took us north towards Shinuiju before branching north-eastwards, inland. Once again my compartment was segregated from the rest of the train, preventing me from wandering its length and perusing its occupants. We three sat in silence for much of the journey. Any curiosity concerning me was stifled, while I could ask nothing of consequence to one without being overheard by the other. The journey was profitable only for exposing North Korea's rural backwardness. Oxcarts, primitive tractors, schoolchildren trudging through the early morning rain. At a marshalling yard we rattled past empty goods wagons, and I stared hard at dishevelled women stepping out and climbing down the sides. Surely hobos did not darken Kim Il Sung's Korean paradise. North Korea's population is less than half the South's, and much of the land is still under-populated. I had heard of rigid constraints on the movement of people, that Pyongyang was a showcase city, off limits to citizens living outside the capital. When I queried this, Hong brushed me off with 'The people can go where they choose.' I must have been aboard a special train, for it stopped nowhere en route, and by a process of deduction was otherwise full of Koreans headed for the same destination. They, I suspected, had as little choice in the matter as I.

At Hyangsan station an imported Japanese saloon awaited us. The driver opened the rear door for me, for in North Korean terms I was a VIP. We drove at speed through a lush valley. It was raining hard and I gestured to the driver to slow down before we aquaplaned into a ravine.

'It's OK,' said Hong, 'he is a good driver.'

'He's an arsehole,' I said. 'Make him slow down or I get out.'

He slowed down.

Far from being a VIP, I felt infuriatingly compromised and helpless, like a pawn in the aggrandisement of Kim Il Sung. The purpose in coming to Mount Myohyang (*myo* = fantastic, *hyang* = fragrance) was

PYONGYANG

to kow-tow before the Great Leader, by means of visiting the grotesque International Friendship Exhibition. At prodigious expense a marble, temperature-controlled, Korean-style palace has been constructed as a personal tribute to the Man Himself. It extends over six stories, and is stuffed with priceless gifts donated by leaders and admirers from around the world. Rather than cosset them away, Kim Il Sung preferred to exhibit them for the People's pleasure, and to demonstrate how jolly popular he was with the whole world. North Koreans are taught that the human race stands in awe of his achievements in every field of human endeavour. For the Great Leader, no problem is so great that it cannot be solved. The very idea, of course, confirms the opposite, for only the insecure need to brag.

The building was fronted by armed soldiers who gesticulated angrily at my camera. Queues of wretched Koreans, come to pay homage, waited outside in the rain. Our little party was ushered inside, where we donned sanitary shoes.

What followed was half a day of pure kitsch. A man in turn ridiculed and reviled throughout the world had at unlimited cost ordered the construction of an edifice that to his unknowing people confirmed his place among the champions of the world. It was like roaming the salons and corridors of Hampton Court or the Palace of Versailles, except that the displays were 'gifts', not the rewards of purchase or plunder.

Lower chambers are commanded by vast white statues of the great man, seated in an armchair with a newspaper in his lap. One chair is mounted upon a marble platform and backed by snow-crested mountain murals. A hushed crowd assembled round a push-button *General Information Map of Presents presented to Comrade Kim Il Sung*, which confirms the universality of his fan club and totals up the number of gifts minute by minute. (Like Idi Amin beforehand, Kim Il Sung boasts any number of self-appointed titles – President, Marshal, General, Respected Leader, Great Leader.) Today, the scoreboard reads 67,331 gifts received from 155 countries. Kim Jong Il, meanwhile, has twenty rooms set aside for him. His gifts totalled a modest 22,086 from 138 countries.

Room by room we padded the air-conditioned corridors to inspect the display cabinets. Here was a stuffed bear from Romania's Ceausescu; a pistol encrusted with god-knows-what from East Germany's Honecker, a Buddhist statue courtesy of Indonesia's Sukarno; a 1950s-vintage, bullet-proof car from Stalin, a crocodile-skin briefcase from Fidel Castro. The Head of State of the Central

~ 233 ~

African Republic had – doubtless to the irritation of conservation groups – bestowed elephant tusks. Indonesian laboratories had created a blood-red flower named 'Kimilsungia', which was claimed to have won the gold medal at the Twelfth International Flower Exhibition in Czechoslovakia in 1988. The younger Kim's gifts included a robot from Austria and a cosmonaut outfit.

One quickly tired of this fraudulent pageant, and only the anticipation of possible British exhibits sustained my enthusiasm. The Korean visitors lingered more willingly than I. Most were dressed so poorly in shapeless jackets and trousers that it was like rounding up the beggars and street urchins of Calcutta and sending them round the Taj Mahal. Like me, these downtrodden souls showed neither wonder nor amusement. Unlike me, they were too fearful to quicken their pace or appear inattentive.

Hong had left me in the charge of Chung, who stayed always at my shoulder. He clearly expected me to show reverence at the exhibits, and was nonplussed by my increasingly sullen demeanour. I brightened only when we reached the display labelled 'United Kingdom'. True, the cabinet was small, just a couple of shelves. One plaque – gifted by the Governor of Dervyshire' [sic] in 1987 – bore the mysterious message 'Bere Consulando'. I admired a glass bowl and a tray, courtesy of two insurance companies. Some chosen words – 'In Shakespeare's Land by A L Rowse' – was mysteriously attributed to an anonymous 'British artist and his entourage'. Equally reticent was the unnamed 'Professor of Glasgow University and his wife', who in 1987 bequeathed a vase. The President of a British tour company was not so coy: he had presented embroidery and a paperweight. The shelf marked 'From the Secretary General of the UK-Korea Friendship Association' was empty.

I could take no more and was escorted to the roof terrace, there to admire the misty, thickly forested slopes of the Myohyang range. Mountain streams, flushed with recent rain, cascaded from all sides. Only foreigners and party flunkeys were permitted up here, not the masses I had left down below.

Myohyang was my first introduction to a North Korean resort. The exhibition was only the centrepiece, for I was afterwards ferried by my maniac driver to nearby Pohyon Temple, which dated back to 1042. It was a relief to see glimpses of a foregone Korea, restored or otherwise, and the four warlike deva kings guarding the temple were, to my eyes, indistinguishable from those in the South. The temple was unusual only in ambience. Inevitably, when common access was regulated, Pohyon was all but deserted, though a cavalcade of black Mercedes proclaimed the arrival of 'the Sons of the First Ambassador of the Mongolian People's Republic and their entourage'.

That I might eat we stopped at the pyramid-shaped Hyangsan Hotel. It was designated a Class A hotel, which meant its interior was stuffed with marble, hexagonal pillared mirrors, incongruous plants. No component fitted harmoniously with another. Guests included the Bulgarian men's volleyball team.

~

It was mid-evening by the time we returned to Pyongyang. Once in my room I rushed to the TV, for North Korean broadcasting is a phenomenon to be savoured. I wondered if any past or present totalitarian regime has successfully imposed thought control on its people to the extent that Kim Il Sung enjoys. There is no alternative to Big Brother, nor any escape from its insidious tentacles. The only culture that North Korea recognises – in music, art and literature – is that which promotes the deification of the god-president. He dare not permit the virus of free thought to invade his country. I became each evening an unashamed telly-addict: all programmes mirrored the regime, each channel preoccupied with glorifying the Great Leader and reliving the Korean War. The 9 o'clock News was delivered by a chubby woman in pink and green *hanbok*. What she lacked in appearance she made up for in passion. She lifted her notes and spoke not in the professionally detached manner of her Western counterparts, but with dramatic emphasis, her voice heavy with emotion and leaden pauses. She might have been delivering an epic ballad of heroism and devotion. At the conclusion of each item she would bow her head and lower her script, as if laying a loved one to rest. News stories showed schoolgirls goose-stepping across the screen, massed army ranks garlanded with flowers clapping frenziedly, and delirious peasants grovelling before Kim Il Sung for improving their agricultural quotas. The Great Leader, I noticed, was never filmed or photographed in right profile, on account of an immense growth protruding from the back of his neck. I might never have known of his affliction but for previous exposure to Chinese TV, whose cameramen were not so constrained.

Following the News, one channel broadcast a documentary of the Korean War, littered with footage of American atrocities and staccato, revolutionary voice-overs. The other showed a Korean War movie, drenched with over-the-top acting, martial music, military choirs and beret-hatted sopranos. They had love in their eyes and mouths that quivered with emotion. Generals and privates held up their heads to utter sculpted paeans of praise. There was no relief from the continuous bombardment of Kim-mania. I wondered what percentage of Koreans bothered to switch on, and what penalties existed for switching off.

North Korea's tunnel vision perceives no other reality than glorious Kimilsungism offset against the iniquitous United States. Public posters are no more eclectic than the media. Black men in the jungle are shown poring over the Great Leader's books, his portrait hanging behind them tacked to a tree. An immense mural dominated the lobby of my hotel. The mural is less stylised than most, showing father and son strolling on a bridge over the Taedong. It is wet and the pavement is shiny with rain. Kim Il Sung wears an unbuttoned brown raincoat that flaps open. His son turns to smile at him. Some pigeons are disturbed at their feet but seem reluctant to fly away, so conscious are they of the quasi-divine figures in their midst.

A photographic exhibition of American bestiality commanded the passageway to the dining room. The captions were bilingual – *Korea should be unified, Nukes out of Korea, Anti-war, anti-Nuclear, Yankee go home*. The crew of the American warship Pueblo, captured in the 1960s, were shown being marched ashore. Much space was given to the beautiful South Korean peace campaigner who, in 1988, was received in Pyongyang and then tried to walk back across the DMZ. She was shown handcuffed to South Korean military police. Rows of shrouded corpses were attributed to the massacre at Kwangju in 1980.

It was much the same outside state department stores. The billboards that in another culture would promote a fete, a concert, a jumble sale, or the plight of John McCarthy, were in Pyongyang exclusively devoted to the promulgation of hatred.

Loose parallels, I reflected, attend the American Civil War. Its traumas invade the consciousness of Southerners to this day, whereas to the Yankee folk of Illinois or Wisconsin the conflict is dead and forgotten. One side remembers, the other forgets. The Korean War is seldom on the lips of South Koreans: it is the North that is obsessed with it, and I wondered whether – as with the Johnny Rebs of Alabama and Georgia – that reflects the spectre of defeat. Pyongyang loudly proclaims that Kim Il Sung defeated the Americans, so why the relentless campaign to prove it? For all Pyongyang's strident peace overtures, reunification would strip its revolutionary government of its mission, effectively annulling itself out of existence.

I equipped myself with a splendid word with which to converse with the people of Pyongyang. Unlike Mandarin, with its infuriatingly incomprehensible tones, the Korean language offers recognisable consonants that filter into the subconscious. I had of course noticed this in South Korea. But here in the North, with its stylised public pronouncements and theatrical presentations, I fancied it was easier to assimilate certain sounds. Among those I picked up from TV was what sounded like 'chigganungg'. The stress lay heavily on the last syllable, and the word lent itself to raised fist and jutting chest. In time I found myself wandering the streets of Pyongyang practising my 'chigganungg'. I found it a wonderfully versatile word, equally adept at greeting passers-by or functioning as a teeth-gritting expletive – not to mention its use as a sophisticated political concept. I had no need of a wider vocabulary when possessed of my all-purpose 'chigganungg'. I doubtless appeared perfectly mad: not only had I no idea of its real meaning, I later learned it had none. My word was pure invention.

~

'Do many visitors come to your country?' I asked Chung, as we drove around Pyongyang's tourist spots. He and I shared the back of the minibus, while Hong, like all good commanders, led from the front. In effect, Hong had washed his hands of me, leaving the guiding to his junior. All I ever saw of Hong was the back of his head and occasional glances at his watch. He yawned often.

'Yes,' said Chung. 'We have very many.'

This surprised me. I couldn't *see* many, and my own entry saga suggested otherwise.

'*How* many?'

Mr Chung thought for a moment. 'This year I have guided ...' he lifted his eyes when counting, '... ten, maybe twelve persons.' He turned to me without a flicker of embarrassment, believing these to be healthy figures for international tourism. But then he had nothing with which to compare them.

For a city of two million people (a fifth the population of Seoul), Pyongyang is undeniably quiet and clean, and the initial impression in consequence finds favour with ear and eye. I wondered if there exists a capital city on earth, Tirana perhaps excepted, with fewer vehicles upon its streets. With the quietness goes an absence of urban angst and exhaust fumes. Instead of the frenetic bustle of Seoul, one encounters a listless, expressionless populace, displaying no conspicuous emotion, going about their daily lives as if lobotomised.

Like Seoul, the city had to be completely rebuilt after the Korean War. Unlike Seoul, Pyongyang does not nestle amid a bed of hills. It is flatter, though uplands disturb the horizon like the rim of a battered wok. The Taedong River, meandering through the city, appears studded with lozenge-shaped islets that impose arteriosclerosis upon its flow. As with the Han, the Taedong's potentially calamitous floodwaters are regulated by dams, or 'barrages' as Koreans are wont to call them. I could conceive of no river more bereft of boats than the Han, until I saw the Taedong. No man-made, movable, floating structure disturbed its surface.

Pyongyang's Central District lies upon the northern shore, snuggled between a bend in the Taedong and a fragmented tributary, the Potong. Central District houses monuments and statues, revolutionary murals, manicured lawns, topiarian shrubberies, prestige architecture and government offices. It is pretty, I suppose, but the prettiness is disturbing and unreal, putting me in mind of Noddy's Toytown. The district is small enough to be explored on foot, though a minibus pandered to foreigners and deterred them from straying.

Towering over the city and visible from all parts is the monstrous skeleton of the 1,000-feet-high Ryugyong Hotel. Pyramidal, tapering upwards into the clouds like some futuristic sky rocket, the hotel was intended to boast three thousand rooms and 105 storeys. Built by army units, the Ryugyong was designed to equip guests with revolving restaurant, swimming pool, cinema, conference room. Alas, no laughter echoes from its rooms, no aromas drift from its kitchens. The drain on the state's coffers proved too great: the money ran out and construction was halted. Instead of a glittering hotel, one shudders at the sight of a grim, grey concrete shell, a testament to folly.

The building was begun in 1987, but its budget was soon consumed. There is talk of subsidence around the hotel, of funds being diverted to meet other prestige projects to celebrate Kim Il Sung's eightieth birthday. Whatever the case, what would have been Asia's tallest hotel has cracks on its outside walls and window cavities sealed with bricks or concrete. I asked Hong if the project had been abandoned. He laughed off the suggestion:

'We are waiting for imports of smoked glass. Then we can finish the exterior.' I wondered why nobody had gifted the glass to the President.

'Gifts' is a strange word to employ for presents authorised, nay commanded, by oneself. But that is how North Koreans describe the colossal monuments erected to Kim Il Sung. Take those celebrating his seventieth birthday, in 1982. They include a replica of Paris's Arc de Triomphe (but ten metres higher), which commemorates the defeat of the Japanese. Nearby stands an immense mural of the President being swamped by ecstatic Koreans. A pennant screams: *Long live General Kim Il Sung – unequalled in the world, patriot of Korean liberation – enthusiastically welcomed back to his native country.*

A twenty-metre-tall, bronze statue of the Great Leader points across the Taedong River to yet another of his seventieth birthday gifts – the 'Tower of Juche Idea'. The 150-metre tower stands as a 'flaming' torch. At its foot stand three statues, bearing a sickle, a hammer, and a torch. In an alcove in the base of the tower one discovers hundreds of plaques presented by international devotees of *juche*. Here, for example, one learns that the works of the Great Leader have been designated an 'ism', like Marxism and Thatcherism. I searched eagerly for a British contribution, and was not disappointed: 'Juche Study Group, England 25th October 1987,' declared a simple white plaque.

There was pride on Hong's face when he said I could visit the Grand People's Study House.

'You are a writer,' he said. 'You will be much pleased by our Library for the People. It has six hundred rooms, five thousand seats, and thirty million books!'

The People's library conveyed books by means of metal track, like a miniature railway. Its reading rooms were long, cavernous, dark and bare. The small wooden desks were arranged in columns, as if in an examination hall. Readers were plagued by echoing footsteps on the uncarpeted floors. Even in broad daylight it was so dark as to strain the eyes. I leant over a reader's shoulder and had to squint to read anything at all.

The Study House's music rooms were fitted with primitive earphones and poor quality plastic records. I saw no evidence of cassette tapes, let alone compact discs. We took the lift to an upper floor. The lift was small and had been transformed into a cosy office for its attendant. Her desk was topped with yellow tasselled table cloth, upon which sat a vase of wax flowers and a blue plastic telephone. The building was also equipped with a two-way escalator, which changed direction at the flick of a switch.

I headed for the lines of card-index trays, for high-tech readers' services are beyond the DPRK's resources. I flicked through a few boxes, but those in English were all written by or about Kim Il Sung and his son.

North Korean books, naturally enough, emanate from the same stable as North Korean television. I located bookshops in the railway station and in my hotel. A nation may be understood by what it reads and watches, and I browsed with the same hypnotic intensity with which I sat glued before my TV. The station bookshop was dominated by a hoarding. It showed Kim Il Sung seated at a desk cluttered with books about himself. Pearls of wisdom from Father and Son framed the portrait. Said Kim Il Sung:

The Book is a Silent Teacher and a companion in life. Young people should carry books with them at all times and read various good books zealously.

This begged the question of what constituted 'good' or 'various' books, especially when the subject was unvarying. Said Kim Jong Il:

The Juche Idea is exerting a great influence on the ideological life of humanity and on the revolutionary changes of the world. It is gaining strong support from people all over the world and giving a powerful impetus to the contemporary historic movement which is aspiring to Chajusong [independence from imperialism].

Typical of the titles on display were: *The Path of Great Love*, in a dove-white cover; *The Immortal Juche Idea* (to whose 101st chapter I had listened on Radio Pyongyang); *The Great Leader Kim Il Sung*; and *The Great Teacher Kim Jong Il*. By way of jacket illustrations I was rewarded by nothing more adventurous than touched-up photographs of father or son. All titles were published by the DPRK Foreign Languages Publishing House.

My eye was caught by a potential classic: Kim Jong Il's *On Improving Film Distribution to Meet the Requirements of Party Ideological Work*. The book was featured (one can hardly say 'reviewed') in the *Pyongyang Times*.

The work points out that because of its revolutionary and socialist content, our cinematic art helps people to hold fast to the Juche revolutionary outlook on the world; it teaches them how they should live, work and fight by highlighting exemplary men of our era. Therefore it serves as a weapon of struggle and as a textbook of life indispensable for Party members and other working people.

It notes that film distributors are charged with an important mission to show the working people our revolutionary films promptly and help them to follow the examples of the heroes of the films and to remould their characters steadily.

It also notes that ideological education to the working people should be intensified through films, and film distributors should play an important role in carrying out the technical and cultural revolutions ... The work was published in English, French, Spanish, Russian, Chinese, Japanese, Arabic and German.

I treasured most of all a Korean-English mini-dictionary I chanced to pick up. It fell open at the entry 'enemy', which was defined: *American imperialism, the most ferocious and cynical aggression and pillage of modern times, and the No 1 common enemy of all the progressive peoples of the world.*

This was a treat, a new insight into the compiling of dictionaries. I flipped through in search of other politically loaded entries. 'Anti-American' constituted a distinct word, defined as: *Let us reinforce the struggle against anti-imperialist and anti-American!* The letter 'L' was rich in insight.

'Love' – *love for the socialist party.*

'Leader' – *Long live Comrade Kim Il Sung, Great Leader.*

'Longevity' – *We wish longevity and good health to Comrade Kim Il Sung, Great Leader.*

~

On the morning of my last day I was ferried around outlying sites. I was whisked over the Taedong, past what Chung identified as the presidential palace (barely visible from the road), to the Revolutionary Martyrs' Cemetery. Parallel lines of bronze busts commemorated those at the forefront of the anti-Japanese struggle.

To the west of the city we passed North Korea's 'Olympic complex'. Furious that the 1988 Games were awarded to Seoul, North Korea not only refused to attend, but devoted a king's ransom on athletics stadia to stand comparison. The 1988 Olympics witnessed no repetition of the mass boycotts by East or West, leaving Kim Il Sung to stage his own shadow-games with whatever dregs of the international community he was able to entice. The stadia included indoor swimming pool, and separate gymnasia for badminton, athletics, combat sports, weight lifting, volleyball, basketball, table tennis, handball and football. The entire complex was ghostly empty, as was the eight-lane highway running alongside. I asked Chung about this. The country was poor, there was no traffic, so why the extravagant road-building?

'For the future,' he said, dumbly, as if sharing the vision of a 21st century DPRK taking its place in the comity of nations, complete with traffic jams and smoggy skies.

We were headed for Mangyongdae. To outsiders the word means nothing. To North Koreans it is Bethlehem, the birthplace of the Saviour, with a dash of Mecca thrown in, for it is all but compulsory for North Koreans to visit and pay their respects, a place of pilgrimage for the masses. The turn-off to the birthplace merited a colour photograph in *Korea Monthly*: 'The fork in the road to Mangyongdae will be remembered forever in the history of our prosperous country.' On my tourist map of Pyongyang the fork itself was listed as a tourist site.

The President's birthplace was a collection of restored thatched cottages, sanitised out of recognition. Solemn organ music drifted on the air. Bent and battered *kimchi* pots supposedly confirmed the poverty of his parents. Like a good disciple, Hong related a parable.

'As a child,' he said, 'Kim Il Sung climbed a tree to catch a rainbow. He couldn't reach it so he climbed a hill instead. Still the rainbow was too far away. But he showed his determination, and this he gives to his people.'

Pilgrims to Mangyongdae were sweetened by an adjoining funfair, with revolutionary museum. One funfair attraction was listed as a 'hand-grenade throwing ground'.

But what of the site of the *General Sherman*? Hong said they'd take me. It wasn't far.

'It is famous because the Korean people defeated the American aggressors without rifles and guns,' he said, solemnly. We soon came to the place. A white monument by the water's edge and a couple of ship's cannon commemorated the slaughter. I gazed out upon the calm water and cocked an ear for the crackle of flames and the screams of the dying. No one had survived. Nevertheless, forty years after the event, F A McKenzie was able to imagine how

the crew of the General Sherman were almost suffocated by the stench and vapour of the burning sulphur and saltpetre. They tried in vain to put out the flames, and ... were forced one by one to jump into the water ... Some of the invaders had white flags, which they waved wildly but waved in vain. Most of them were hacked to pieces before they reached the shore. Others were brought to land, where they tried by friendly smiles and soft words to win the goodwill of the people. But they were not allowed many minutes to live. They were pinioned and then cut down, mutilated in abominable fashion, and the bodies torn to bits. Parts were taken off to be used as medicine, and the remainder burnt. The General Sherman itself was consumed by flames to the water's edge.

In South Korea I had watched a televised dramatisation of the *General Sherman*. I wondered whether the South's present friendship with America blunted past enmity, and if so whether the plight of the crew was treated with present-day sympathy. Not a bit of it. The *General Sherman* was clearly a *cause célèbre* for all Koreans.

Hong looked at his watch and yawned. This was an unscheduled stop and he wished to press on.

'We will take you to the craft shop to buy souvenirs,' he said.

I was fast tiring of my official itinerary, for I was seeing nothing of the Pyongyang behind the tourist veil. That, of course, was entirely to my escorts' liking. At first my protestations were nominal.

'I would like to see the Museum of the Korean War.'

'It is closed.'

'How can it be closed?'

'We must give seven days notice to visit the museum.'

'In that case can we go to the Pyongyang subway? I have heard much about it; that it is more beautiful even than Moscow's.'

Hong exchanged brisk words with Chung. Yes, I could visit the subway.

An electronic map by the ticket office showed the extent of the twin, X-shaped lines. The low, arch-roofed escalator burrowed deep into the earth, for stations doubled as air-raid shelters. The gradient was steep, the light gloomy, and without the distraction of advertisements the descent was like gliding down an open pit shaft. As with a well-chosen aperitif, however, the sensory deprivation sharpened the sensation that awaited. Stepping from the escalator I turned down some marble steps. They opened not so much upon a platform as upon an immense ball-room, illuminated by firework clusters of orange bulbs in the cathedral-like ceiling. A scenic mural of Kim Il Sung commanded the ballroom from the far end of the platform. Most striking of all were the tunnel walls. In London or Paris or Tokyo they would be peppered with route maps and advertisements. In Pyongyang they were devoted to mosaics.

They ran the length of the platform and depicted the scene above ground, in this case the banks of the Taedong near the Tower of Juche Idea.

'Each station is different,' said Chung.

'You mean each station has a different mosaic?'

'It is more. Each station is completely different.'

'Show me. Let's take the train to the next station.'

Hong looked annoyed and gave another glance at his watch. I don't know why, for the day was supposed to be at my disposal.

'Just one more station,' he said curtly.

The train itself was an anticlimax, for I imagined carriages gliding into view encrusted with jewels and trailing ermine. Instead a rickety blue cigar tube trundled to a stop. The seats were wooden and hard, and the carriages, deprived of advertisements, lacked compensatory appeal.

The second station was no less wondrous than the first, but I was by now distracted by notions of escape. The minibus had been driven round to meet us. It was overdue, and I wondered whether to take advantage by losing myself from my escorts. The opportunity soon passed, but another was not long in coming.

14

A BID FOR FREEDOM
Escape from My Minders

Travelling in these [Diamond] mountains is far from luxurious,
but its hardships are not unaccompanied by retrieving merits, and
seldom have I seen a quainter sight than the yard of a farm at
night. The sheds in which our animals drank up their mess of
beans and hot water, ran round three sides of a square, in the centre of which blazed a bright fire to scare wild beasts and robbers.
Round the fire sat some half-dozen Koreans, totally regardless of
the intense cold, chattering and smoking, and occasionally replen-
ishing the flames with a pile of reeds or brushwood which sent up
a blaze of light the moment it was kindled. Squatted as they were
on a manure heap, they seemed, with the bright stars above them
to be more favoured than we in our low kennel ... Now and again
the silence was broken by the screams of a fractious stallion, bit-
ing and kicking his neighbours, who in their turn plunged and
squealed, until blows had brought them into order. How such
nights of sleeplessness and riot brought any refreshment to man or
beast seemed a marvel.

W R Carles – *Recent Journeys in Korea* – (1886)

K IM HYUN HEE is just about the most famous woman in South
Korea. She is beautiful, brave, intelligent, unmarried. She is
also North Korean, being the agent who blew up a KAL
airliner over Burma in 1987. After planting the bomb she and
her elderly accomplice were detained in Bahrain. He dutifully took his
life. She tried to take hers, failed, and was handed over to Seoul, where
she was memorably filmed being led down the aircraft steps with her
mouth bound with sticky tape. Realising her propaganda value, the
authorities eventually pardoned her. She lives today under constant
guard against North Korean assassins, has written best-selling memoirs, and from time to time graces television screens to give shy but
graphic accounts of her former life in Pyongyang. South Korean men

are said to be besotted with her, and many have offered their hand in marriage.

She was a frequent studio guest in 1992, when South Korea took the unprecedented step of broadcasting excerpts from North Korean television. We learned of the Pyongyang traffic policeman who died on duty trying to 'exterminate' traffic accidents, and who was commended posthumously by Kim Jong Il; of the textile factory thrilled with his guidance ('he knows everything'); and of the state's enthusiasm for rugby. It had never occurred to me that North Koreans might partake of this most English and class-oriented game. It was introduced earlier this century and survived the division of Korea. I watched astonished as well-behaved players gave chase to an oval ball on a soccer pitch. The tackling appeared strictly legal, not to say soft. A team from Pyongyang University proved too much for the representatives of a fertiliser company. Rugby, North Korean viewers were informed, promotes a sound body and a sound mind.

1992 was a signal year for North Korea-watchers. On 16 February Kim Jong Il turned fifty and on 15 April Kim Il Sung reached eighty. There was much speculation that the elder Kim would finally hand over to the younger, but he did not. Koreans traditionally consider old age to begin at sixty, so the Great Leader's longevity is taken as confirming his quasi-divinity. The birthdays of father and son provoked celebrations in Pyongyang on a scale gargantuan even by North Korean standards. I was at the time in Seoul writing this book, and on 15 April was hill-walking in the countryside. From the sky above me a card fluttered to earth at my feet. I picked it up. It measured about five inches by three. On one side a family clutched a pennant showing the sun rising over Kim Il Sung's birthplace. On the other, doves flew over the earth among hundreds of balloons trailing streamers. The streamers proclaimed this most hallowed of all dates, and the magnificent age of the Great Leader.

I pondered the origins of the card and whether I could be shot for possessing it. Only later did the truth dawn. North Korean balloons drifting overhead had dropped their cargo of adoring proclamation. So, there exists one means of direct communication between North and South – favourable wind permitting.

25 June 1992 marked the forty-second anniversary of the start of the Korean War. North Korean television excelled itself in the promotion of creative hatred. A 'struggle day' was proclaimed, and citizens reminded of how the United States, even in 1950, was the world's

mightiest power. 'Victory' for the North provided proof of the virtues of *juche*. Speech contests now encouraged the masses to excoriate America. One soldier's entry was titled 'Cry With Rage'. He howled into the microphone:

> If American troops attack you, our history won't forgive. You [Americans] will be destroyed. You are the irreconcilable enemy. North Korea is invincible. Don't be proud of your power, we will break your arrogant nose. American bitch. One North Korean soldier can beat one hundred US soldiers. North Korea is a nation of heaven.

The soldier was upstaged by a blue-shirted worker. His lips foamed and his shoulders heaved:

> Let us imagine when we reunify. The Great Leader will be smil-ing. He will meet factory workers from Paekdo to Hallasan. US jackals use sticks to beat North Korea and now have nuclear bombs. Let's kick out American soldiers and reunify!

A line of chorus girls clamoured 'Unify! Unify! Unify!', like some pubescent display of gushing teeny-boppers.

~

I was becoming increasingly frustrated by my suffocating minders. In the hours remaining to me in North Korea I wished to roam suburban Pyongyang.

'We will now take you to the craft exhibition,' said Hong.

'I don't want to go to the craft exhibition.'

'Where do you want to go?' He sounded miffed.

I pulled out my tourist map of the city. It confined itself to essentials, giving a good idea of scale and size, and the whereabouts of tourist sites, which it highlighted with little diagrams. It was useless as an aid to wandering among the suburbs.

'Please drive me over the bridge, away from all these monuments and into a housing estate,' I said.

Insofar as I could read his expression, Hong dismissed me as mad. He spoke sharply to the driver and we headed east, across the Taedong and into the suburbs. I had of course no control over our route, for Hong doubtless kept me away from what might be worth seeing. Once or twice I managed to direct the driver left at this junction, right at the next, just to see how Hong would react. Beside me in the back Chung grew ever more agitated, for I had taken to routing my requests through him, which he then had to pass forward. As my demands became ever more unpredictable he turned and asked me in a hushed whisper to state them directly to Hong.

'Pull up here, please,' I said.

'Why?' asked Hong.

'So I can get out and walk.' We were deep in a sea of grimy apartment blocks, interspersed with the occasional children's playground. No military secrets likely to be exposed here.

'It is very difficult to stop here.'

'I shall only be a little while. I shall come back in fifteen minutes.'

'It is against the law to stop here,' said Hong, playing his trump card.

I looked around for yellow lines or other indications to support his protest. The road was wide and empty. We had the street to ourselves.

'Of course you can stop. Just here please, on that corner. According to this map I can catch public bus No 3 back to my hotel.' (Presuming I could get on board. Pyongyang's buses seemed no more common than other kinds of vehicle, and were accordingly packed to the point of suffocation. Women with children were given priority, and queued separately.)

'You cannot take the public bus. You have no money.'

This was true. I wasn't allowed any. Hong barked at the driver and we wheeled back to the city. I felt maddeningly incarcerated.

'That's the Mayday Stadium. I'd like to see it,' I said, gritting my teeth and pointing to the gleaming, parachute-roofed edifice that my map located to be on an islet in the Taedong.

'We cannot go there. The road is closed.'

'No it's not. Look! You can see a car going along the bridge.'

'The road is closed,' repeated Hong, insolently, expecting the matter to be finished.

'You say the road is closed. I say it isn't. I'll get out here and see you later.'

We had stopped at a crossroads. Before Hong could stop me I pulled open the sliding door and stepped from the minibus, which vanished in a cloud of fury around the corner.

It would be wrong to imply that it is illegal for a Westerner to wander unchaperoned far from his hotel. That I could do so had been established from the outset. Likewise my freedom to photograph what I chose. I never feared official retribution for my private excursions, though, like now, they were sometimes hard to realise.

'We are here to help you,' Chung had remarked, and he probably meant it.

It was nevertheless exhilarating to be alone in this strange city. I lingered awhile after the minibus had vanished to savour a pretty traffic warden. In white hats and tunics and dark skirts these girls police the city's intersections, where they click their heels and swivel to the right, 90° at a time, waving their zebra batons like wands. Having no traffic to direct adds an air of tedium, not to say mystique, to their work, and I wondered how many circles they trod in the course of each working day. The girls were apparently selected for their good looks, to ease motorists' frustrations, which, in the absence of drivers to appreciate them, was rather like inviting beauty queens to fish in a dried up pond.

Paying due care and attention, peering studiously left, right, and left again, I began to cross. There came a furious blast of a whistle. I looked up to find the traffic girl waving me frantically back to the kerb. I retreated, looking about me to confirm that the road was clear. The girl did another four-stage circuit on her podium. When once again facing me – no vehicles having troubled her in the meantime – she jabbed her baton to my left, where I located a flight of steps leading down to an underpass. I was meant to cross by that means. Emerging from the other side I turned and bowed my thanks.

The cleanliness of Pyongyang's roads is not a simple consequence of their emptiness. The city employs squads of female road sweepers. In their protected environment they have developed no safety reflex. They do not glance constantly over their shoulder or keep a nervous lookout for speeding or inattentive motorists. Heads down they brush and they sweep, sweep and brush, with the abandon of gardeners.

The regimented apartment blocks about me sported balconies encased in iron railings. Red streamers dangled from roofs stating 'Long live *juche*'. Curious about rationed foodstuffs, and knowing that public markets do not exist, I ventured inside a fruit and vegetable store. (Not long after I left North Korea the economy deteriorated to such an extent that the populace was urged to eat less. 'Lets eat two meals a day' screamed the banners.) The shop boasted a long marble counter and was framed by paintings of luscious apples and pears. But there was just one customer, and the scanty produce was better suited to display than consumption. Fifteen apples were laid out upon a tray like snooker reds – five in the bottom row, four in the second, and so on. The customer bought an apple with a coupon. The apple was taken from the top of the pyramid, handed over, and the sale logged by pencil in a battered ledger. If it was like this in the showpiece capital, what must life be like in the provinces, where foreigners could not hope to penetrate?

A department store beckoned. I lingered by the toy shelves, intrigued to find DPRK products with names in English, presumably for export to unimaginable destinations. Toys included 'Mangyongdae Fountain Pens', 'High-Speed Passenger Ships', and miniature 'Child Pianos'. No less surprising were the solar-panelled baseball hats powering small fans over the brow.

The clothes stalls were enlightening. The boutiques of Seoul parade the latest Western fashions, skimpy skirts, high hems, lace blouses, feathered hats. The mannequins stand with hands on hips in come-on poses. Those here in Pyongyang were short, dumpy, bob-haired. The dresses would be mocked in the West, and favoured only by the wives of vicars. Take this calf-length, green-spotted specimen. It is box-pleated, dirndl-waisted, and comes with white spray.

Not far from the store I found an inviting dirt lane, down which I discovered traditional, low, slate-roofed houses surrounded by high walls. The dwellings were perfectly concealed, and the neighbourhood exposed me for the only time in North Korea to naked hostility. In comparable homes in the South, families would be cooking, cleaning, laughing, waving. Here, I searched in vain for signs of domesticity within, and I began to wonder if my presence was suspected. Turning a blind corner I collided with an old man whose face lit up in horror. Maybe it was my intrusion into a Korean sanctuary that upset him, or maybe it was my camera, clicking at this and that. Koreans tradition-ally fear cameras as presenting threats to the soul, though here I sensed they feared threats to the state. Whatever the source of his fear, the man turned and ran in the direction I was headed, calling out warnings unintelligible to me. An approaching couple likewise turned and scat-tered as if at the sight of a gun. Word spread so fast that rounding every corner I saw figures fleeing from my looming presence.

The lane led eventually to an unpaved square. It was this that I was intended not to discover, for in the middle was a tanker dispensing water to headscarfed old women wrestling with buckets and basins. Such indignities were not for the eyes of foreigners, and, though I was outwardly unrestricted in my movements, Hong and Chung surely doubted I would end up here. I wished to photograph the panicking faces, but the angst was palpable, and as alarm had evidently preceded me I feared at any moment the sound of police sirens.

Like a surrounded tiger I backed away, down yet more lanes which with a traveller's instinct I sensed looked promising. In due course I came upon a scrawny soldier guarding a line of shabby huts. Before I could come close he raised his hand to shoo me away. I did not expect North Korea's young conscripts to be housed in luxury, and they evidently were not. Emerging from the warren I stumbled upon a platoon of squaddies sprawled upon a verge. I conjured up my biggest smile and strolled over. I had no idea what reaction my presence would provoke. Like the riot police in the South, the defenders of *juche* grinned and beseeched me to sit amongst them. I introduced myself and braced myself for the crunch-line. I told them my country. My utterance of '*yong-guk*' drew no hostility. This puzzled me, considering that these very soldiers had probably lost grandfathers at British hands. True, a German does not nowadays provoke paroxysms of rage among the British solely on account of his nationality. But Britain, unlike North Korea, does not daily address herself to past and present grievances.

Unlike the townsfolk from whom I had recently fled, the soldiers were perfectly at ease and amiable. They seemed so young and small, midgets in comparison with their better nourished cousins in the South. Their faces were callow and blotchy and their fingers stained yellow with nicotine. They laughed at the enormity of my (size 12) shoes. The soles of their own boots had worn through, or were crudely patched, and in truth these guardians of the Great Leader looked pathetic specimens of the military art. I was confident they would not obstruct my wish for a photograph, but in this as in much else I was mistaken. As one, the soldiers shook their heads. Cameras are the work of the devil.

So are floods. Though sceptical of the reasons for my changed itinerary, the evidence of recent inundation was clear. When the elements threaten, Kim Il Sung calls upon a youthful civil defence force. The nation's children are his salvation. Month after month, in parks and public squares, rehearsals for this or that anniversary are carried on with mighty contingents. Thousands of sunhatted, tracksuited schoolchildren go through their repertoires. The boys in navy and the girls in red bend and twist in fantastic contortions. The 'flowers in spring' routine involves an inner ring of boys slowly stretching upwards, while an outer ring of girls arch over backwards until their hands touch the ground. The children have mastered the sideways split, legs splayed and chins upon the ground. Teachers with microphones choreograph every sequence.

Almost from my arrival in Pyongyang I had been bewitched by armies of older children parading through the streets. They marched in school uniforms of navy and white, sporting the red kerchiefs of the 'young pioneers', and bearing satchels in one hand and brushes, buckets, or spades in the other. At their head strides a student with a red flag. Only the military band is missing, substituted by coordinated whoops of allegiance and defiance.

Now, nearing the Mayday Stadium, I chanced upon the product of the students' labours. The nearby bridge across the Taedong was open – isolated cars and buses straggled across it – making me wonder afresh why Hong had insisted otherwise. The islet beneath the bridge, at the far end of which stood the stadium, had been reduced to a swamp. Legions of ant-like children scurried hither and thither, bending low with their spades or dragging sandbags through the mire.

~

I bemoaned my inability to meet ordinary North Koreans. Only once did my presence invite charity. On street corners ice cream stalls pandered to luxury. A woman in army uniform was about to buy. Seeing me curious and envious, she bought a second and strode towards me, hand outstretched. I received with a smile a dollop of ice cream upon a small, shallow, saucered wafer.

Cut off from Pyongyang's citizens – by language on my part and prohibition on theirs – I was restricted to Hong and Chung for personal insights. Hong I ruled out: he was altogether too smug and self-righteous. In any case, as a result of my walkout he had virtually ceased to communicate with me. Chung, I sensed, might be more responsive. From him I had already learned that North Korea permits no bourgeois pets, such as domesticated cats and dogs, and no telephone directories. Meat, he admitted, was increasingly difficult to obtain, but rationing was not a reaction to shortages but a policy to treat everyone alike. He insisted, too, that the wearing of the Kim Il Sung lapel badge was not compulsory.

'People can choose to wear one.' This was tantamount to saying everybody wanted to; even actors wore them on TV costume dramas.

Miners, said Chung, earned ten times his salary, and road sweepers double. Shop assistants, however, and army conscripts earned 'very little'.

In order to probe deeper I needed to detach Chung from his superior. No opportunity presented itself until we found ourselves in the waiting room at Pyongyang station. I was about to leave North Korea. Hong had drifted away. It was Chung who broke the ice.

'You have been to South Korea.'

So they knew all along. 'Did you know that from my passport?'

'Yes. Soon our country will be united and I shall see it for myself. What is it like?'

I encapsulated my impressions, that South Korea was in some respects like modern Japan, while North Korea reminded me of China in the 1960s. I added:

'East German people will learn that West Germans are much more aggressive. I think North Koreans will discover the same about South Koreans.

'Koreans are all the same.'

'Maybe. But Germany did not fight a civil war like Korea did. Therefore Germany's scars are not so deep and will heal more quickly. Reunification will be very difficult for Korea, I think.'

'Koreans are different from other people,' said Chung, dreamily. 'I have heard that South Korea is rich, but Seoul is not as beautiful as Pyongyang. Most visitors think Pyongyang is very beautiful,' he added, sensing that I did not. 'My last tourists were from Poland, and they said many kind things.'

'Do you hate America?' I asked.

'No. We Koreans hate Japan more than America.' I had unearthed the one issue that united the two Koreas – their shared antipathy to Japan.

'Then why is Kim Il Sung negotiating loans from Japan?'

'It is Japan that begs to do business with us. The Japanese are criminals, but we must help them.'

'What do you do with criminals in your country? Are there many prisons?'

'There is no crime in my country?'

'None at all?'

'Very little. The people do not know the laws. The criminal code is secret.'

'Well, what would happen to you if you stole my wallet?'

'Nobody steals things here. Kim Il Sung has created an honest society.' I had noticed that neither Hong nor Chung ever spoke of the President as 'Dear Leader', but always by his name.

'What do you really think about Kim Il Sung?' I asked, playing devil's advocate. 'Most of the world, including many Chinese, think he's mad.'

Chung didn't take umbrage. He kept his eyes straight as he said: 'Nobody dares to criticise Kim Il Sung.' He looked at me, and the look said more than his words. Chung, I sensed, knew better than to think he was governed by a divine genius. Nevertheless, so much that I learned from Chung reinforced rather than contradicted the picture in my mind of Koreans as a whole – the depth of feeling against Japan, the capacity for hard work, the endurance of suffering, the pride taken in prestige 'white elephants', the innate superiority of the Korean race, and the almost mystical belief in a future unified Korea paved with gold.

It had been for me a personal challenge to see North Korea. Month by month, week by week, shifts in global politics eat away at her prospects for survival. Her agents are allegedly desperate to get their hands on Kremlin documents which, if released, could undermine Kim Il Sung's insistence that the South started the Korean War. Without friends, even North Korea must change. Even as I write, Pyongyang has acquired its first karaoke bar (South Korean songs erased), funded by Japanese sources. I was thankful to have breathed North Korea's invigorating if paranoid air while I could. It was not without a sense of regret that I boarded my train in Pyongyang, for I felt I was saying goodbye to something unique, and that were I ever to return it would be to a country unrecognisable from that which I was leaving. The ticket inspector welcomed me in faltering English:

'Thank you for visiting our country.'

North Korea might be a pariah, but she was a polite pariah. I threw a final glance over my shoulder and called to Mr Hong.

'Do you ever dream of pigs?'

His face did not relax its stony glare.

'I dream only of *juche*.'

Glossary

Suffixes

do	island/province
dong	village
po	port
sa	temple
san	mountain

Food and drink

anju	snack provided with alcohol in bar
boricha	cold barley tea
kalbi	marinated ribs
kimchi	spicy vegetable side-dish
makkoli	milky coloured rice wine
mul	water
pipim-pap	mixed vegetables with egg and rice
ramyon	instant noodles
ranaska	pickled yellow vegetable
soju	colourless distilled spirit
sam-gae-tang	chicken and ginseng stew

General

adjima	aunt, married or middle aged woman
AFKN	American Forces Korea Network
anio	no
annyong hashimnikka	hello
chajusong	independence, autonomy
changgo	hour-glass drum
char-yot	attention
chidokha	dreadful
chigae	A-shaped frame carried on back
chikheng	limited express bus
haenyo	Cheju's diving women
hanbok	traditional dress
hanguk-mal	Korean speech
hangul	Korean script
harubang	grandfather (Cheju sculptures)

hwa-too	flower card game
ibul	quilt
insam	ginseng
juche	North Korean ideology of self-reliance
kibun	Confucian term for 'mood' or 'feeling'
kisaeng	equivalent to Japanese geisha women
Kobukson	Turtle Ship
kombay	'cheers!'
kosok	express bus
kut	exorcism
kyong-un-ki	tractor
maedip	knotted and tassled wall-hangings
mian hamnida	'I am sorry'
minbak	homestay/unlicensed yoinsook
mogyoktang	bathhouse
moktak	Buddhist wooden hollowed pot/drum
mutang	sorceress
neh	yes
ondol	traditional underfloor heating
paduk	board game (Go in Japanese)
Paekche Kingdom	kingdom of south-west Korea 18BC to AD660
piri	thin musical pipe
pokpo	waterfall
poktanju	beer and whisky mixed
pungsu	geomancy
pyogae	pillow, usually of wood
Silla Dynasty	unified Korea AD660 to 1910
ssirum	traditional wrestling
tabang	tea house/coffee shop
Taekukki	South Korean national flag
taramji	squirrel
won	Korean currency
yangnom	'foreigner', 'outsider'
yo	thin mattress
yogwan	Korean hotel
yoinsook	Korean hostel
yong-guk	Britain
yong-guk saram imnida	'I am British'
yut	game sticks used like dice